"This is the book I have been waiting to recommend on applying Bowen Family Systems Theory in congregational life. Bowen theory makes sense of the emotional forces that arise when people live and work together. Creech understands the challenges churches face amid rapid change, urban crowding, rural decline, and social upheaval. His work addresses leadership with a perspective that includes proclamation, pastoral care, spiritual formation, and life in Christian community. Throughout, he reflects on the theological implications of taking a systems approach. This is an insightful, comprehensive, yet highly readable book."

—**Katie Long**, editor-in-chief, Family Systems Forum,
Center for the Study of Natural Systems and the Family

"Creech masterfully connects Bowen theory with particular ministerial tasks, illustrating how the theory can inform and shape Christian service. I always learn from Creech's insights and you will too."

—**Peter Steinke**, author of *Uproar: Calm Leadership in Anxious Times*

"This book is a rare gem, a gift to leaders. Robert's unique approach guides the reader beyond theory and even practical how-tos toward identifying one's own road map and inner compass. Pastoral leaders will be inspired to chart a life-giving course for their personal life and ministry, leaving behind winding paths that often lead to confusion, frustration, or dysfunction. I don't know a more authentic and trustworthy guide than Robert. This work represents his personal journey of transformation; I'm confident it can be a catalyst for others as well."

—**Elizabeth Wourms**, Heart to Honduras

Family Systems and Congregational *Life*

A MAP FOR MINISTRY

R. ROBERT CREECH

B
Baker Academic
a division of Baker Publishing Group
Grand Rapids, Michigan

© 2019 by R. Robert Creech

Published by Baker Academic
a division of Baker Publishing Group
PO Box 6287, Grand Rapids, MI 49516-6287
www.bakeracademic.com

Printed in the United States of America

Library of Congress Cataloging-in-Publication Data
Names: Creech, R. Robert (Richard Robert), author.
Title: Family systems and congregational life : a map for ministry / R. Robert Creech.
Description: Grand Rapids, MI : Baker Academic, [2019] | Includes bibliographical references and index.
Identifiers: LCCN 2018020572 | ISBN 9781540960375 (pbk.)
Subjects: LCSH: Pastoral theology. | Systemic therapy (Family therapy) | Christian leadership.
Classification: LCC BV4011.3 .C738 2019 | DDC 253—dc23
LC record available at https://lccn.loc.gov/2018020572

ISBN 978-1-5409-6157-0 (casebound)

Material from Murray Bowen, *Family Therapy in Clinical Practice*, 1994, a Jason Aronson book, is reprinted with permission of Rowman & Littlefield.

The poem "Maps" by Holly Ordway is used with permission. Originally published in Malcolm Guite, *Word in the Wilderness* (Norwich, UK: Hymns Ancient & Modern, 2014), 36.

Unless otherwise indicated, Scripture quotations are from the New Revised Standard Version of the Bible, copyright © 1989, by the Division of Christian Education of the National Council of the Churches of Christ in the United States of America. Used by permission. All rights reserved.

Scripture quotations labeled ESV are from The Holy Bible, English Standard Version® (ESV®), copyright © 2001 by Crossway, a publishing ministry of Good News Publishers. Used by permission. All rights reserved. ESV Text Edition: 2011.

Scripture quotations labeled KJV are from the King James Version of the Bible.

Scripture quotations labeled NIV are from the Holy Bible, New International Version®. NIV®. Copyright © 1973, 1978, 1984, 2011 by Biblica, Inc.™ Used by permission of Zondervan. All rights reserved worldwide. www.zondervan.com

19 20 21 22 23 24 25   7 6 5 4 3 2 1

To Melinda,
who has walked patiently and lovingly with me in marriage,
a partner in ministry,
a faithful friend,
a scholar in her own right,
a mother and grandmother extraordinaire,
without whom . . .

MAPS

Antique maps, with curlicues of ink
As borders, framing what we know, like pages
From a book of travelers' tales: look,
Here in the margin, tiny ships at sail.
No-nonsense maps from family trips: each state
Traced out in color-coded numbered highways,
A web of roads with labeled city-dots
Punctuating the route and its slow stories.
Now GPS puts me right at the centre,
A Ptolemaic shift in my perspective.
Pinned where I am, right now, somewhere, I turn
And turn to orient myself. I have
Directions calculated, maps at hand:
Hopelessly lost till I look up at last.

—Holly Ordway

Contents

Preface   ix

Acknowledgments   xiii

PART 1: ORIENTING THE MAP

1. Always Take a Map: The Value of Bowen Family Systems Theory   3
2. Reading the Map: An Overview of Bowen Family Systems Theory   13

PART 2: A MAP FOR PRACTICAL THEOLOGY

3. Third-Way Leadership: More Than Principles and Practices   31
4. The Future of Congregational Leadership: Leading in Chaotic Times   49
5. Proclamation: Preaching as Pastor and as Prophet   63
6. Pastoral Care: Helping without Hurting   77
7. Spiritual Formation: Growing in Christlikeness   89
8. Christian Community: Journeying with Others   101

PART 3: A MAP FOR READING SCRIPTURE

9. Bowen Family Systems Theory and Biblical Interpretation: The Rules of the Game   117
10. Mapping the Family of Abraham: Family Systems, 2000 BC   125

11. Mapping the Character of Jesus: Differentiation and
    Christlikeness   137
12. Mapping the Teaching of Paul: New Life in Christ and
    Community   151

    Appendix A Mapping the Family of David: Family Systems,
       1000 BC   163
    Appendix B Bowen Theory and Theological Language   177
    Appendix C Important Terms in Bowen Family Systems Theory   185
    Appendix D Bowen-Based Training Programs   191
    Appendix E Bowen Family Systems Theory and Ministry:
       A Bibliography   197
    Notes   203
    Index   223

Preface

Writing clarifies thinking like few other activities. Francis Bacon famously claimed that "writing maketh an exact man."[1] That, as much as anything, accounts for why I sat down to write this work. I wanted to know more clearly what I think about offering congregational ministry from the perspective of Bowen Family Systems Theory (BFST). I also suspected that it might make a difference to others engaged in that work.

A colleague first introduced me to the theory in 1987, soon after I had accepted the call to be senior pastor at the University Baptist Church in Houston, Texas. He asked me if I had read *Generation to Generation*, by Rabbi Edwin Friedman. I had not. I found a copy of the book and read it through, unclear about what to make of this family systems perspective on congregational life. On the one hand, it made good sense to me. Friedman's stories demonstrated the power of such an approach. On the other hand, I was clueless as to what to do with it in my own family and congregation, and I did not know where to find out. So I placed the book on my shelf and forgot about it.

A few years later a round of congregational chaos and a simultaneous series of family crises sent me back to the book. Friedman's perspective, as I recalled it, might have something to say about the confusion swirling around me. I pulled *Generation to Generation* off the shelf and reread it. Motivated by my own misery, I sought out a Bowen-trained coach and educational program in my city and slowly learned to see my part in the mess and began, by God's grace and much effort, to modify the situation. I attended clinical conferences on Bowen theory in Houston and Washington, DC, read Bowen's *Family Therapy in Clinical Practice*, studied books and articles about the theory, kept journals, developed a family diagram, engaged research on my own family, visited the Bowen Center in Georgetown, watched many hours of Bowen on video, and met regularly with a coach. Bowen's understanding of human behavior began to make more sense to me as I tried to engage it in my life.

The move from applying the theory in my own family to applying it in the congregation I served was a natural one. What I was learning was shaping my way of doing pastoral work. Eventually, I offered these ideas to others in a pastoral training program in Houston called LeadersEdge. A collaborative project with colleagues Jim Herrington and Trisha Taylor resulted in a book dealing with BFST: *The Leader's Journey*, in which we encourage congregational leaders to seek personal transformation as they work at leading change in their churches.[2]

My own attempts to understand and apply BFST now span two decades. I have had opportunities to present my thinking before both clergy and academic biblical scholars, as well as therapists and scientists who are interested in the theory. Through this exchange, my ideas about the theory have been questioned, expanded, modified, and enriched.

The work of writing this book is really an attempt to clarify my own thinking about BFST and the work of ministry. I intend the book itself to fill a gap I perceive in the literature. Most books for clergy have focused on understanding congregational systems from the perspective of leadership. However, I have discovered that when one begins to use this theory to think through the work of ministry, it affects everything we do: from strategic planning to bereavement visits to preparing next week's sermon. BFST can help us better understand spiritual formation and may even offer insights into our reading of the Bible. This book provides clergy with a more comprehensive connection between BFST and the work we do each week.

The book comprises three parts. The first part, "Orienting the Map," introduces BFST as a tool for ministry, surveys the role it has come to play in clergy training over the past thirty years, and projects its usefulness in the future. I describe the theory in enough detail in chapter 2 to introduce a newcomer or to refresh the memories of those who may not have thought about it much since a seminary class. The chapters in part 2, "A Map for Practical Theology," apply systems thinking to the central aspects of pastoral ministry: leadership, proclamation, pastoral care, spiritual formation, and the life of the community of faith. Part 3, "A Map for Reading Scripture," addresses the possibility of employing BFST as a tool to provide a fresh perspective on biblical texts. After outlining the challenge of applying a psychological theory to biblical texts, I explore the stories of the patriarchs, the life of Jesus, and the teachings of Paul from a natural systems perspective.

Appendix A offers an additional biblical case study in the story of King David. Appendix B addresses the question of integrating BFST and Christian theology. In appendix C you will find key terms to know in BFST, and appendix D provides information on BFST training programs in North America. Finally, appendix E contains a thorough bibliography of works related to BFST and congregational life for your further study.

A set of reflection questions follows each chapter. I encourage you to use these questions to consider what the theory says about the territory you are attempting to negotiate, or perhaps about times in your ministry that continue to puzzle you.

Acknowledgments

Although a book may bear the name of one author, it is seldom the work of a single mind. I am grateful for Victoria Harrison's patient guidance, shared wisdom, and pointed challenges. She has played the roles of coach, teacher, gadfly, colleague, and friend for many years. The time, energy, and money she has personally invested in coaching and in developing educational programs through the Center for the Study of Natural Systems and the Family in Houston has affected the lives of many families over time, including my own. I am especially grateful for her interest in the issues faced by clergy, both in their families and in their congregations.

I have also learned much from others associated with the Bowen Center in workshops, clinical conferences, and conversations. Randall Frost, Roberta Gilbert, Michael Kerr, Anne McKnight, Dan Papero, Louise Rauseo, as well as many fellow students of theory along the way have enriched my understanding of both theory and life. The works of writers and thinkers such as Edwin Friedman, Israel Galindo, Margaret Marcuson, Ronald Richardson, and Peter Steinke have been a help. I appreciate their contribution to my understanding of this theory.

My own students at the George W. Truett Theological Seminary and pastoral colleagues in a variety of training settings have taught me with their questions and insights. Katie Long generously applied her pastoral wisdom, her knowledge of BFST, and her skills as an editor to the early versions of this work, making it clearer, more concise, more accurate, and more practical. The errors that remain in my thinking or writing are no fault of any of these good folks—I will take full credit. In addition, I want to thank Baker Publishing Group for their support, advice, and editorial guidance. I am especially grateful to executive acquisitions editor Robert N. Hosack, whose advocacy and confidence made this project possible.

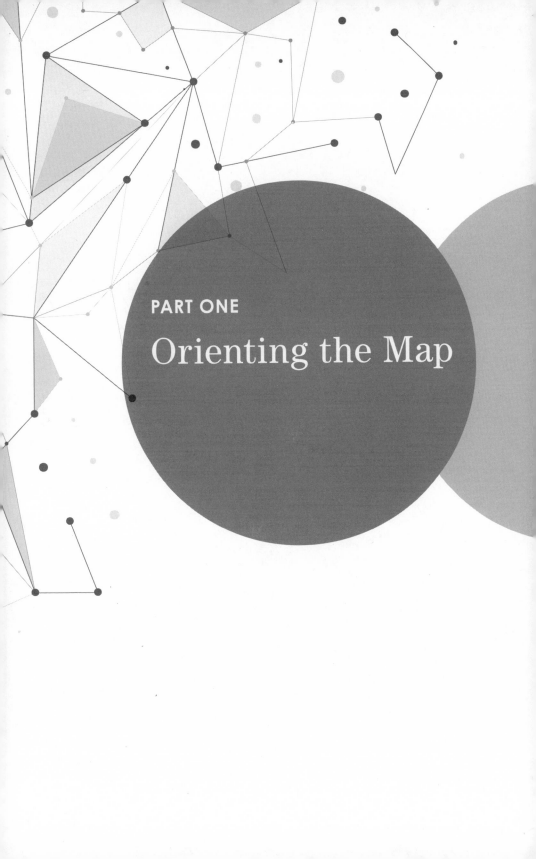

PART ONE

Orienting the Map

1

Always Take a Map

The Value of Bowen Family Systems Theory

Then thought I with myself, who that goeth on Pilgrimage but would
have one of these Maps about him, that he may look when he is at
a stand, which is the way he must take.

—John Bunyan, *The Pilgrim's Progress*

"Always take a map." That was one of a dozen "notes to self" that my
wife and I made after a near-disastrous canoe trip down Arkansas's
Buffalo National River. The Buffalo flows unhindered for 135 miles,
without any bridges, roads, fences, dams, or people around. For a day and a
half, Melinda and I floated in solitude down this picturesque stream, enjoying
the mountains, fishing for smallmouth bass, and absorbing the beauty and
quietness of the surroundings.

Halfway through the second day, the shallow river, about fifty feet wide,
suddenly narrowed to an S-shaped chute about ten feet wide and four feet
deep. The water rushed through in a noisy, powerful current. No one had
warned us of any dangerous places. The canoe rental agency billed this
route as a "float trip" for families, not a whitewater adventure. We could
have taken our canoe out of the water and, with some effort, carried it
around this spot, but after surveying the scene, we agreed to navigate the

chute. The only hazard appeared to be a large stump, about three feet in diameter—the remainder of a tree on the bank of the river. The soil had eroded around it, leaving an enormous root system hanging down. We needed to enter the chute, evade the stump, and negotiate a ninety-degree turn. Then we would be back on a wide and gentle part of the river. It looked like fun.

We entered the chute but found the current so swift that we were unable to steer. We crashed into the roots. The impact knocked Melinda down into the canoe. We were unharmed, but the bow of the canoe had lodged in the roots. As we tried to pry it loose with our paddles, without warning the canoe turned sideways in the fast stream and capsized. Both of us spilled into the rapid flow with a lot of debris. All our possessions floated down the river. The canoe wedged sideways in the root system, held there by the powerful stream. Suddenly a huge piece of the tree broke loose and fell on me, pushing me to the river bottom. I thought I might die.

The current finally pushed the stump off me, and I surfaced. The canoe broke loose from the roots, sending Melinda downstream, pinning her leg against a protruding log. A canoe full of rapidly rushing water held her tight. She thought her leg was breaking. We struggled to move the canoe enough to free her leg. She was uninjured except for bruises. But the strong current still trapped our canoe fast against the log.

Miles from civilization, we did not know where to find help. With excruciating effort, we turned the canoe enough so that the water worked with us, straightening it out. We beached the vessel, emptied it, pounded out a dent created by the log, and gathered our remaining gear.

We were both exhausted from battling the canoe and the current and by the quick drop of the adrenaline rush from our bodies. With no idea how far we were from our end point, we began to paddle what proved to be but a short distance to our take-out spot.

Driving back home to Texas, we brainstormed what we had learned that would help if we attempted such a journey again (which we did, with friends, a couple of years later). We recently came across that scrawled list. At the top was the admonition, "Always take a map."

Anytime we engage unfamiliar territory, a map is a useful companion. Someone has been there before us. We can navigate unfamiliar territory by using their observations and experience. The map is not the territory, but if it is accurate, we have a way to think about the territory and to make our way through it. We can circumvent obstacles. We can avoid dead ends. We may discover shortcuts. The territory is less formidable.

Mapping the Territory of Congregational Ministry

The territory of ministry is often unfamiliar terrain, even to the experienced. More than one minister facing a difficult, unforeseen scenario has lamented, "They didn't teach me about this in seminary." In fact, the territory of congregational life is so diverse and so unpredictable that no education could prepare one for every possibility. Pastors require a map, a way of thinking about that territory, so that we can find our way through it successfully.

We can think of navigating some of the territory of congregational ministry in terms of competencies, skills, or programs. We usually feel prepared to offer these. And the more we practice them, in reflective ways, the more confidently we apply them in the future. We can float down these parts of the river.

The whitewater of congregational life, however, occurs in the rapids of relationships. This truth is not self-evident. Pastors may enter congregational ministry like newlyweds, starry-eyed and convinced that "love is all you need." It is not. What congregational life and marriage have in common is that they both require a lot more than warm feelings, communication techniques, and good intentions when anxiety rises like a flash flood. These relationships, so beautiful and satisfying when the system is calm, can become terrifying in a moment. Clergy may point to the church's governance system, or a building program, or the budget as a problem. That is a bit like blaming the canoe for the rapids. We can navigate these intense relational events successfully in most cases, but seldom will we accomplish this accidentally.

If the territory in ministry that is most unpredictable—and potentially the most dangerous—is human relationships, what map might we rely on? How do we learn to think about our relationships in a way that, despite the uniqueness of each one, allows us to understand ourselves and others?

Bowen Family Systems Theory (BFST) has served as such a map for me for nearly two decades. Honestly, I did not engage the study of Bowen theory because it seemed like a nifty idea or because I wanted to become a more effective pastor or because it was trendy. My family was suffering symptoms of extended stress and anxiety, and I wanted to find a way forward. A strong wave of emotional process threatened what was most dear to me and held us in its current. I was ready to do whatever was necessary to get free. What I learned was lifesaving. Only later did I discover the obvious: what was true about managing myself in the anxiety and emotional process of my own family was also true about managing myself in the emotional current of the congregation I served as pastor. Bowen theory became for me a map, a way of thinking about myself and about how relationships worked. That map, when I managed to follow it, helped me find my way through the twists and turns of each new part of the exciting, treacherous, and rewarding territory of human relationships.

This book is about that map and how we can use it to make our way through those aspects of ministry in which relationships most impinge on us, in which emotional currents bind us, preventing us from moving forward: how we lead our congregations, how we preach, how we offer pastoral care, and how we read and understand Scripture. We may know the skills involved in each of these. But knowing how to paddle a canoe is different from knowing how to steer when it threatens to capsize amid dangerous debris and a strong current. The rapids of relationships can also easily overturn a ministry.

Bowen Theory Meets Congregational Life (1985–2018)

Since the publication of Edwin Friedman's *Generation to Generation: Family Process in Church and Synagogue* in 1985, many pastors have discovered that the eight concepts of BFST help them understand their own lives and families as well as those of their flocks. Friedman, a student of Murray Bowen, demonstrated how the emotional system of the clergy's own nuclear and extended family interconnects with the emotional systems of the families *of* the congregation as well as the family that *is* the congregation. Friedman applied BFST in a way that made sense to many who were engaging congregational life daily.

Clergy training programs in BFST soon spread across North America, beginning in 1990 with Friedman's own organization, the Center for Family Process, in Bethesda, Maryland. Larry Matthews's Leadership in Ministry workshops, Roberta Gilbert's Extraordinary Leadership Seminar, Peter Steinke's Healthy Congregations, and Doug Hester's Ministry Leadership Concepts are a handful of some of the more well-known programs.

Other congregational leaders turned to educational programs not specifically designed for clergy, such as the postgraduate program of the Bowen Center for the Study of the Family in Washington, DC, and others. The Center for the Study of Natural Systems and the Family provided Defining Leaders, a three-year program in the Houston area geared toward ministry leadership. (See appendix D for information on these and other programs across the country.)

Mainline seminaries frequently include at least some exposure to the theory as part of theological education. Clinical pastoral education programs often incorporate it into their training regimen as well. In addition, a modest collection of resources is available, as practitioners and scholars continue to engage the intersection of Bowen's theory and the life and ministry of the clergy. Writers such as Roberta Gilbert, Israel Galindo, Peter Steinke, Ron Richardson, Margaret Marcuson, R. Paul Stevens, Jim Herrington, Trisha Taylor, and myself have addressed aspects of clergy leadership, congregational emotional systems, and the clergyperson's family. For nearly three decades, Bowen's thinking has influenced the way many pastors function in proclamation, pastoral care, and leadership.

So why yet another book on the subject? Other books on BFST and ministry tend to focus on *explaining* the theory in the context of congregational life so that clergy may understand it. Those that focus on application of the theory tend to address the topic of pastoral leadership. The application of BFST to such pastoral tasks as biblical interpretation, spiritual formation, proclamation, and pastoral care is more often ignored. Additionally, the focus on leading in a regressed society (one of Bowen's eight concepts, and in his mind one of the most important) is omitted from most works on BFST and leadership. This book is an effort at a more comprehensive engagement of BFST and congregational life—from issues of leadership, especially during crises and times of societal regression, to issues of pastoral care, spiritual formation, proclamation, and biblical interpretation.

The Popularity of Bowen Theory among Clergy

Why have congregational leaders found this theory so attractive? I have no scientific survey of clergy responses to that question. However, based on observations from my own engagement with the theory as a pastor and from working with scores of students and colleagues in classes and workshops, I offer the following:

1. Thanks to the programs and resources mentioned earlier, the theory is *readily available* to clergy in forms directly applicable to their work.
2. The theory is *understandable*. Pastors can learn and practice these ideas.
3. The theory is *compatible* with the biblical perspectives and theological categories held by mainline religious traditions.
4. The theory *helps clergy focus on self*, rather than on others, whom they cannot control.
5. The theory provides ways for clergy to think about a variety of issues in the congregation, *without having to develop separate expertise* in counseling, management, conflict resolution, or other fields.

6. Clergy daily encounter family and congregational issues that are *relational*. Bowen theory applies directly to questions we face.
7. Clergy find that the theory provides a way of thinking about life in congregations and families that makes a *practical difference*.

During this same period (1985–2018), clergy of every tradition have witnessed seismic changes in congregations and society. Technological, geopolitical, environmental, moral/ethical, and economic issues have rocked the world, and their consequences have not spared the church. Bowen's theory provides clergy a map for negotiating the terrain of social change as well. Thoughtful practitioners have engaged the theory to manage themselves amid anxiety generated in society, families, and congregations. Leadership in anxious times requires a way of thinking about both the world and oneself, and Bowen theory has offered a way forward. That Friedman's offering of the theory to fellow congregational leaders coincided with the onslaught of such challenging times may have been a major factor in making the theory so attractive.

Bowen Theory, Congregations, and the Future

What of the future? Given scenarios of a surging world population, the growth of megacities, and the potential ecological crises we will face in the next forty years, how important might Bowen theory be for pastoral leaders in the mid-twenty-first century? The changes and challenges that lie before us appear to tower over those we have faced previously. What will the world of 2050 look like? To what will congregations and their leaders need to adapt?

The technology that will be part of the world forty years from now is unimaginable. Who can look ahead accurately when knowledge is doubling every year and a half to five years, depending on which field is considered and whom you believe? Although my imagination will not take me there, I know these technological changes will be a factor to which pastors will be constantly adapting.

Some aspects of the future are more predictable, such as demographics and ecology. More than 7.5 billion people occupy our world today, nearly twice as many as when I graduated from seminary in 1976. By 2050, that figure will likely reach 9.8 billion.[1] The current US population of 310 million will swell to 438 million by 2050, twice as many as when I received my seminary degree.[2] Where will most of them live, these 9–10 billion people worldwide, 438 million of them in the US? In cities. In huge, overcrowded cities. In 1900, only 150 million people in the world lived in cities. In 2007, for the first time, the world had more urban people than rural, with more than 3 billion. In 2050, more than 6 billion people, 7 out of 10 on the planet, will live in huge cities under unimaginably crowded conditions. The number of cities of more than a million has exploded over the past century, from a mere dozen in 1900 to 83 in 1950 to more than 400 today. Eighteen megacities now have populations over 10 million.[3]

The challenges that go with urban crowding are well known: crime, disease, quality of life, transportation, food supply, adequate water, waste management, energy demands, and other social problems. These will grow exponentially. Most clergy in 2050 will minister in large, densely populated, urban settings.

Urban property will be scarce and therefore expensive. Models of church life dependent on large pieces of real estate and massive buildings likely will be unsustainable. How long before an increasingly secular culture decides that churches duly owe local and state governments the potential tax revenue from church property? Churches may no longer get a free ride. Owning property and facilities may become too burdensome for many congregations.

Environmental concerns add to the issues of population growth. Lack of adequate clean water, an increasingly serious problem worldwide, will become more so with the growth of cities. Food supply systems that depend on cheap oil leave large cities vulnerable. Global climate change remains a wild card for coastal cities. With up to 70 percent of the world crowded into cities, living in a world surrounded by asphalt, concrete, and glass, people will increasingly experience alienation from creation and from each other.

At the same time, rural populations will have their own challenges, as will their pastors and congregations. The "unsettling of America" that began in the postwar era began a move from the countryside to the cities that has now left small towns and rural areas depleted of economic resources, population, and a future.[4] Well-educated, full-time clergy are less and less an option for these churches. Anxiety rises in the face of fears for survival, and yet these struggling and likely apprehensive congregations are often the first stop for a young seminary student starting out in ministry. The pastor's survival may depend more on the ability to understand emotional systems than on skilled exegesis or preaching.

These parts of the future are predictable. Those who lead congregations will require a way of thinking that helps them keep their heads amid the swirl of reactivity, anxiety, and fear such changes inevitably generate. BFST can be a valuable and useful map for congregational ministry and leadership in a world growing progressively more anxious.

An applied knowledge of Bowen theory will be an asset for clergy, first, because the theory describes "human" behavior that remains valid across time and cultures. Approaches to ministry and leadership arise and disappear quickly in an anxious, often leaderless environment such as ours. The pressure to develop and employ quick, relatively painless "fixes" generates leadership snake oil by the trainload, and congregational leaders, like other anxious men and women, often eagerly pay for a bottle of the latest brew. The sheer multiplicity of "solutions" bears witness to their ineffectiveness. If there were a single dependable method to fix the problems, we would have adopted it long ago. We are often surprised when a strategy that appeared to work in one place does not seem to fit in ours. Or the approach we once employed effectively has become anemic, limp, and useless. To wait anxiously and dependently for the next new approach in the leadership market leaves congregational ministers without a way to anticipate the future, think their way into it, or learn their way through it. Dependence on leadership gurus leaves us vulnerable.

Bowen theory is not a leadership theory per se. Bowen attempted to study and describe human behavior scientifically and so did not limit his thinking to a current philosophical theory or perspective. We can illustrate his eight concepts from the study of ancient texts and stories as well as from contemporary human experience across cultures. Unlimited by time or culture, BFST has the potential to be one of the few aspects of clergy training that can accompany us into the future of the church and society. Church structures and practices certainly will change in the next forty years. Human reactivity and emotional processes will not. BFST will continue to offer accurate ways to understand ourselves despite radical contextual changes.

Second, as anxiety rises, Bowen theory provides a way of thinking about and understanding that anxiety. Congregations with high-functioning leaders stand a better chance of thriving despite the anxious environment.

Bowen himself used the term "societal regression" to anticipate the times in which we live, marked by overpopulation and the threats it creates. In a 1974 lecture he said, "I believe man is moving into crises of unparalleled proportions, that the crises will be different than those he has faced before, that they will come with increasing frequency for several decades, that he will go as far as he can in dealing symptomatically with each crisis, and that a final major crisis will come as soon as the middle of next century. The type of man who survives that will be one who can live in better harmony with nature." He continued: "This prediction is based on knowledge about the nature of man as an instinctual being, and on stretching existing thinking as far as it can go. There are many questions about what man can do about his environmental crisis. The thesis here is that he might modify his future course if he can gain some control over his reaction to anxiety and his 'instinctual' emotional reactiveness, and begin taking constructive action based on his fund of knowledge and on logical thinking."[5] Bowen theory offers a way of thinking about the crisis itself, about the anxiety it generates, and about managing oneself as a leader in such regressive times.

Third, Bowen theory provides a way of thinking about the future that will help discerning men and women respond to and adapt to the changes around them rather than merely reacting instinctively. Leadership is inherently about the future. Leaders are "midwives" helping others give birth to their future. Congregations that do well through the next forty years, that learn to function at a high level amid changes and challenges, who manage to make it through these times with minimal destructive conflict or simple disintegration, will be those who can respond to their environment rather than react. These congregations will require leaders who can help them understand their unique calling, draw on their faith traditions, think and pray together about their future, hold on to their values, and remain faithful to their identity. If leaders are learning to work on themselves in these areas, to take responsibility for self, and to manage their own reactivity, they will be a powerful asset to these churches. Pastors who know their own values and faith, those who can think and pray through their challenges, will be in a better position to assist congregations in giving birth to the future.

Conclusion

The most perilous places in ministry lie in the realm of relationships. Clergy who "always take a map" will have an advantage in church budget meetings when finances are down, in conversations with parishioners about their life struggles, in the pulpit when a prophetic word is called for, in congregational planning sessions when the future is unclear, in the immediate aftermath of an unforeseen crisis, and in many other treacherous features of the terrain of congregational life. BFST can help us navigate successfully through this territory. Remember: "Always take a map."

●— Questions for Reflection

1. What is currently serving as your "map" for negotiating the important relationships in your life? What maps have you absorbed from family or others along the way? What thoughtful theoretical perspective have you used?

2. What has been the most intense experience of "whitewater" in your own relationships, either in your marriage, your family, or your congregation? What was it like to be caught up in the current? How did you find your way out? What do you wish you knew then that you know now?

3. What are your biggest concerns about the future of congregational ministry that you anticipate facing as a pastoral leader?

2

Reading the Map

An Overview of Bowen Family Systems Theory

Those who explore an unknown world are travelers without a map: the map is the result of the exploration. The position of their destination is not known to them, and the direct path that leads to it is not yet made.

—Hideki Yukawa, Japanese theoretical physicist

The first time I opened a US Geological Survey topographical map, its contour lines, shading, and multitude of cryptic symbols, so different from the highway maps of Texas I had studied as a child, bewildered me. The map showed everything—buildings, radio towers, streams, ponds, changes in the terrain—not just the main roads. If I could decipher the meanings of all those lines, I could use such a map to walk straight across the countryside. But learning to read the map required some effort.

Encountering Murray Bowen's distinctive way of thinking about human behavior is like that. Systems thinking is not the way we have come to understand ourselves and others. Our linear thinking has us looking for cause and effect, for others to blame for the problems in our relationships. We hope to diagnose the "patient" in our families or congregations. Systems thinking is not our ordinary perspective. Trying to see familiar things in a different way is a challenge. But the effort is worth it.

You may have encountered Bowen Family Systems Theory (BFST) in your seminary training or as part of a unit of clinical pastoral education (CPE). Perhaps you stumbled on a book that included the theory or, like me, had a friend recommend one to you. On the other hand, this may be your first encounter with this approach. Whether it has been a while since you have spent time with the theory or this is your first venture into it, this chapter can acquaint you with this map before moving into the territory. Like the many symbols and lines on the topographical map, BFST has a set of terms and concepts that require some proficiency before we can usefully employ them. They are few, and they are not complex, but they are important to grasp.

Development of Bowen Family Systems Theory

To describe Bowen's thinking as a "theory" is to make a claim about it. Murray Bowen set out to develop a *scientific theory* of human behavior.[1] Though we commonly use the word "theory" to mean a guess, a mere conjecture, the term in science is more precise. It is "a set of statements or principles devised to explain a group of facts or phenomena, especially one that has been repeatedly tested or is widely accepted and can be used to make predictions about natural phenomena."[2] Israel Galindo describes the nature of theories:

- Theories describe phenomena as we perceive them. (They are descriptive, not prescriptive.)
- Theories are grounded in a discipline (in the case of BFST, clinical psychology).
- Theories are universally applicable to the focus of their concern (for BFST, all "relationship systems" regardless of their context).
- Theories are open to being disproved.[3]

To speak of Bowen Family Systems *Theory* is to assert that these concepts are the result of such a process of scientific inquiry.

Bowen developed the eight interlocking concepts of BFST over a period of approximately twenty-five years, as he worked with families in the Menninger Clinic in Kansas (1946–54), the National Institute for Mental Health (1954–59), and the Georgetown University Medical Center (1960–90). They are the product of years of observation and reflection, not the result of deductive conclusions. Consequently, Bowen claimed that these concepts described *human* behavior, rooted deeply in our biological connection with all living beings over many millennia. He believed that these concepts transcend both time and human cultures.[4]

Through his observations, Bowen began to see in a new way how human beings functioned in relationship to one another. He noticed, for example, that the symptoms of hospitalized people diagnosed with serious mental illness varied in response to their family members' presence and behavior with them. These variations followed set and predictable patterns Bowen could observe and eventually predict. He discerned the same patterns in less extreme forms in families he was seeing in his clinical practice. Bowen came to understand that families function as "emotional systems," not simply as assemblies of individuals, and the emotional system became the focus of his work with them.

What Is an Emotional System?

Understanding a family or a congregation as an emotional system is unfamiliar territory for most of us. We attend to individuals and their behaviors, diagnosing them, labeling them, and trying to figure out ways of working with or around them. When human beings work or live together, an emotional system forms. This means that we unconsciously monitor those around us and automatically react or respond without thinking, as anxiety makes its way around the system.

Consider, for example, a family with a father, a mother, two sons, and a daughter. Suppose Dad comes home from a good day at work. Things have gone his way all day. He left early, avoiding the evening traffic. When he arrives, the boys are shooting basketball in the driveway. Their sister is working on her homework and texting her friends. He makes a cup of coffee, finds the newspaper, and sits in the living room to relax.

Mom's day has not been so pleasant. As a high school counselor, she has faced angry parents, disrespectful students, and a demanding principal. Extra paperwork kept her at her desk longer than usual, and traffic from an accident on the freeway delayed her trip home. When she pulls into the driveway, she is frazzled. She walks to the back door without speaking to her sons. When she enters the house, both her husband and her daughter look up, but she does not make eye contact. Mom walks to the kitchen and sees that no one has begun dinner preparation. She rattles pots and pans and closes the pantry door with more force than necessary. The boys come inside and get into an argument. Dad takes his reading to the study. The daughter puts down her homework and instinctively moves to the kitchen to calm her mother by helping.

Everyone has a part to play in this drama, and they step into their roles without a thought. This is an emotional system at work. Each one is monitoring the others. Who is depending on me? On whom am I depending? Who is expecting something from me? What am I expecting from others? Are they meeting my expectations? Who is in distress? Are others aware of my distress? Whose attention am I seeking? Who is looking for my attention? Below the level of awareness, our emotional capacities are attending to and reacting to all the others in the system all the time.

Congregations form emotional systems as well, perhaps not as formidable as our nuclear families, yet intense at times. Friedman writes: "All clergymen and clergywomen, irrespective of faith, are simultaneously involved in three distinct families, whose emotional forces interlock: the families within the congregation, our congregations, and our own. Because the emotional process in these systems is identical, unresolved issues in any one of them can produce symptoms in the others, and an increased understanding of any one creates more effective functioning in all three."[5]

A systems perspective offers both good and bad news. The bad news is that if anything chronic is occurring in a system in which I participate, I play some part in keeping the symptom in place. The bad news is that I cannot place blame on others. The good news is that if anything chronic is occurring in a system in which I participate, I can make changes in the part I play that will have some impact on the system. I am not simply a victim of others' behaviors.

Two Invisible Forces

Bowen postulated that two forces are constantly at work in an emotional system. Like gravity, these invisible forces reveal themselves to us by their effects. He called these the "togetherness force" and the "individuality force."[6] They represent the pressure we experience in relationships to be "we" and the pressure we experience to be "me." Each person knows the tug of these forces. During times when anxiety is high in an emotional system, we feel the togetherness force more strongly. The system pulls its members into a common center to conform to common thinking, to agree to common practices, to speak a common language, even if that means compromising principles or values espoused by individuals. This pressure can be unbearably strong at times. The togetherness force is not necessarily a bad thing. When the threat is real, it can be a means of survival. The problem with the togetherness force is that it also operates when the threat is imaginary or exaggerated, inhibiting clear thinking by individuals and thus robbing the emotional system of important resources.

People experience the individuality force as the internal pressure to be a self despite the group's demands. Michael Kerr describes it as "a biologically rooted life force (more basic than being just a function of the brain) that propels an organism to follow its own directive, to be an independent and distinct entity."[7] These two counterbalancing forces operate unseen in every emotional system with powerful effect.

Anxiety and Reactivity

"Anxiety" is an important term in BFST. It represents the automatic biological reaction to threat that is hardwired into our brains. Feelings may or may not accompany the anxiety. Our experience of anxiety sometimes lies outside the realm of our awareness, showing up in such physiological responses as sweaty palms, lowered skin temperature, or changes in breathing, heart rate, or blood pressure. We may not even perceive the changes taking place in our bodies during such moments, but they are present. Anxiety is not the same thing as "feeling nervous." It is a God-given, automatic response to a perceived threat that produces a series of chemical effects in the body.[8]

Bowen used the term "emotional reactivity" nearly synonymously with anxiety. Emotional reactivity is our capacity to react to threats without thinking. It can save both time and lives. When under immediate threat, we may not have time to take out a yellow legal pad, draw two columns, and thoughtfully consider the pros and cons of possible responses. Rather, we automatically respond with immediate action. This is emotional reactivity.

But not all reactivity or anxiety is the same. What Bowen called "acute anxiety" is the type just described. It is our automatic reaction to a threat that is both real and time-limited. For example, when driving down the interstate highway at seventy-five miles an hour (yes, that is legal in Texas), you depend on rapid response times. You are surrounded by the potential threat of eighteen-wheelers whose drivers cannot see you in their mirrors. New drivers may be nervously making their way down the road at slow speeds. Intoxicated drivers may be unable to perceive their environment properly. Your car or someone else's could malfunction, owing to an unseen mechanical problem. These are just a few of the possible dangers—so it makes sense that any drive produces some anxiety.

If a driver suddenly swerves in front of you, your emotional reactivity will engage. You will instantly monitor the vehicles around you, select the best route to avoid a collision, and apply appropriate pressure on the brakes to try to protect yourself and those with you. In that split second, a chain of chemical reactions takes place in your body. Blood flow moves from the internal parts of your body, such as the digestive tract, to the large muscles. You develop temporary tunnel vision, focused clearly on the threat before you. Heart rate and breathing change. In those few seconds your brain files this experience away so that if something like it occurs again, you will be able to respond even more quickly.

Depending on how close the call was, you may need to pull over at the next exit to calm down. But you will calm down as the threat passes. Gradually your chemical state will return to a more nominal condition. That is the experience of *acute anxiety*.

Chronic anxiety, on the other hand, is the response to a threat that is either imagined or exaggerated. It is not time-limited. We experience the same chemical changes in our bodies, but they do not revert quickly to a more normal level. Rather, we live with those chemicals in our bloodstream constantly and with the consequences they bring.[9] Our brains do not know, at the level of reactivity, the difference between a real threat and an imagined one, and so they respond as programmed.

The same physiological changes occur in our bodies in response to our emotional reactivity to people in our family or our congregation. An anxious congregant can easily pass that anxiety on to the pastor, who reacts automatically, experiencing the chemical changes that accompany the threat response. The congregant notices the pastor's anxiety, often unconsciously, and will likely react by becoming even more anxious. The cycle can continue back and forth, resulting in a variety of symptoms in the relationship. Anxiety is contagious. The pastor can easily catch the anxiety and take it home, spreading it among family members. All this usually happens below the level of our awareness.

Two Variables in an Emotional System

All of us live with some level of chronic anxiety all the time. As Bowen observed how emotional systems varied in their manifestation of symptoms and in their ability to function in times of higher anxiety, he identified two variables: the level of emotional maturity (or differentiation of self) and the level of anxiety. You might think of these variables in terms of the capacity and content of a cup. An eight-ounce cup can contain only eight ounces of coffee before it spills over the edge. A sixteen-ounce cup can easily handle several ounces more without a mess. Systems with more emotionally mature members (capacity) can manage more anxiety (content) before producing

a symptom. Less emotionally mature members of the system are more vulnerable to symptoms when anxiety rises. Individuals and families vary in
our capacity to handle the anxiety that arises from time to time. However,
given enough anxiety, even a more emotionally mature person can become
symptomatic.

Anxiety might show itself in physical symptoms (cancers, allergies, etc.).
It could manifest itself in emotional symptoms such as depression or manic
episodes or in such social symptoms as alcoholism, drug addiction, or criminal
behavior. Although we commonly understand symptoms as belonging to the
individual who becomes symptomatic, Bowen came to see them as symptoms
of the anxiety present in the emotional system.[10]

Key Concepts of Bowen Family Systems Theory

During twenty-five years of observations, Bowen produced a theory with eight
interlocking concepts.[11] (Late in life he proposed a ninth concept but never
fully developed it.) To speak of these concepts as "interlocking" means that
they do not stand alone. We require each of them to understand the others
fully.[12] We could start with any of the concepts and then move to the others,
but I will present them in the order in which he developed them. This is also
the order in which he presents them in his writings.

Concept 1: Emotional Triangles

When any two parts of a system become uncomfortable with one another,
they will "triangle in" or focus on and draw in a third person or group as
a way of stabilizing their relationship with each other.[13] Bowen noticed this
first in the relationships among his patients and other family members. Soon
it was clear that this is a typical human response to increased anxiety in a
relationship. Emotional triangles appear around us constantly. One parent,
following a conflict with a teenager, declares: "Wait till your mother (or father)
gets home!" Parishioners corner their new pastor to lobby for the pastor's
support on an issue for which they have unsuccessfully advocated for years.
People take sides about the pastor's orthodoxy following Sunday's sermon.
In Luke 10:40, Martha bursts from the kitchen and demands that Jesus tell
Mary to help her.

Emotional triangles are neither good nor evil—they just are. They are part
of human behavior. However, getting caught in one, taking sides on an issue
between two other people, can leave the triangled person bearing the stress
that more appropriately belongs to the other two. Bowen called triangles

the "molecules of the emotional system." They are the building blocks of a system. Learning to observe them and developing the capacity to avoid being ensnared in them is a challenge.[14]

Bowen used the term "detriangling" to describe the effort to avoid becoming involved in the emotional process and anxiety of two others. The goal in detriangling is to remain in good emotional contact with each of the others without taking sides on the issue between them. It is the attempt to control "one's own automatic emotional participation in the emotional process."[15]

Concept 2: The Scale of Differentiation

Bowen observed that some individuals do better than others when anxiety rises. Some seem to be more fused with others and more reactive to their environment and to people around them. Others appear to remain more thoughtful in the presence of others' anxiety. Families differ in this respect. And congregations and other organizations reflect the same variability. How can we account for that?

Bowen called this capacity for a person to balance emotion and intellect "differentiation of self" or "emotional maturity."[16] He placed individuals on a hypothetical scale ranging from 0 to 100. Zero would represent people who are entirely reactive to the world around them. They would possess no ability to think for themselves. They would completely fuse with another in each of their important relationships. Such a person would scarcely be able to survive. Bowen did not imagine that anyone existed at this level.

At the other end of his hypothetical scale would be perfect individuals, whose ability to stay connected to important others in their lives would include the capacity always to think for themselves and act on their own principles. Their emotional and intellectual capacities would both function fully. Bowen did not think that anyone achieved this level of differentiation either.

Most people, he believed, would fall below 50 on his scale. This means that more than half the time even the more emotionally mature among us succumb to our reactivity to one another rather than engaging thoughtful responses. A few individuals, he claimed, might achieve a level as high as 75, but these would be rare.

Although he postulated this scale of differentiation of self, he did not believe that any test could ascertain a person's level of emotional maturity.[17] Such an assessment would require a broad knowledge of an individual's life and relationships over time. Bowen did, however, attempt to describe what life and relationships would be like for people in the four quartiles of the scale (0–25, 25–50, 50–75, and 75–100).[18]

Bowen believed that we emerge into adulthood with a given level of differentiation, derived from our family of origin. In our families we have learned such things as how threatening the world is, how free we are to take risks, how much we depend on others for our well-being, and how much they depend on us. Typically, our level of differentiation will be about the same as that of our parents. When we have been the anxious focus of our parents (see "Concept 5: Family Projection Process"), we might step out into the world with a slightly lower level. If another in our family has absorbed that focus, we might be just a bit higher on the scale. According to Bowen, this level remains unchanged throughout our lives unless we make serious, deliberate, and sustained efforts to improve it.

Regardless, if we choose to marry, we will seek a spouse who is at the same basic level of differentiation as we are.[19] We would experience someone lower on the scale as "too needy" for us. Someone higher would see us that way, and we might view them as cold or distant. We will look for someone willing to invest as much in the fusion of our lives together as we are. For example, someone at a level of 35 on Bowen's scale would need to invest about 65 percent of self in the relationship and would expect the other to reciprocate.[20] A "perfect" marriage, in Bowen's thinking, would be two people at 100 on the scale. Both people would (1) be willing and able to talk about any subject whatsoever without becoming reactive to the other; (2) treat the other as an equal in every way, with neither dominating the marriage with their own agenda; and (3) have the capacity to emotionally connect to the other without taking on the partner's anxiety. Such marriages do not exist.[21]

In chapter 7 we will consider the relationship between differentiation and spiritual formation. This will raise questions about how we might intentionally change our level of differentiation over time. In chapter 11 we will look at the well-differentiated life that Jesus lived as one who is fully human.

Concept 3: Family Emotional Process

Working with families and individuals in his practice, Murray Bowen observed that human beings consistently exhibit only a handful of basic emotional responses to increased anxiety. When we feel stressed, anxious, or threatened, we automatically revert to reactions that thousands of years of experience have deeply embedded in our brains. Our repertoire is small: we fight, we flee, we overfunction or underfunction, or we engage emotional triangles. That is it. Bowen called this concept in his theory "the family emotional process" or the "nuclear family emotional system."[22]

Conflict is one automatic response. When anxiety rises, people sometimes become "edgy." They get "a chip on their shoulder." They seem to want to pick a fight. They insist on their own way and attack those who differ from them. Conflict is usually messy, often noisy, and sometimes frightening. When it emerges in the face of rising anxiety in a family or other emotional unit, its very presence increases the anxiety. So things can quickly begin to spiral out of control. To control this behavior, family counselors and organizational consultants often attempt "conflict management." However, since anxiety drives conflict, even if we suppress the conflict around the current issue, another issue will soon arise to take its place. Or the anxiety will manifest itself with one of the other responses.

Sometimes people respond to rising anxiety by fleeing. Bowen called this reaction "distancing." Although this behavior is quieter, it is an anxious response and generates further anxiety as well. People withdraw from relationships, responsibilities, and communication. Conversations become superficial. People avoid topics that might produce conflict. People "walk on eggshells" to avoid upsetting others. Although emotional systems characterized by distance may appear harmonious, they are anxious systems too.

Bowen terms a third automatic response to rising anxiety "reciprocal functioning" or "overfunctioning/underfunctioning." Someone in the system may take over, doing for others what they can do for themselves, deciding for others, thinking for others, telling others what and how to think. They become overly responsible. This overfunctioning is always reciprocated by other people who abdicate their responsibility, becoming needier, refusing to think or do for themselves, depending on the overfunctioner to fill in for them. Overfunctioners may complain about underfunctioners, but they keep overfunctioning. Underfunctioners may agree that they are the problem, but they remain irresponsible.

Underfunctioning can take the form of physical, emotional, or social symptoms. Alcoholism is an example. The alcoholic underfunctions, missing work, losing jobs, wounding relationships. Nevertheless, a spouse or parent may call the alcoholic's boss to make excuses, take on an extra job, or do without necessities. Both parties may agree that the problem is the alcoholic, but both play a part in maintaining the anxious system. Overfunctioners may view themselves as sacrificial and loving, but they play a part in allowing the underfunctioner to persist in underfunctioning.

The fourth potential reaction to anxiety, "projection," is a form of the emotional triangles mentioned earlier. When reactivity rises, a family might focus its worried attention on a child, for example, who then becomes symptomatic. The anxious focus on the child keeps the parents from having to face the anxiety in their own relationship, as the child is "triangled in." The parents keep their attention on the child, and the child pays the price. Again, the child's symptoms may be physical, emotional, social, or some combination. The emergence of the symptom ensures the parents' continued attention and anxiety.

In a congregation, worried focus may show up in other ways. As the church's financial support diminishes, for example, people may blame the pastor or the youth ministry. In this way, the system shifts its anxiety to one of its members. They seem surprised when the person they have focused on develops a symptom—an illness (physical), absconding with funds (social), or burnout in ministry (emotional).

Bowen observed that when systems did not "specialize" in one or another of the four responses (sometimes they fought, sometimes they grew distant, etc.), they seemed to do better over time. When a family resorted to one response to the exclusion of others, however, the reactions tended to be much more intense. Conflict could escalate to violence, distancing could end in divorce or cutoff, or the underfunctioning could be paralyzing. The projection could result in devastating symptoms in the one on whom the system focused its anxiety.

Note that these four emotional processes are automatic. We have a choice in the matter, but left to ourselves, we will exhibit one or more of them when anxiety rises. The higher the level of differentiation of self, the more flexible the system. When anxiety rises, it is possible for those in the system to look thoughtfully for more appropriate responses rather than automatically yielding to these reactive modes.

Concept 4: Multigenerational Transmission Process

The "multigenerational transmission process" helps to explain how it is that we come by our emotional responses and our level of differentiation.[23]

Bowen noted that each nuclear family is the product of sixty-four nuclear families in the five generations that precede it. Over nine generations, more than one thousand nuclear families play a part.[24] More passes between these generations than DNA. Finding their way through the family are beliefs and attitudes—such as ideas about sex and reproduction, about death and dying, about money and work, about the dominance of men or women, and about ways of reacting when anxiety rises. Addictions seem to pop up in certain families generation after generation, as does susceptibility to diseases such as cancer or cardiovascular disease.[25] Families pass on their strengths as well as their weaknesses.

The multigenerational transmission process accounts for the reality that within the same family, over generations, some branches of the family seem to function better than others. Marriages are more stable, couples reproduce without difficulty, individuals function successfully in life (acquiring an education, for example, or making contributions through their work or gifts), and people remain relatively healthy. Other branches, however, seem to face more than their share of life's problems. How might we understand that?

As Bowen described the process, each child leaves home slightly more or slightly less well-differentiated than the parents. If that child marries, the spouse will be someone at the same level of emotional maturity. If the couple has children, those children will leave home slightly more or slightly less emotionally mature than their parents and marry people at their same level of differentiation. Over generations, these differences magnify, producing nuclear families with considerably different levels of differentiation of self, and consequently families that function in life at very different levels.

We can understand the multigenerational transmission process best in our own extended families by developing a family diagram of at least five generations.[26] The research and thought that goes into producing a detailed family diagram can lead to insights about how your own family has contributed both strengths and vulnerabilities to your life, giving you opportunities to think about what alternatives might be available to you as you face life's challenges. "Family trees," as Friedman puts it, "are always trees of knowledge and often they are also trees of life."[27]

Concept 5: Family Projection Process

Have you ever wondered how two children from the same parents, same environment, same gene pool, can turn out so differently? How is it that one offspring may function well in life and another not so well? "Family projection process" helps clarify this.

We encountered this concept when we learned about the family emotional process. When anxiety arises, one of the automatic human responses—besides conflict, distance, overfunctioning, and underfunctioning—is projection. The members of the emotional system, under stress, often focus their attention on one member of the system, or one part of the system, projecting their anxiety, fear, or blame onto that member.

Families typically direct this projection toward a child in the form of an anxious or worried focus.[28] Children within a nuclear family are not usually subject to equal amounts of this focus. For one reason or another, one child seems to be "selected," though not consciously, to receive this attention.

Perhaps the child's gestation or birth was difficult for the mother. Perhaps the child was born with a physical condition. Perhaps the family was dealing with an unusual level of anxiety, such as the loss of a grandparent, at the time the child was born. Perhaps previous generations struggled with the "first son" or "second daughter," and unconsciously this birth portended such difficulties. The conditions may vary, but in one way or another, children may attract this special attention.

Depending on how strong the focus is and how high the level of chronic anxiety in the family, to some degree the process is likely to impair the child in life. The child learns to depend on the parents for certain things rather than learning to take responsibility for self. The child takes this dependence out into life in a lower level of differentiation of self than either of the parents or of siblings who were spared such focus.

The consequence of the family projection process is that two children from the same family may have very different trajectories in life. The child who received extra focus may demonstrate more emotional, social, or physical symptoms along the way or face far more difficulties in such life tasks as maintaining jobs or entering and sustaining relationships. Meanwhile, a brother or sister on whom there is not so much focus may enter life with a bit more emotional maturity than the siblings or parents.

Concept 6: Sibling Position

This concept describes the uniqueness of each child in a family. Bowen adapted the concept of "sibling position" in whole from the work of Walter Toman, who identified ten basic types of sibling relationships in a "family constellation."[29] He described how one's position in the birth order of a family affects such aspects of life as how we learn to relate to those of our same sex, to the opposite sex, to those who have more power, and to those over whom we have power or authority. The birth order of spouses is important to understanding the way marriages function. While an "older brother of sisters" married to a "younger sister of brothers" is likely to have fewer gender or power conflicts, the union of two firstborns may face those issues regularly.

Bowen concluded that "all things being equal," one's sibling position (and that of one's spouse) helped him understand many aspects of a nuclear family's behavior.[30] "All things being equal" means that birth order is not deterministic. Other variables may enter the equation, such as levels of emotional maturity or other circumstances or patterns in the family that might trump the impact of birth order. Relationships do not have to run on automatic all the time. As people become aware of some of these facets of their family or of themselves, they can learn to make more thoughtful choices.

Concept 7: Emotional Cutoff

The concept of "emotional cutoff" developed out of Bowen's observation that many families experience an extreme version of the emotional process earlier identified as "distance." He called this intense expression of distancing "emotional cutoff," or sometimes simply "cutoff,"[31] and described it primarily as a reaction that occurs between generations (as children cut off from parents). A physical relocation can accomplish cutoff, whether by a move across town or across the country. But one can cut off emotionally and continue to live in the same house or neighborhood as one's parents. Cutoff does not necessarily follow a family feud (although it may). It can develop gradually as members of one generation seek to manage their anxiety by quietly withdrawing from the previous ones.

Cutoff means that one lives without knowledge of and relationship with the previous generations of one's family. A variety of consequences often accompany the experience of cutoff. Families that maintain good contact with the previous generations, even if living at a great distance, tend to have access to more resources, both physical and emotional, as they make their way through the challenges of life, while those who cut themselves off often struggle on their own. They may find it easier than others to simply walk away from relationships in life or to reject relationships with people in their lives who could be important to them. And, Bowen discovered, the cutoff experienced in one generation tends to recur with even greater intensity in succeeding ones.[32]

Maintaining or reestablishing family relationships can be difficult work, but it may be worth the effort. Increasing contact with one's family through visits, phone calls, or email can help. Being present for important family events—weddings, births, funerals, reunions, significant birthdays or anniversaries—can help keep relationships alive. Work on a comprehensive family diagram often reveals the places where emotional cutoff is at work in a family. The fact that one does not know basic facts about some family members may be a giveaway that cutoff is at work.

Concept 8: Societal Emotional Process

Bowen considered "societal emotional process" to be distinctive in his approach to family systems thinking. He also believed it to be "about the least understood concept" in his theory.[33] Bowen postulated that the same emotional processes observable in families were also at work in the larger emotional system of society. Just as a human family could enter a downward spiral of regression, given a high-enough level of anxiety and a low-enough level of emotional maturity, so could a human society. The processes, he contended, were identical.

The anxiety operative in society, Bowen observed, makes its way from the external environment into families and back again to society's institutions by means of triangles. Parents, educators, and the justice system, for example, often become corners of triangles with teenagers who are behaving irresponsibly. The anxiety in the home and the anxiety in society feed each other in a seemingly endless loop of reactivity. Churches and pastors can play their part in this parade of anxiety as well. One pastor reported entering the church office on a Monday morning and noticing the anxiety crackling among her associates. She then realized that it was standardized testing day at the local high school. Some of the staff had children in school, and others were married to teachers or administrators.[34]

Concept 9: The Supernatural

Bowen Family Systems Theory comprises these eight interlocking concepts. Near the end of his life, however, Bowen began to talk about a possible ninth concept, which he called "the supernatural." He recognized a "functional fact" that human beings often embrace some concept of the supernatural as part of their beliefs, and that such beliefs affected their functioning in life. This, he believed, we could study and incorporate into the theory. Bowen himself did not take this idea further but left it to those who followed him to do so.[35]

Conclusion

The basic concepts of BFST are not difficult to learn. We can easily become intellectually acquainted with a few key terms and the eight concepts. The difficulty is in changing the way we see the world through its lens and the effort it takes to work on our own differentiation in the important relationships of our lives—with our parents, spouse, children, parishioners, and friends.

Learning to read a map is one thing. One need only become proficient in deciphering a handful of symbols. But using the map to cross treacherous territory is another issue entirely. That journey involves effort, perseverance, challenge, courage, and overcoming occasional setbacks. Becoming competent in the concepts is necessary.[36] But intellectual acquisition of these ideas is insufficient to produce the kind of life change and effective ministry they can generate. Those results require us to incorporate work on differentiation into our lives. We must learn to lean into our own immaturity. We must develop the capacity to recognize emotional reactivity in ourselves and others. We must practice inserting a pause before automatically reacting to others, so that we can make a thoughtful response instead. We must become curious about our own family over the generations, both nuclear and extended, learning all we can about it. We must learn to be an important member of that family, a person the family can trust, who is "present and accounted for" in anxious times. We will probably need the wisdom and direction of a coach to help us do our best work with this. These and other practices can equip us for more meaningful relationships and for more effective congregational ministry.

●— Questions for Reflection

1. Can you recall a recent experience of anxiety in one of your own emotional systems—your family or your congregation, for example? What got the anxiety going? What kept it going? What reactions do you remember in yourself or others? How did it end?
2. Who in your own extended family do you think of as the most emotionally mature? Who would you turn to for wisdom?
3. What is your own sibling position? How do you see that position in your family constellation shaping you?

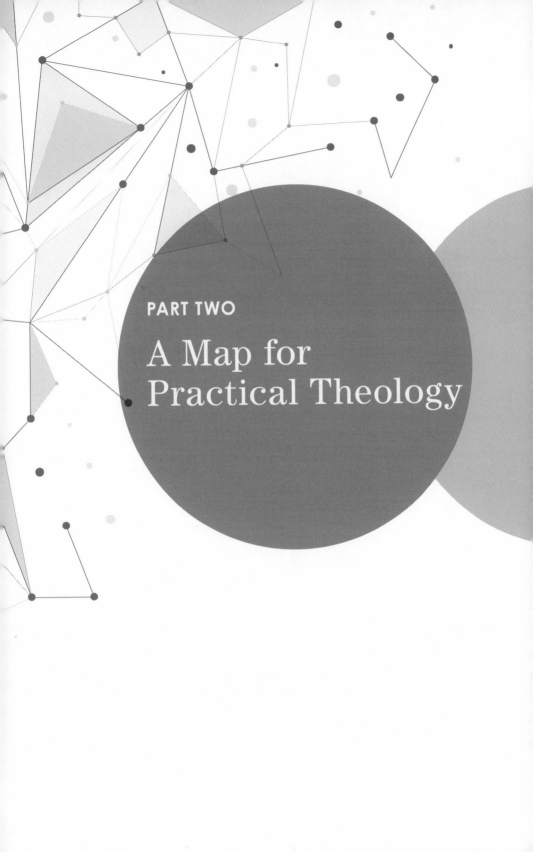

PART TWO

A Map for Practical Theology

3

Third-Way Leadership

More Than Principles and Practices

It was . . . disconcerting to examine your charts before a proposed flight only to find that in many cases the bulk of the terrain over which you had to fly was bluntly marked: "UNSURVEYED." It was as if the mapmakers had said, "We are aware that between this spot and that one, there are several hundred thousands of acres, but until you make a forced landing there, we won't know whether it is mud, desert, or jungle—and the chances are we won't know then!"

—Beryl Markham, *West with the Night*

Bowen Family Systems Theory and Practical Theology

Practical theology deals with the way we think about our work as pastors while considering the truth of the gospel—how we *theologize* about our *practice*. We do practical theology when we attempt to make sense of our individual ministry experiences by considering them in relationship to God's revelation in Jesus Christ. We think through this morning's hospital visit with a dying mother of three, yesterday's pastoral conversation with newlyweds surviving their first serious argument, last night's committee meeting that fell flat. Richard Osmer defines the tasks of practical theology in terms of its efforts to answer four questions about ministry experiences: What is going on? Why is this going on? What ought to be going on? How might we respond?[1] We can bring these questions to bear not only on the individual experiences of ministry but also on broader issues of *how* we offer ministry to others in Christ's name on behalf of the church.

Miroslav Volf and Dorothy Bass focus on how our beliefs (theology) and practices interact in the church's life.[2] The focus on practices requires us to pay attention to "specific people doing specific things together within a specific frame of shared meaning."[3] That Christians have learned and settled on certain practices through the centuries implies a set of beliefs that has generated such common activities. Within the church a variety of traditions and theological emphases have produced some diversity in practice—Amish, Anglicans, Baptists, Catholics, Methodists, Eastern Orthodox, and Pentecostals differ in beliefs, which shapes differences in preaching, worship, and polity. Differences in theology also shape distinctives in practice. Theologies and practices may differ, but all traditions hold this in common: their theology and practice, faith and life together, are joined. Practices shape our beliefs and beliefs generate practices. Practical theology is a reflective approach to this union.

Eugene Peterson uses the term "spiritual theology" to describe "the specifically Christian attempt to address the lived experience revealed in our Holy Scriptures and the rich understandings and practices of our ancestors as we work this experience out in our contemporary world of diffuse and unfocused 'hunger and thirst for righteousness.'"[4] Spiritual theology is, for Peterson, "the attention we give to living what we know and believe about God."[5]

Engaging practical theology—or more broadly, spiritual theology—requires pastors to be able to reflect on the work we do in ways that bring our best thinking about our work into conversation with the gospel. Bowen Family Systems Theory (BFST) can contribute to that fuller understanding of our tasks as we do the necessary work of theological reflection. What does BFST bring to our more complete understanding of such pastoral tasks and practices as the work of leadership, proclamation, pastoral care, spiritual formation, and Christian life in the community of the church? We begin with the sometimes-daunting task of congregational leadership.

Introducing Third-Way Leadership

Bookstores offer a buffet of information on the nature and practice of leadership. Academic and popular journals address the topic constantly. A simple internet search for "leadership" will produce millions of hits. Universities

include leadership studies across the curriculum—from business, to education, to religious studies. Our preoccupation with the topic of leadership
suggests that we do not yet have it figured out. We are still grappling with the
meaning and practice of leadership.

Leadership training, such as that offered in John Maxwell and Steven
Covey's *21 Irrefutable Laws of Leadership*, often focuses on techniques that
purport to equip leaders with practices to imitate or rules to apply as they make
decisions, manage conflict, make plans, work with organizations, or engage
individuals in their organization.[6] Techniques and principles are valuable as
far as they go. They can give leaders fresh ideas and suggest new, potentially
useful practices. One problem, however, is just remembering them well enough
to think through which practice is appropriate or which rule applies. Which one
of the "twenty-one irrefutable laws" fits this situation? Can I even remember
twenty-one laws? Another, bigger problem is that laws and techniques do not
address the underlying anxiety that is part of every congregation and the life of
every leader. A bag of leadership tricks will not address the emotional process
that runs behind the scenes while congregations work on "managing" their
conflict, discerning a future, or struggling with a budget shortfall.

BFST is not a leadership theory, and Friedman notes this distinction: "To
the extent leaders of any family or institution are willing to make a lifetime
commitment to their own continual self-regulated growth, they can make any
leadership theory or technique look brilliant. And conversely, to the extent
they avoid that commitment, no theory or technique is likely to succeed for
very long."[7] BFST offers a third way for leaders in congregations—neither
a set of principles nor a bag of tricks, but a way of thinking about human
relationships. A reasonably firm grasp of Bowen's eight concepts accompanied
by intentional work on one's own differentiation of self offers a way to think
about human behavior and relationships that can make a pastoral leader more
effective, even when anxiety is high in the congregation.

The leader who is working on differentiation will be better able to provide
a steady hand to a congregation facing significant changes and adaptations
to its ministry context, discerning its future, managing intermittent conflict
among its members, or engaging an unexpected crisis that suddenly calls the
congregation's future into question. Such leaders will offer their congregations
a better chance to thrive and serve effectively during times when the culture
surrounding them is anxiously spinning into a regressive reactivity. These
leaders will also demonstrate an ability to sustain an active, effective ministry
over the course of a lifetime, avoiding burnout, blackout,[8] or moral failure.

Third-way leadership is leadership that flows from learning how to apply
BFST principles in our lives and ministries. One does not need a long list of

"leadership principles." The map that BFST offers allows pastors to think and pray their way through a wide variety of congregational issues that call for wise leadership.

The Tasks of Congregational Leadership

The pastoral leader's role in a church is both complex and demanding. On the one hand, pastors bear responsibility for assuring that the congregation is seeking to know and do the will of God in its witness to the world. However, the leader's task is not necessarily to answer the question, "What is the will of God for us?" For a pastor to attempt to think for people in that way, assuming the Moses position in the triangle between God and God's people (Exod. 32:30–34), may be anxious overfunctioning. On the other hand, for a pastor to fail to lead the people to discern an answer to that question would be to underfunction, neglecting a critical leadership responsibility. Being present and accounted for as a leader requires a pastor to assure that there is an answer to the question of the congregation's mission. It is a moral obligation, something legitimately owed to the flock over which God has given the pastor oversight (1 Pet. 5:1–2).

The work of leadership, however, will inevitably generate emotional turmoil as it becomes clear that moving into the future means *moving*—making changes to go someplace new or different. Once the pastor and congregational lay leaders have prayerfully and thoughtfully discerned a new direction, the pastoral leader then has an additional role. The leader must communicate those changes and help implement them in a way that produces as little negative emotional impact on the congregation as possible. This will mean, among other things, that the pastor must function well in relationships in the congregation, especially with those not yet convinced of the way forward. Leadership is not merely presenting brilliant ideas with a striking PowerPoint presentation. It includes sound and solid preaching week after week so that the congregation gains trust in the pastor's life and character. It requires competent and reliable pastoral care before, during, and after the changes, so that the congregation is confident in the pastor's affection for them. Day after day, third-way leadership beats a bag of leadership tricks in this work, but it is far more demanding.

Leading as a Relational Task

Leadership, like proclamation and pastoral care, is an intensely relational dimension of pastoral ministry. We preach to people with whom we are in community. We care for people who are part of our lives and congregation. And we work with those same people in determining a future together as a congregation.

Leadership is inherently about the future. Management or administration is about the present: How do we get organized? What are our policies? Management is about helping congregations do things right. Leadership, however, is about helping them do the right thing.[9] We do not manage a congregation into the future. Attempting to continue to do what we have always done in a changing environment, regardless of how well we have done it, guarantees that eventually we will fail. A changing environment requires adaptation and growth as the horizon of the future moves toward us. A leader must make those adjustments successfully.

To say that leadership focuses on the future, however, is not to define *how* one leads. Depending on the context of the congregation, its resources, the abilities and capacities of its members, and how fast change is taking place around it, pastors and congregations may determine the appropriate route to the future in a variety of ways. Where there is time to consider the future thoughtfully, a leader may gather the prayerful thinking of as many members of the congregation as possible, help them sift through their options, and then wisely choose a direction. When a congregation is facing an immediate crisis that jeopardizes its future and requires a decision, the leader may need to make a thoughtful choice about the next step without benefit of such consultation. When the building is on fire, someone needs to take charge. That same element of urgency likely will not be present in developing a strategic plan for the coming three years.

Whether the leader is helping to develop a ministry budget, to raise funds for a building campaign, to call a new staff member, or to find a new place for growing numbers of middle-school students to meet on Sunday mornings, the focus is on the future. The corollary to that statement is that leadership is inherently about change. If we were already doing what we sense we need to do, we would not require a leader. Managers could get the job done. But we need leaders to take us to places we have not been before. Leaders are necessarily agents of change. And change never fails to generate anxiety among those we lead.

Friedman, addressing the therapeutic work of counselors, observes the inherent human resistance to change: "There is something basic to all human efforts to change or to resist being changed, irrespective of the context. In the therapeutic form of the paradox, the counselee comes in and says, 'I have such and such a problem. I want you to help me with it but . . .'—this is the part of the contract that is never spelled out—'I will do everything I can to prevent you from succeeding.'"[10]

This same sort of tacit opposition shows up in other settings. We choose our leaders to help us move to what we describe as a preferred future, but below the level of consciousness, we whisper, "I will do everything I can to prevent you from succeeding." Pastoral leaders should remind themselves that this emotional reality holds for pastoral search committees and congregations as well: "We want to grow, reach young families, and minister to our community, just so we don't really have to change anything." If what the congregation currently is doing were accomplishing those goals, they would not need to change. The fact that the future they profess to prefer is different from the present implies that changes and adjustments will be necessary. The adage is true: the system is perfectly designed for the present results. If we like the results we are getting, we ought not consider changing a thing. If we want different results, however, something must change. But we humans do not much like suggestions of change. It makes us break out in an anxious sweat.

We know something about anxious people and anxious systems. When people grow anxious, they become more reactive to one another, more on edge, and more easily offended. Conflict erupts more easily. People can become distant from one another. Some begin to take over, and others allow them to do so—with each group at least a bit resentful of the other. Finger-pointing increases. Anxious worry over certain parts of the system proliferates. Gossip increases. Change inevitably yields anxiety, and anxiety produces such fruit as this. These processes are not "out there" in the congregation only; they operate just as automatically in the lives of pastoral leaders.

Leadership, therefore, is not merely rational. It is inherently relational. The invisible emotional dimension of congregations is as real and powerful as any organizational chart.[11] To take up leadership is to choose to stir the congregation's anxiety to some degree, making possible all the consequent symptoms. To lead is to paddle directly into the whitewater of relationships.

One of the worst assumptions leaders can make is that because they have a good idea, they are about to receive a standing ovation. If that "good idea" represents change, and if the pain of changing now seems greater than the pain of not changing, then the system will automatically throw its weight into maintaining the homeostasis of the present. Changes in a congregation are like grasping one piece of a complex mobile hanging from the ceiling. Moving that one piece to a new position affects the positioning of the whole mobile. But when you let go of the piece, the forces of physics restore the whole thing to its original arrangement. In the same way, the emotional system of a family or congregation will attempt to return to its former array with all its weight. But an emotional system differs from the mobile. Real change is possible if leaders can hold that new position in place long enough for the rest of the system to adjust to it. Leaders need to be able to stay connected to that anxious congregation, managing their own anxiety to the degree possible, so that change has a chance to succeed. Eventually others in the system will adjust.[12]

In his lengthy study of the way innovations, whether ideas or products, make their way through a population, Everett M. Rogers argues that, regardless of the reasonable nature of the proposed change, most human beings are reluctant to accept it immediately.[13] Rogers's theory, first introduced in 1962, has continued to be applied in a variety of systems. He described a given innovation as moving toward acceptance incrementally. A bell curve divides the population into Innovators (2.5 percent), Early Adopters (13.5 percent), Early Majority (34 percent), Late Majority (34 percent), and Laggards (16 percent).[14] On a given innovation, a person might belong to one group or another. The Early Adopter of a technological change, such as a smartphone, might be a Laggard on the use of electronic screens rather than hymnals in a worship service. The point for leaders to grasp is that the best ideas, if they require a change, seldom receive full support when first introduced. Instead, they usually generate anxiety and resistance initially. Leaders who prepare for that response stand a better chance of calmly holding on to what they believe to be the right thing to do, rather than surrendering to the pressures of the group.

The relationships in which pastors are entwined in a congregation exert significant power on their capacity to lead. When leaders introduce change and anxiety rises, the togetherness forces increase their pull on the pastor and others advocating change (exercising leadership) to return to the orbit of the status quo. As a space vehicle needs sufficient speed to leave Earth's gravitational pull, a leader must have a level of differentiation strong enough to resist the pull of the system. This is not simply a matter of techniques or leadership principles. It is third-way leadership. The tug of relationships often occurs at a level below our consciousness, as automatic as our breathing. Having the capacity to stay in relationship with the people we serve while resisting the pressure they unconsciously exert on us requires a level of differentiation sufficient to cope with the force of the system. Knowing the right thing to do is different from having the ability to do the right thing under pressure.

The Relational Vulnerability of the Leader

Because leadership is intensely relational, pastors are vulnerable to the impact of the relational system on their functioning. One's "pastoral affection" for the congregation's members may impede leadership when the pastor has a low threshold for their pain. When the leader introduces change, and people for whom the pastor cares begin to whimper, the system will pressure the leader to retreat, to ease the pain, and to quiet the cries. Developing a greater capacity to endure the pain of others will eventually help them to function less dependently in the relationship. Friedman writes, "If one family member can successfully increase his or her threshold for another's pain, the other's own threshold will also increase, thus expanding his or her range of functioning. . . . Where members of a family are too quick to spare another pain, the resulting dependency tends to make the other's threshold fall. In addition, he or she will become addicted to having pain relieved through someone else's functioning."[15] Pastoral affection, if it is a form of emotional fusion, can inhibit effective leadership.

Leaders who function at lower levels of differentiation can find that relationships impinge on their leadership capacity in another way. If one of their goals is to receive congregational approval, then frowns and grumblings of disapproval will affect their decision making more than will a clear vision of the congregation's future. The pastor may yield to the pressure of the togetherness force and abandon leadership for something more relationally comfortable.

Relationships can obstruct leadership when the opponents of change weaponize the pastor's financial dependence on the congregation—or when the pastor fears they might. A serious shortfall in the church's operating budget, for example, as disgruntled members withhold their offerings or designate them to special funds, can serve as a kind of emotional blackmail to pull a pastor back in line. The more serious threat of dismissal may threaten the pastor's family and career. In chronically anxious families or congregations, we tend to organize ourselves around the least mature members.[16] Leadership is difficult when money purchases the agenda of a less emotionally and spiritually mature faction of the congregation.

The Value of a Less Anxious Presence

Friedman popularized the concept of a "nonanxious presence." He wrote, "What is vital to changing any kind of 'family' is not knowledge of technique or even of pathology but, rather, the capacity of the family leader to define his or her own goals and values while trying to maintain a nonanxious presence within the system."[17] Pastors sometimes hear this as simply working to calm ourselves down, but what Friedman had in mind was much more than that. The "presence" he refers to includes the earlier phrase, "defining his or her own goals and values." It means that one is fully present as a self, with all one's beliefs, values, principles, and goals clear amid an anxious system that attempts to challenge or sabotage leadership. It means being fully present in the system, remaining connected to the important others who are part of it as well. The nonanxious aspect refers to the capacity of leaders to regulate their own reactivity to the anxiety.

Nonanxious presence may be too high a goal for the pastoral leaders I know (including myself). If anxiety is an organism's reaction to its environment, the only truly nonanxious people may be in cemeteries. Lowering the bar to aspire to being a less anxious presence will serve most of us well most of the time. Some of Bowen's students informally credit him with encouraging them to be helpful to others by simply being the calmest person in the room. That is a worthy goal for most of us.

A pastor can work at becoming the least anxious person in the room, thus offering space for people to think more clearly in times of higher stress. The impact of a leader who can stay calm around others became clear for me one Sunday morning. I was halfway through the sermon when the fire alarm went off in the building. Because I have diminished hearing, especially at high frequencies, I could not hear the alarm at all. I noticed people in the congregation squirming about nervously but had no idea what was stirring them. I kept on preaching. The text that morning was Mark 4:35–41, the story of Jesus's stilling of the storm on the Sea of Galilee. I was focused on his question to the disciples in verse 40: "Why are you so afraid? Have you still no faith?" (ESV). Gradually the congregation calmed down, some thinking I might have been playing a trick on them with the alarm. They went from being "alarmed" to being "unalarmed" in a brief span of time in the presence of a less anxious leader. Fortunately, a person from outside the sanctuary came in and approached me with the information that someone had triggered the fire alarm and we needed to calmly evacuate the building, which we did. Had there actually been a fire, this less anxious leader could have seen his flock go up in smoke. But the experience drove the lesson home: the congregation looks to its leaders, and a calmer leader can help others react less anxiously.

Although my lower anxiety in this situation was due to hearing impairment and thus ignorance of the potential threat, leaders can deliberately work on their own reactivity and make a difference in their congregations. When people are anxious, thinking gives way to automatic reactions. Reactivity generates chemical reactions in the brain that make reasoned responses far less likely than automatic emotional ones, such as fight, flight, or freezing. A calmer leader can think, helping create an environment in which others can think as well. To the degree that people are thinking rather than simply reacting, they stand a better chance of solving problems, discerning God's will, or recovering from a crisis.

The calm voice of the captain on a commercial airliner is important to the success of a flight. Passengers hear that voice welcome them, thank them for choosing the airline, and confirm their destination. The captain explains the route they will travel, at what speed and altitude, for how long, and what the weather will be like when they arrive. This communication has not provided travelers with information they could not have attained in other ways. What they have heard is the voice of the person who will be their leader for the next few hours, saying with a calm confidence, "I know where we are going. I know how to get there. I know what it is like. This is our future together. You can trust me." Along the way, the captain's calm voice usually speaks again, following a chime, giving more information, perhaps telling the passengers they are free to move about the cabin, or warning them to remain seated and buckled for an upcoming bumpy ride. Later, the calm voice will announce their imminent arrival at their destination.

Should an emergency develop along the way, however, the captain will speak into that as well, with the same calm confidence, so the passengers can rest assured that the captain and the crew are doing everything necessary for the safety and security of everyone. We can only imagine what it would be like in the passenger cabin if the captain screamed in panic when the flight was about to be rough! The influence of a calmer pastor is no less reassuring when a congregation's ride gets bumpy.

Strategic Leadership versus Crisis Leadership

Pastors and congregational leaders can handle *strategic leadership* deliberately, thoughtfully, and prayerfully over time. Pastors can meet with key leaders to conduct helpful studies of the congregation and the community, engage outside consultants, read useful resources together, and pray for direction. The process will likely generate a degree of anxiety among these leaders as they see things from different perspectives or feel threatened by an idea or proposal that makes its way into the discussion. But over a few months, their thinking about the congregation's future can begin to take concrete form in plans and goals for the horizon before them. They can consider together how to communicate these proposals to the congregation in a way that generates minimal reactivity. In this kind of strategic leadership, the less anxious pastor seeks to manage the emotional and intellectual process, not to determine the outcome. A pastor capable of this kind of leadership blesses the congregation.

Crisis leadership, however, requires a different repertoire from the pastor. A crisis is a time that calls the congregation's future into question. Gene Klann describes the nature of a crisis:

> A crisis is generally characterized by a high degree of instability and carries the potential for extremely negative results that can endanger the continuity of the organization. It's a key moment or critical period that brings both surprise and dramatic change. In this way a crisis can be described as a turning point in the affairs of an individual or an organization. It's significant because the consequences of the situation will be decisive in determining the future of that individual or organization. . . . A crisis has the potential to divide an organization's past from its future, to replace security with insecurity, and to separate effective leaders from ineffective ones. A crisis also has the potential to swap routine for creativity and to shift an organization from "business as usual" into significant change.[18]

A crisis is a time of emotional upheaval and chaos that will significantly stir human emotions, reactivity, and anxiety, not only in the congregation but also in the life of the pastor.

A season of crisis usually appears with little warning. A fire consumes the church's facilities overnight. A tornado, hurricane, or flood destroys not just the church building but the entire community. A drunken driver crashes into a van carrying church members on a mission trip. Violence erupts when a shooter enters the church's sanctuary during worship. Other crises may seem to appear suddenly, although they actually could have been developing for some time, while the pastor and congregation either ignored the signs or simply could not see them. Budget crises, embezzlement, or clergy sexual abuse, for example, may have been predictable if leaders had been paying closer attention. Sometimes we expend a lot of energy not to know what is happening right before us.

Regardless, once a crisis makes landfall, congregations need leaders who can keep their heads and help the church negotiate the storm. The goal during such times is to lead in such a way as to minimize the emotional impact on the congregation.[19] Thinking in terms of systems alerts us to the potential emotional impact. We can expect to witness all the reactive behaviors, often more extreme than usual: conflict, distance, overfunctioning/underfunctioning, and projection in its various forms (blame, worry, triangling, gossip, rumors). These behaviors, however bizarre or extreme, should not surprise us.[20] Less anxious pastors can help congregations endure the storm with minimal damage and then recover and rebuild.

A crisis does not create the leader's character and capacities—it reveals what is already there. When the crisis arrives, it is too late to develop wisdom, character, spirituality, or differentiation. Those resources will either already be in place or they will not be resources at our disposal. During a crisis a competent leader will be one who has been doing the right things beforehand.

Klann offers a concept of crisis *leadership*, as opposed to crisis *management*, focusing on the way leaders' relationships with the people they lead influence how the organization endures.[21] He identifies three key elements that leaders must address before, during, and after a crisis: communication, connection with vision and values, and caring relationships. I would add a fourth element, preliminary to the other three: a crisis plan.

Many congregations do not have plans for handling crises, but most would benefit from them. Congregations can best develop plans when the emotional system is in a state of relative calm and people can think clearly. They can thoughtfully construct brief written plans for a variety of possible crises so that leaders do not have to create a plan from scratch when emotions are intense and thinking is more difficult. The calm explanation of the flight attendant about seat belts, oxygen masks, exits, and flotation devices before a flight is nothing more than a crisis plan, so that, if a crisis occurs, we will have a better chance to survive. Crisis plans might address how the congregation would respond to various natural disasters, clergy sexual abuse, abuse of a child by a church volunteer, an active shooter episode, or a serious accident at the church or on a church trip, for example. Churches of all sizes experience such events. Plans could include immediate actions to take, longer-term actions that might be necessary, having easy access to important phone numbers such as those of the church's attorney and insurance company, and a plan for communication with the congregation and other constituencies, including the media.[22] Not preparing such plans means that congregational leaders must create them on the spot, during the crisis, when clear thinking is far more of a challenge. This need not be an elaborate or extensive process. It simply requires thinking ahead of time about the kinds of crises the congregation could face, whom to contact and how, where to turn, and what initial steps to take.

Klann underscores the importance of regular communication during periods of relative calm. The congregation needs to know the shepherd's voice. Like the airline pilot calmly addressing the passenger cabin when all is well, the pastor's familiar voice from the pulpit and in a variety of forms of written communication can help keep the level of anxiety in the congregation a bit lower. Wise pastors communicate to their people God's truth and important information about the congregation's life, as well as their own affection and care.

During times of crisis and anxiety, people seek information for their security. Observe our tendency to glue ourselves to news broadcasts when a national crisis occurs. Even if information is slow to come in, we will listen to reporters tell us the same facts repeatedly. If people do not get good information, they may simply create their own report and pass that around as truth. Crisis plans should include strategies to communicate as fully as possible with the congregation, using all forms of contact available, but giving priority to face-to-face communication. Less anxious leaders will attend to the words they choose, their tone of voice, and their demeanor as they address the congregation. In general, the greater the effort at communication, the less the emotional impact of a crisis on an organization.

Additionally, communication with outsiders is often necessary during crises. The third-way leader will take initiative to communicate with the community and the media when necessary, being as visible and as available as possible. The congregation should offer a formal press release produced soon after an event, reviewed by the church's attorney if necessary. The pastor, as the voice of the congregation, will seek to be truthful, accurate, honest, and simple. It will be important to explain as clearly as possible what has happened, what the church is doing, and what is yet planned. The leader will accept responsibility (not liability) for the crisis, communicating, "I'm going to do everything necessary to see us through this."

When no crisis threatens the future, the leader will regularly connect decisions and plans to the congregation's thoughtfully and prayerfully considered vision and values. The effort that goes into a congregation's answering the questions of vision and values is worthy of a pastor's time and energy. This is where the congregation defines itself, saying, "This is what we believe we are called to do" (vision) and "These are the important principles we try to keep in mind as we pursue that future" (values). When vision and values are solidly in place, the leader's task is to consistently hold those up to people making congregational decisions and overseeing ministry. Over time, the pastor, staff, and some key leaders may tire of repeating these elements so often, but keeping the focus is important. Congregations may need to hear these ideas repeated, explained, and applied many, many times before they fully sink in.

During a crisis, the leader will be careful to connect the actions and responses of the congregation to the vision and values that have become familiar to them. The message is clear: "This is how a church with this vision and these values responds to an event like this." These connections are more valuable if they are specific and clear: "Because our church holds a value of service, we are organizing teams to assist with the mud-out efforts in homes in our flooded neighborhood." The leader will also model the values by participating in the response to the crisis wherever possible.

Before a crisis occurs, pastors need to attend to the fourth element as well—the extension of competent pastoral care to the congregation. This, of course, includes such ordinary acts as weddings, funerals, pastoral conversations, and spiritual direction. In addition, lay leaders experience this care as the pastor equips them for ministry, providing support and feedback, listening to them, keeping promises to them, and assuring that they have full information about what is going on in their church.

A period of crisis is a time to expand expressions of care. This will mean being more visible and available than usual, expressing care authentically, being involved with those most affected, sharing the experience. Care for others during an extended period of crisis will also require pastors to take responsibility for their own care to maintain their resilience and allow themselves to be the less anxious presence needed. Conflicts will occur and problems will arise during the crisis. The caring leader will make plans to address these when the storm has passed.

These four components of crisis leadership also are part of third-way leadership during the normal life of the congregation. When a crisis occurs, they are the core of crisis leadership. In other words, we do the same thing during the crisis that we have been doing before, but with the volume turned up significantly. We retrieve the crisis plan and look it over carefully, amending it as needed for this situation. Then we begin to implement it as planned. We focus on intensifying our communication, providing as many people as possible as much information as possible. We hold up the church's vision, and we care for our flock.

When the crisis has subsided, the same four elements will receive the attention of the third-way leader. Congregational leaders will review and revise the crisis plan, the communication plan, and the church's vision and values, consulting as many stakeholders as possible. How well did these serve us? What was missing? What did not work? What proved to be essential? Given what the congregation has just endured, how well did those principles guide them through the crisis? Does the congregation need to revise any statements? Do they need to amend any policies or procedures? Finally, pastoral leaders will take initiative in rebuilding or restoring bruised or broken relationships. Leaders will recognize and thank people who contributed to survival in extraordinary ways. The congregation may plan to provide follow-up counseling for those most wounded by the event.

The key element is the leader's ability to sustain a relatively calm posture with those in the congregation. When anxiety is high, the leader's level of functioning will have a direct impact on the functioning of those who take their emotional cues from their leader. The leader's anxiety or lack of it will be equally contagious. Thoughtful preparation for crises and personal work on differentiation of self will provide a congregation with a better chance to survive a severe crisis and reimagine its future.

Becoming a Less Anxious Presence

The process of becoming a less anxious leader is not simply a matter of deep-breathing exercises. (Although if that helps, by all means, breathe deeply!) The kind of personal change, or differentiation of self, that helps us learn to manage our automatic reactivity is challenging and takes time. All of us enter adulthood with a level of emotional maturity or differentiation that is primarily the product of the nuclear and extended families in which we grew up. Our level of differentiation will be close to that of our parents, since it is in our nuclear family that we experienced the degree of attachment or dependence that determines how much we will tend to fuse in our other relationships—that is, how much we are emotionally dependent on others.[23]

Work on differentiation of self is a lifelong project of becoming progressively less emotionally fused to others so that we can remain in relationship with them while exchanging less and less of one another's anxiety. We can have more of our own thoughts, beliefs, and feelings, rather than having those determined by the relationships of which we are part. We become a bit more objective about what is taking place in important relationships. We also become less reactive to the anxiety of others, so that we can provide a less anxious presence. Bowen believed that with a great deal of effort over time, individuals might be able to increase their own level of differentiation slightly, yet even small changes would have a significant effect on the course of one's life and relationships.[24]

Becoming a less anxious presence is the product of becoming a better-differentiated person. It is not something we just decide to do in the moment. An effort toward differentiation will increase our capacity to be with others when anxiety is high, while retaining our ability to observe the emotional processes of the system, to see the part we are playing, and to notice and manage our own reactivity. The project of differentiation calls for intentional work over time—the rest of our lives, actually. Being a less anxious presence is more than just calming down. In chapter 7 we will take up the kind of work required to increase our capacity for being such a presence.

Conclusion

Because pastoral leadership is a relational domain of ministry, like preaching and pastoral care, it does not occur in a vacuum. We bring to the work of leadership the reality of the emotional system that is the congregation and the reality of our own level of basic self and the patterns of reactive behavior we have learned from our own families. We lead out of who we are and who we are becoming. One who has neglected the hard work of spiritual, emotional, and intellectual growth will bring a good deal of immaturity. Those who are working on learning to love God wholeheartedly and their neighbor unselfishly, on pursuing spiritual practices, and on being present and accounted for in their relationships and responsibilities will bring a more mature, principled self to leadership. We exercise leadership both in the emotional ecology of the congregation and in that of our own families.

It follows that a pastor who is working on differentiation of self will be able to offer a more authentic and effective ministry of leadership.[25] The better differentiated the pastor, the more thoughtful and principled leadership will be possible. The more emotionally mature the pastor, the more that leader is open to hear the thoughts and needs of others, as well as to express one's own thinking. Better differentiated pastors will be of greater help to the congregation when anxiety is intense, such as in a crisis. They will make a more powerful impact when the congregation needs to think and respond to issues rather than simply react.

Conversely, a thoughtful approach to the task of leadership will offer opportunities for the pastor to work on differentiation of self. The relational nature of this domain will call on leaders to clarify their thinking, stay connected to others, and manage their own reactivity. This is part of work on differentiation. The congregation provides a laboratory for the pastor to carry on that work outside his or her own family system.

●— **Questions for Reflection** ─────────────────────────────

1. How do you understand the significance of the term "third-way leadership"? What are the other two ways? What approach to leadership has most consistently guided your thinking about that pastoral role?

2. How do you think about the goal of being the "least anxious presence" in the congregation? What practices are helping you move in that direction?

What would the project of working on your own differentiation look like?

3. In your thinking, how does crisis leadership differ from strategic leadership? What crises have you faced as a pastor? What did you do during a crisis that most helped the congregation make its way through? What could you have done differently?

4

The Future of
Congregational Leadership

Leading in Chaotic Times

Now when I was a little chap I had a passion for maps. I would look
for hours at South America, or Africa, or Australia, and lose myself in all
the glories of exploration. At that time, there were many blank spaces
on the earth, and when I saw one that looked particularly inviting on
a map (but they all look like that) I would put my finger on it and say,
"When I grow up I will go there."

—Joseph Conrad, *Heart of Darkness*

The twenty-first century in the United States erupted with a volley of social
crises, shifts in moral perspectives, and chaotic economic and political
events. A presidential election went undecided for weeks. Terrorists at-
tacked on 9/11. We began two wars. Wall Street collapsed. A severe economic
recession led to government bailouts of banks, insurance companies, and
automakers. Major hurricanes struck Texas, Louisiana, Mississippi, Florida,
and North Carolina. A catastrophic oil spill threatened livelihoods along the
Gulf Coast. The questions of abortion, same-sex marriage, immigration, gun
control, taxes, and health care divided the nation. Ongoing concerns about
international terrorism, domestic violence, crime, drugs, and public education

grew. Political polarization left fewer and fewer people in the middle. We entered the century as recipients of the proverbial curse: May you live in interesting times!

The symptoms of an anxious society swirl about us. Distance grows to the point of cutoff as media figures, partisan political leaders, and politically active citizens choose to speak about—rather than to—each other. Social media has developed as a platform for both the public expression of views and the rapid spread of misinformation and disinformation. Adults focus on upcoming generations, projecting their anxiety onto their children and grand-children. They worry about falling test scores, nutrition, safety, and rights. Reactive legislation attempts quick fixes, but test scores drop, teachers are blamed, obesity grows, and behavior problems around sex, drugs, alcohol, suicide, and violence continue among teens and preteens. Our congregations worship and serve in a society that is observably anxious.

Trying to make sense of events and trends that appear irrational and cha-otic can leave pastoral leaders baffled. Cause-and-effect thinking, blame, and focus on relieving symptoms do not solve problems but only contribute to the anxiety. Leaders at all levels of society—political, corporate, and religious—seem clueless in the face of problems that have been growing since at least the early 1960s.

As we watch our world spiral deeper and deeper into a regression, we leaders can hunker down in fear, standing in the pulpit and shouting at the world from the safety of our sanctuaries, or we can charge out the door to try to fix the symptoms on our own. Or might we find a way to lead wisely both inside and outside the congregation? Like the two hundred chiefs of the tribe of Issachar who served King David, congregational leaders need to have "understanding of the times, to know what Israel ought to do" (1 Chron. 12:32). This kind of wisdom requires a different way of thinking about what is happening.

Bowen's Eighth Concept: Societal Emotional Process

Bowen argued that from the late 1940s through 1972, society had regressed about 20 percent on his scale of differentiation.[1] He reached his conclusion without benefit of the internet, deriving his claims from observations and personal knowledge of public officials in his local area; from following the national scene through newspapers, magazines, and the literature; and from files he kept on landmark court decisions and cases in which there was enough information on the key people to make a valid estimation. Bowen based his assessment on issues known to influence regression in families and small social groups. He excluded changes he considered might have direct connection with the sweeping progressive change in society. He also tried to exclude issues polarized between liberal and conservative forces.

The symptoms of regression Bowen identified included increases in violence, crime, drug use, divorce rates, and the sexual revolution in its various expressions. He also observed a pronounced increase in people's focus on "rights" rather than "responsibility," an increase in the togetherness force in society, more frequent decisions to allay the anxiety of the moment, and an increase in cause-effect thinking.[2]

What is different in the twenty-first century, as we fret over the future of our society, is the data. We no longer are dependent on hunches and anecdotal evidence to surmise that things are moving in a downward spiral. Evidence points heavily toward the reality of an extended regressive period in American society, beginning at least by the 1960s and continuing into this century.

Congregational leaders occupy places of distinct influence in this social system. With more than 53 million Americans attending one of 331,000 houses of worship each week, led by an inestimable number of clergy, pastors have the potential for formidable influence.[3]

Although most congregational leaders would prefer to be part of the solution to this troubling condition, we often yield to pressure to focus on the symptoms and issues of the regression, inadvertently contributing to the level of anxiety rather than reducing it. Pastoral leaders are susceptible to the same fears and anxieties as others. It is unsurprising, then, that many clergy join the ranks of the reactive, focusing their rhetoric, leadership, and political involvement on a few emotionally laden social and political issues, such as abortion or same-sex marriage. Use of the language of a "culture war" further polarizes views on such issues and defines those who think differently as enemies.

The polarized representatives of partisan politics frequently co-opt religion for their own purposes. Reactive religious leaders hastily join parades led by political figures, right or left, to support quick-fix, ineffective solutions focused on society's symptoms. This reaction simply reinforces congregants' fears and anxieties, and regressive societal behaviors continue unabated. The very institutions, including churches, that could contribute to society's progress, instead add to its regression.

Pastoral leaders have every reason to be interested in societal emotional process. Our theology speaks of hope for a redeemed world. Our commitment to justice draws us out of our personal or organizational concerns to those of the world around us. Although we have difficulty simply ignoring the regressive symptoms of our society, we may remain unsure of what to do with them. Judging from the rhetoric from some of our pulpits, our congregations and their leaders live with as much fear and anxiety about our world as those who profess no religious commitments at all.

We have reasons to lead thoughtfully during these troubled times, dealing also with matters that go beyond the huge issues facing our culture. A systems perspective recognizes that the anxiety generated from a regressive society quickly and easily finds its way into the clergy family, the families of the congregation, and the family that is the congregation. Congregational ministry does not occur in a vacuum. The interlocking triangles of these emotional systems assure that the anxiety and reactivity permeating the world in which we live influences the effectiveness of our congregations in mission and ministry. Churches that find themselves enmeshed in conflict, paralyzed in their decision making, or struggling to survive may not make the connection between the anxious world in which they live and the challenges they face, but dots do connect. Our congregations will benefit from pastors who have the maturity to lead wisely in such times.

Leading with a New Way of Thinking

In the face of an anxious society, Bowen Family Systems Theory (BFST) suggests a different way to see the problems, to identify one's own part in them, and to choose new ways to respond.[4] Pastors can influence their own systems toward emotional maturity and progress. Higher functioning congregations, clear on their mission and purpose and vitally connected to their communities, can extend their influence to families, schools, civic organizations, businesses, corporations, and even into the legal system. Systems thinking about leadership and about regression moves beyond decrying the symptoms and blaming others: it includes taking responsibility for the witness of the congregation and one's own life as a leader.

The possibility of this quality of leadership offers hope to congregations, to their communities, and to the society at large. However, the regression itself challenges efforts to become such a leader. Anxious systems and anxious societies are not the soil from which leaders easily arise. Anxious systems tend to look for leaders who will provide palliative care, alleviating the pain of the symptoms without addressing the underlying anxiety with long-term solutions. Edwin Friedman spoke of a "leadership-toxic" climate "so reactive that it cannot choose leaders who might calm its anxiety."[5] Yet hope in such a regressive time may lie in the development of a critical mass of leaders who operate out of differentiation of self, who think independently rather than submitting to the pressures of the system, while maintaining a connection to the group and investing in its welfare. To the extent that such leaders arise, we might consider that society to be less regressed.[6]

Pastors have claim to a legacy left by the Hebrew prophets; during times of societal regression, they called their nation back to the principles of the covenant that bound them to their God. Few of these representatives received a hearing from the political or religious leaders of the day, who were offering quick-fix advice. As Jeremiah put it, these so-called leaders

> have treated the wound of my people carelessly,
>   saying, "Peace, peace,"
>   when there is no peace. (Jer. 6:14)

Karl Menninger spends eleven pages of his book *Whatever Became of Sin?* exhorting the clergy to directly address the issues of sin and its destructiveness, calling for confession and repentance.[7]

This kind of prophetic posture is not a mere railing against the sins of the day but a holding up of the principles of what is right, whole, and healthy by both life and word. Led by principled men and women, faith communities that can model a principled way may influence their immediate environment and create impulses that permeate the broader context. What would characterize such leaders and communities? While the list is potentially quite long, three points of focus seem especially tied to the concepts of BFST: a responsible focus on self, a thoughtful focus on principles, and an intentional focus on the care of creation.

A Responsible Focus on Self

Women and men who carry out effective leadership will be those who work to focus on their own lives, their own thinking, their own roles and responsibilities, their own part to play, the log in their own eye, rather than on the failures of others. They will learn to manage their own reactivity to the anxiety of society and of the people they lead. Such self-management is indispensable for a leader in anxious settings. Bowen described a family leader as one "with the courage to define self, who is as invested in the welfare of the family as in self, who is neither angry nor dogmatic, whose energy goes into changing self rather than telling others what they should do, who can know and respect the multiple opinions of others, who can modify self in response to the strengths of the group and who is not influenced by the irresponsible opinions of others."[8] This also describes the high-functioning leadership that might offer hope to congregations and communities.

Bowen suggested that regression in a family is stemmed when one family member finally has enough and rises out of the mess with an "I-position," saying in one way or another, "I believe this family can do better." When such a person enunciates clearly and calmly what he or she will and will not do and holds that position even in the face of pressure to return to the previous togetherness of the group, that eventually leads to higher functioning in the rest of the family. Bowen's eighth concept states that the same process would operate in society. As one leader after another has the courage to function differently out of differentiation of self, bit by bit various portions of society stand a chance of functioning at a higher level.[9]

Again, the pressure in times of rising chronic anxiety is for the pastoral leader to share the fears and anxieties of others, to yield to their demands for a quick fix, to abandon beliefs and principles, to blame others for problems, and to demand that others change their behavior. Better-differentiated leaders, working from a systems perspective, will focus on self, on our part in the situation, on our own responsibilities in it, on the mission or purpose of the congregation, and on better understanding the anxieties that underlie the presenting problems or symptoms. Friedman asserted that the "way out" of the regression involves "shifting our orientation to the way we think about relationships, from one that focuses on techniques that motivate others to one that focuses on the leader's own presence and being."[10]

A Thoughtful Focus on Principles

The common reactive tendency of both families and the larger society is joining in a focus on symptoms. That focus is not helpful, however. Friedman observed that when families concentrate on their symptoms rather than on emotional processes, they find the issues reappearing in other forms, no matter how much expert advice they receive. He writes: "The same is the case when an entire society stays focused on the acute symptoms of its chronic anxiety—violence, drugs, crime, ethnic and gender polarization, economic factors such as inflation and unemployment, bureaucratic obstruction, an entangling tax code, and so on—rather than on the emotional processes that promote those symptoms and keep them chronic. In that case, the society will continue to recycle its problems."[11] The same behaviors that characterize a chronically anxious family abound in a chronically anxious society, including heightened reactivity, increased herding, blaming others, a quick-fix mentality, and a failure of nerve in leadership. These traits subvert our capacity to adapt as humans and drag society downward.[12]

Leaders in such times must move their focus away from symptoms to their own convictions and beliefs. Friedman calls for leaders who have the capacity to separate themselves from the surrounding emotional process, the capacity to be clear about their own principles and vision, the willingness to take risks, the persistence to face inertial resistance, and the self-regulation to stand in the face of reactive sabotage.[13] These capacities occur in well-differentiated, high-functioning leaders.

Differentiation of self requires us to become clearer about our own beliefs, values, and principles. What beliefs are we not willing to negotiate under pressure? What do we both profess and consistently attempt to live? Many of us have simply absorbed our beliefs from the world around us, or have had our beliefs forcibly imposed by others. Bowen observed that a high percentage of people attempting to define a self will reach out to some set of social norms, such as the Ten Commandments, to state "their beliefs." "They don't believe what they believe," he says, "they believe what they are told they must believe."[14] Few of us believe what we do as the result of clearly thinking it through. Leaders, especially during times of regression, need to be clear about their most important principles and must live by them, even under pressure to compromise.

During regressive times, leaders need to think through their own ethical and moral perspectives, what they believe about right and wrong. They must include their principles of behavior, how they ought to live in relationship to others. And they must include their theological beliefs, what they believe about God, about humanity, about sin, and about redemption. Their effort should include clarifying their own goals for life as well. The work of thinking through these beliefs for themselves, neither absorbing the dogma others have given them nor simply reacting against it, is a challenging move against the current of togetherness that would dictate what those beliefs should be. Consequently, such thinking is an act of differentiation.

A well-differentiated leader operates more often based on thought-out principles, beliefs, and values. These core beliefs provide the basis for making solid decisions rather than reacting emotionally to the anxiety of a group demanding a quick fix or to the pressures for togetherness. Pastoral leaders come to our task with principles and beliefs that include our own understanding and commitment to various theological and ethical concepts in our traditions. To the degree that we have personally and thoughtfully appropriated these concepts, they provide a means for calling the congregation to consider its own mission, purpose, and values. Otherwise, invoking them is likely to be another emotional reaction to the anxiety of the moment.

Pastoral leaders cannot afford to set aside core theological and ethical beliefs while attempting to provide wise leadership in these interesting times. What, for example, is the meaning of "hope" in a world that is regressing in its functioning decade after decade? How might our concept of hope guide our decisions about preaching, leadership, and ministry in this time? What is the future we believe God holds out to the world? What are our responsibilities to begin to live into that future now? How will we concretely live this belief? If they take to heart Kierkegaard's oft-cited definition of hope as "a passion for what is possible," well-differentiated leaders might find themselves describing a vision for a different kind of future, one marked by the congregation living more responsibly in the present.

What of our understanding of justice? When the regression impinges on the lives of those whose poverty or powerlessness leaves them in jeopardy, what responsible actions must we take? Is it sufficient, for example, to rant against abortion while providing no alternatives for those mothers or for the physical or social well-being of children brought into the world? How will we put this belief into practice?

What does the concept of mercy look like in a high-functioning congregation? How shall we engage those whose lives are diminished by the regression's symptoms (victims of drugs, violence, sexual abuse, poverty, family issues, etc.) without succumbing to the temptation merely to treat the symptoms? How shall we foster practices that engage a belief in compassionate ministry to the least, the last, and the lost?

What shape does peace (*shalom*) take when understood in its full biblical sense of wholeness and health? How will congregations be guided by a principled attempt to be peacemakers (Matt. 5:9) as part of their mission and purpose? How do we move beyond reactive war protest to responsible peacemaking?

What form does the concept of repentance take? Does the Hebrew *shub* (to turn), or the Greek *metanoein* (to think anew), offer possibilities to a leader working on differentiation? How do we think through theological categories in such a way that they become our own? How does a congregation come to possess authentically (or be possessed by) their own ethical and theological convictions?

Pastors who remain connected to their congregations, who think through their own beliefs, who seek to live principled lives, and who encourage and coach others in that process as well—such leaders can create waves of growth toward maturity capable of spreading through the congregation and the surrounding community. Many theological and ethical categories can help the thoughtful leader and congregation take responsibility for changing their part in the anxiety and regression of their own communities by defining their purpose, thinking through their beliefs, and living into them with increasing integrity.

An Intentional Focus on the Care of Creation

The third focal point for leadership during an anxious age of regression may not be as obvious as the first two, but it emerges directly out of Bowen's thinking. As he analyzed the current regression, Bowen pointed primarily to environmental sources of the underlying anxiety of the times. He believed that conflicts between and among human beings, such as war, are not the source of the anxiety driving the regression but are symptoms. Rather, he concluded, the conflict between the human and creation lies at the root of the regression. He surmised that an exploding human population, with its attendant environmental impact, is near the source of the problem. Human beings are instinctively aware of the limited resources to sustain life on Earth and of the possibility that the rapidly increasing human population may soon exhaust such things as arable land, clean water, and fossil fuels. At the same time, we notice the absence of new frontiers beyond which to spread, and we begin to feel more "fenced in." Additionally, we begin to recognize that our ecosystem cannot continue to absorb the waste products of our unsustainable, consumer-driven lifestyle. Society began to address this growing awareness in the 1960s and 1970s, but we did not solve the problems, and so the issue has carried over to the twenty-first century. Whether or not we intellectually accept the conclusion of 97 percent of the actively publishing climate scientists that Earth is warming more rapidly due to human activity, we sense the threat to the world around us and to ourselves as well.[15]

Occasional reminders of the fragility of the environment and the finite nature of Earth's resources, such as a major oil spill, make the news for a time. We occupy ourselves with finger-pointing and new legislation. But we seldom see the role our own lifestyles play in the ongoing demand for cheap energy. We ignore constant threats to the planet through the elimination of large portions of rain forests, the extinction of hundreds of species, the spewing of nitrogen-based agricultural products into our waters, and the atmospheric effects of the carbon-based lifestyles of developed nations. Denying the threat at the conscious level does not fool the emotional system, however. Human beings perceive the threat to our environment as a threat to our own future and survival, and anxiety rises.

Bowen suggested that pulling out of the regression would require "a human being who can live in better harmony with nature."[16] What efforts on the part of leaders might move in that direction? How might high-functioning congregational leaders respond to this underlying source of societal anxiety? Creative, thinking leaders might identify many directions forward. None, however, is a quick fix. Traveling such routes runs counter to those currently pursued by the culture. Thinking, conviction, beliefs, and principles must precede our actions. Leaders need to incorporate such commitments into their lives, not merely advocate for them in words.

E. O. Wilson—entomologist, biologist, self-designated secular humanist, and author—wrote a book titled, ironically, *The Creation*. As a literary device, he writes the book as an impassioned letter to an unnamed recipient, a Southern Baptist pastor. He assumes the pastor to be reasonable, devout, and committed to conservative religious beliefs. Wilson attempts to persuade this pastor that both the writer and the pastor have reason to hold a common goal: saving life on Earth. Apparently Wilson hopes to engage the leadership of conservative, evangelical Protestants in the effort to live in greater harmony with the creation.

Wilson raises the issue of the importance of religious leaders' involving themselves in the stewardship of Earth: "You may well ask at this point, Why me? Because religion and science are the two most powerful forces in the world today, including especially the United States. If religion and science could be united on the common ground of biological conservation, the problem would soon be solved."[17] Wilson puzzles over why so many religious leaders have hesitated to make protection of creation part of their witness and message. He ponders whether the only things that matter to them are human-centered ethics and the afterlife. An eschatology that simply believes God provided sufficient resources on Earth to last until the second coming of Christ perplexes him. The fate of about ten million life-forms other than the human seems to matter to Christians not at all.

Wilson rightly charges that "this and other similar doctrines are not gospels of hope and compassion. They are gospels of cruelty and despair. They were not born of the heart of Christianity." Then he pleads, "Pastor, tell me I am wrong!"[18] He tells his imaginary reader: "You are well prepared to present the theological and moral arguments for saving the Creation. I am heartened by the movement growing within Christian denominations to support global conservation. The stream of thought has arisen from many sources, from evangelical to Unitarian. Today it is but a rivulet. Tomorrow it will be a flood."[19]

Responsible religious leaders who accept the environmental analysis of the regression as accurate will employ their role as teacher/preacher to educate their congregants regarding the issues of stewardship of Earth. They will think through their own theology of ecology and apply biblical teaching to the current issues. Genesis 1:26–30 and 2:15 are suggestive of the human responsibility to "till . . . and keep" the garden in which God has placed us. Genesis 3 narrates the separation between humanity and the creation that is a consequence of human sin. Many agricultural instructions of the Mosaic law imply responsibility to care for the land. In fact, the concept of the Holy Land itself as a gift of God to Israel is a central theme in the Hebrew Scriptures.[20] American congregations can learn to appreciate anew the holiness of creation from a biblical perspective.

Wendell Berry writes of how an honest reading of Scripture points to a view of Earth that confesses God's ownership of it all, our responsibilities in stewardship of it, and the holiness of creation and all of life in it.[21] Berry notices the disconnectedness or disharmony between human beings and creation. This shows up not least in our disconnectedness from the soil, which provides our sustenance. Berry describes the "industrial eater" as one who "does not know that eating is an agricultural act, who no longer knows or imagines the connections between eating and the land, and who is therefore necessarily passive and uncritical—in short, a victim. When food, in the minds of eaters, is no longer associated with farming and with the land, then the eaters are suffering a kind of cultural amnesia that is misleading and dangerous."[22]

As an antidote to this disconnection, a way of living in greater harmony with creation, Berry urges a kind of "urban agrarianism," in which one acts more deliberately and consciously regarding food. He suggests, for example, that we prepare our own food, learn the origins of our food and buy what is produced closest to our home; that whenever possible we deal directly with a local farmer, gardener, or orchardist; that we learn what is involved in the best farming and gardening; and that we learn as much as we can, by observation and direct experience if possible, about the life histories of food species. Berry also suggests that to the extent possible we participate in food production.

> If you have a yard or even just a porch box or a pot in a sunny window, grow something to eat in it. Make a little compost of your kitchen scraps and use it for fertilizer. Only by growing some food for yourself can you become acquainted with the beautiful energy cycle that revolves from soil to seed to flower to fruit to food to offal to decay, and around again. You will be fully responsible for

any food that you grow for yourself, and you will know all about it. You will appreciate it fully, having known it all its life.[23]

Bridging the disconnection between the human and creation might begin with being more mindful about what most of us do thoughtlessly three times each day: eat a meal.

Reconnecting with creation may be particularly challenging in urban and suburban settings, where the disconnection is most pronounced.[24] As the human population has exploded, so have the extraordinarily large cities around the globe. In 1900 only 14 percent of the population lived in cities. Today half the people of the world do. By 2050, 70 percent of our population will live in cities.[25] It is easy to imagine how creation becomes a mere fairy tale to people living where concrete, glass, and asphalt fill the landscape of their daily lives.

Yet the need to reconnect harmoniously with creation is most dire in these very settings. Many symptoms of the regression are especially prominent in cities. We may assume that this disconnect with creation would generate even higher levels of chronic societal anxiety in urban contexts. People in urban and suburban environments may need connections with the soil even more.

In a presentation on societal regression in 2009, Dan Papero of the Bowen Center noted that during a regression, signs of progress may also appear.[26] One encouraging trend is a movement, especially popular among urban and suburban young adults, to eat SLOW (Seasonal, Local, Organic, and Whole). Small and large urban farmers' markets and Community Supported Agriculture organizations offering locally grown produce are increasingly common in cities. Schools, churches, hospitals, and community associations in cities and towns are developing community gardens. Organic production is on the increase because of consumer demand. Multitudes of small farms across the country are reclaiming sustainable agricultural practices. The writings of Wendell Berry, Wes Jackson, Jane Goodall, Barbara Kingsolver, Michael Pollan, Joel Salatin, and others have helped to place an alternative way of thinking about food before an urban and suburban audience. These and other signs of greater environmental responsibility, cropping up in media and in practice, mark some progress. Leaders are arising out of the morass of the regression to offer alternative ways to relate to creation more harmoniously.

How might commitments to historical Christian practices reshape the way clergy and congregants live in a world where disconnection between the human and Earth results in irresponsibly consumptive lifestyles? The classical disciplines of prayer, worship, solitude, and simplicity provide resources for living in greater harmony with the created order. Other responsible ways of living involve using less energy, taking up less land for waste disposal, being frugal with scarce resources such as water, and recycling. Additionally, recreation that puts us into contact with creation is a thoughtful response. Clean parks in urban, inner-city areas might be the nearest some people ever come to being "out in creation." Congregations could find ways to help make this connection possible.

What can clergy contribute—out of our thoughtful beliefs and convictions, by example in our own lives, by our preaching and teaching, and by our leadership—to help reconnect our congregations with the creation and with life lived in greater harmony with it? Whatever we can do might well have an impact, not only on Earth and the other life-forms with whom we share it, but also on the level of anxiety in our communities and our culture.

A Way Forward

The current regression did not arise quickly. It developed over decades as anxiety increased, as reactivity heightened, as symptoms appeared, as society reacted to those symptoms with wars on drugs, poverty, and terrorism, as well as with denial, superficial agendas, loud rhetoric, knee-jerk legislation, and a failure of nerve to stand for what is needed. We abandoned our principles to silence the demands of the least mature. Over those years we elected leaders who promised to fix what was wrong. When they did not or could not, we ousted them for others who promised to take care of things. We demanded our rights as consumers and forsook our responsibilities as stewards. We acted out of our appetites and instincts rather than out of our reason. We exploited the resources of Earth and exploded in numbers. Congregations and their leaders and members were often part of this same soup. All of this took time.

The current regression will not end quickly. But that fact does not relieve congregational leaders from the task of responsible influence. Focusing on differentiation, becoming the best version of ourselves emotionally and spiritually that we can, is not optional for leaders during such times. Clarifying and developing our thinking about our core principles, beliefs, and values is necessary, for we will be asked to enunciate those, take a stand on those, and live consistently in light of them. Asking and answering key theological and ethical questions with our congregations will be part of the process. If we accept the environmental thesis of Bowen and others as the best explanation of the source of the societal anxiety underlying this regression, then we will learn to connect with creation more responsibly as stewards, living in greater harmony with the created order as leaders and as congregations.

●— **Questions for Reflection** ————————————————————

1. What aspects of the reactivity prevalent in the world around us do you find most directly having an impact on the congregation you serve? How might you relate differently to people who grow especially anxious because of those issues?

2. What form ought Christian preaching take in a time of increased societal regression? How do you address the issues without participating in the reactivity? How do you affirm Christian doctrine in ways that might counter the anxiety?

3. Does it seem odd to you to connect your pastoral leadership to issues of creation care, such as food production, eating practices, and simpler living? Are these things genuinely related to the anxiety in society that finds its way into the life of the church? What could your congregation do to engage the issue of stewardship of Earth more fully?

5

Proclamation

Preaching as Pastor and as Prophet

Who can map out the various forces at play in one soul? Man is a great depth, O Lord. The hairs of his head are easier by far to count than his feelings, the movements of his heart.

—Augustine of Hippo, *Confessions*

Preaching and teaching lie at the heart of religious traditions that emerged from the Reformation. Other traditions hold the role of proclamation in high regard as well. Along with baptism and the Eucharist, preaching remains one of the universal expressions of Christian worship. But what an audacious act it is for a man or woman to stand in a pulpit and attempt to speak the Word of God to the people of God! Preaching is fraught with temptations that range from hubris to cowardice. Ministerial reflection on the work of proclamation is vital in keeping our heads and hearts in the right place as we respond to our calling to preach. Bowen Family Systems Theory (BFST) provides concepts and perspectives that can help us gain clarity about what we are doing when we preach, about what dangers and challenges accompany the effort, and about how we might perform the work with greater integrity and less danger to our own souls and the souls of our congregations.

Preaching as a Relational Task

Professors of preaching and pastoral theologians wrestle with the definition of preaching, offering descriptions that range from deeply theological to objective and practical. For example, the late John Stott defined the act specifically in terms of God's revelation to God's people: "To expound Scripture is to open up the inspired text with such faithfulness and sensitivity that God's voice is heard and his people obey him."[1] Ronald E. Osborne, on the other hand, offers a more functional definition that could be used in research in the field. He describes preaching as "a human activity characterized by specific marks," identified according to ten characteristics. It is (1) a sustained mode of public address, (2) dealing with a religious or ethical theme, (3) bearing witness to the faith of a community, (4) rooted in a holy tradition, (5) occurring within an assumptive world of rationalized belief, (6) communicated through the person of the speaker, (7) employing the form of verbal art, (8) possessing the character of immediacy, (9) intended to convert the listener, and (10) conveying powers of renewal to those who hear.[2] One element that remains constant in definitions across the spectrum, however, is that preaching involves a relationship. It is not merely giving a talk.

A graduate of our seminary serves as a pastor in central Texas. One morning he sat in his favorite local coffee shop preparing a sermon for the upcoming Sunday. A woman saw him with his Bible open, his laptop running, and an intense, thoughtful look on his face. Curious, she leaned over from her table and asked him what he was doing. "I'm a pastor," he said. "I'm working on my sermon for next Sunday."

"What will you be preaching about?" she inquired. The pastor pointed to the biblical passage and described the text to her. "Do you think," the woman asked, "that your sermon will be the best that anyone ever preached about that?"

The pastor responded without having to take long to think, "No. Certainly not."

She asked, "Why don't you just find the best one and use that, then?"

Her question made a kind of logical sense, but it assumed a theology of preaching that the pastor did not hold. He explained to her how he understood his responsibility as a preacher: to listen to the biblical text, to attend to the life of the congregation, to consult the voices of Christian thinkers, living and dead, and to seek to design and deliver a message to this local congregation at this moment in their life together. He understood preaching as intrinsically relational.

Israel Galindo says that preaching is not "a performance grounded in textual exposition" but "a pastoral function grounded in a congregational context mediated by the relationship between pastor and flock." Describing "a good systems sermon," Galindo writes, "A sermon delivered by the pastor of a congregation is not merely a well-honed homily, a polished hermeneutical, or a theological exposition of a text. It has a function by virtue of who is preaching (the pastor-leader), who is being addressed (the congregation, who make up the community—the system), and the context that mediates their relationship (the church, a community of faith)."[3]

William H. Willimon acknowledges that any Christian may and should read and study the Bible. The pastor's role in preaching, however, remains distinct: "Yet when the pastor reads, he or she does so as priest, as one who listens to the text for the whole church, who interprets Scripture in light of the reading of the whole church down through the ages. The pastor's reading reminds the church that the Bible is produced by the community of faith and must be interpreted within that community under the inspiration of the Holy Spirit."[4]

The pastor's task is relational: to bring the congregation to attention before God, into a listening posture before the biblical text, the Christian tradition, and the Holy Spirit. The mere fact that preaching involves language makes the act inherently relational. The relational dimension of preaching is both what gives it abiding power in the life of the church and what makes it a place of vulnerability in the life of the preacher.

Because preaching is relational, we preachers bring our entire being to the task, just as we do in every relationship. Who we are physically, emotionally, spiritually, and intellectually is who sits contemplatively in the study and who steps into the pulpit. Who we are in relationship to each and all in our congregation is who ponders the text during the week and proclaims it during worship. Phillips Brooks observed that preaching is "truth communicated through personality." Brooks did not have in mind the contemporary stage or screen personality of popular preachers. By "personality" he contemplated the person, or the character, of the preacher: "Truth through Personality is our description of real preaching. The truth must come really through the person, not merely over his lips, not merely into his understanding and out of his pen. It must come through his character, his affections, his whole intellectual and moral being. It must come genuinely through him."[5]

Stage actors or politicians may be able to stand before an audience and pretend to be something other than who they really are. That effort does not work for authentic preaching. Our level of emotional and spiritual maturity, whatever it may be, accompanies us into the pulpit.

Our relationships with those in our congregations are what make us effective as preachers. Those same relationships can make us vulnerable to the togetherness force of the congregation's emotional system and inhibit our ability to proclaim the gospel as we ought. One challenge we face is the tension between authentic and appropriate affection for those we serve and the occasional need to speak to them with prophetic courage.

Pastoral affection is not only appropriate; it is also indispensable in an effective ministry. Paul's word to the Philippian church reflects that connection between Paul as a Christian leader and this congregation he dearly loves: "It is right for me to feel this way about you all, because I hold you in my heart, for you are all partakers with me of grace, both in my imprisonment and in the defense and confirmation of the gospel. For God is my witness, how I yearn for you all with the affection of Christ Jesus" (Phil. 1:7–8 ESV; cf. Gal. 4:19–20; 1 Thess. 2:7–8). Such pastoral affection grows out of the pastor's intimate and personal knowledge of the people and the cumulative fruit of their life and ministry shared together over time.[6]

Given the relative emotional reactivity of which we all are capable when anxiety rises, however, these important relationships can become a chink in our armor, a place of vulnerability. BFST observes that when anxiety rises, the togetherness force dominates an emotional system. Our herding instinct takes over, and we work to achieve a comfortable "oneness," in which individual thought and behavior are increasingly suppressed.[7] At the very time anxiety rises in the congregation, from whatever source—whether societal partisan politics, natural disasters, terrorist attacks, international crises, or financial or relational crises in the congregation—the pastor's capacity to speak a courageous, prophetic word may be inhibited by the desire to seek a "homey togetherness."[8] Confronting the congregation's beliefs, behaviors, or values with a biblical and prophetic stance may take a backseat to the more secure approach of seeking a shallow but secure sense of unity. Pastors may experience this as a hesitancy to offend or wound those they "love."

Another aspect of relational vulnerability we bring to preaching is the desire for approval. We can become emotionally dependent on others telling us how we are doing rather than being able to assess that for ourselves with some degree of objectivity. That dependence on others is a mark of our emotional immaturity, and it is a common one for pastors. Our fusion in relationships with those whose approval we desire—our parents, our spouse, our children, or our parishioners—leaves us vulnerable to their reactions and will inevitably inhibit our "speaking the truth in love" (Eph. 4:15).[9] Working on differentiation of self could help us become more faithful preachers.

Another dimension of our relationship to our congregations that leaves us susceptible to a "failure of nerve" in preaching is our financial dependence on them.[10] Wendell Berry criticizes pastors in the Deep South for their failure over the years to address issues of slavery and racism on this very basis. In his book-length essay *The Hidden Wound*, he pictures a pre–Civil War southern congregation in which slave owners and slaves often worshiped together. The "master," to avoid the painful question of how he could presume to own the body and life of a man he considered to be a recipient of the same salvation he claimed, had to play mind games. "To keep this question from articulating itself in his thought and demanding an answer," Berry says, "he had to perfect an empty space in his mind, a silence between heavenly concerns and earthly concerns, between body and spirit."[11] But what of the preacher in the pulpit? How could he manage that tension? Berry writes:

> But also consider this congregation of masters and slaves from the point of view of the pulpit. How, facing that mixture, and dependent on the white half of it for your livelihood, would you handle such a text as the Sermon on the Mount? . . . If a man wanted to remain a preacher he would have to honor that division in the hearts and minds of the congregation between heaven and earth, body and soul. His concern obviously had to be with things heavenly; unless he was a saint or a fool he would leave earthly things to the care of those who stood to benefit from them.[12]

The consequence of this compromise was a southern religion that increasingly focused on the question of salvation and factored issues of justice and truth out of the equation of Christian living. Berry calls this theology a "bogus mysticism" that allows one to "secure the benefits of eternal bliss without having to give up the benefits of temporal vice: corrupt your soul and save it too!"[13]

Pastors may fail to address racism, corruption, economic injustices, care for refugees and strangers, consumptive lifestyles, or creation care, particularly when political polarization sends fault lines through most congregations. When congregational finances suffer, pastors may find themselves "tiptoeing through the tithers," careful not to offend church members politically, economically, or theologically.[14]

Proclamation and Emotional Triangles

Bowen described emotional triangles as the molecules of human emotional systems.[15] With that metaphor in mind, we may compare the pastor's time in the study and the pulpit to pouring a catalyst into a beaker in a lab, encouraging chemical reactions that sometimes powerfully realign congregational molecular structures. The essential triangle at work in a congregation is that of the spiritual leader, the congregation, and the God they worship and serve. This triangle shows up in the biblical account of Moses and the people of Israel at Mount Sinai. The people discovered that interaction with the holy God who had delivered them from Egypt was too frightening to endure. "You speak to us," they told Moses, "and we will listen; but do not let God speak to us, or we will die" (Exod. 20:19). Moses agreed to this arrangement. From that point forward, "the people stood at a distance, while Moses drew near to the thick darkness where God was" (v. 21). The people's discomfort with God drove them to turn to Moses as a mediator. He found himself managing his own relationship not only with Yahweh (33:11–13) but with the people of Israel as well (32:30–34). Moses's experience bears out the observation of Friedman regarding triangles: "To the extent a third party to an emotional triangle tries unsuccessfully to change the relationship of the other two, the more likely it is that the third party will wind up with the stress for the other two."[16]

This triangle is as basic to the life of the congregation as the father-mother-child triangle is to the nuclear family.[17] We pastors can easily find ourselves in a Moses-like predicament, where congregations expect us to be professional Christians, mediating for them with God. As a result, preaching can take on this triangular emotional process in which the congregation expects to hear from God through the pastor, and the congregation then deals with the preacher and the sermonic words rather than with their relationship to God. They can decide what to do with what the preacher says without having to encounter the impact of God's Word on them. This can be stressful for the pastor.

Triangles can catch the preacher off guard in other ways as well. People in a congregation hold a variety of beliefs or opinions about issues that matter to them. Pastors can inadvertently "take sides" on an issue between two others simply by a text selection or a sermon illustration. A husband and wife may have argued about a matter on the way to worship that morning, and the pastor's opening illustration seems to side with the wife. As they walk out of the sanctuary, she smiles and greets the pastor. Her husband glares. The pastor has been triangled in without knowing what has transpired. Such a process underscores the way the act of preaching can affect the molecular structure of the congregational emotional system.[18]

When a pastor knows of issues between congregants or factions in the congregation and addresses the *content* rather than the emotional *process*, the triangles can become divisive and destructive. Bowen observed that each triangle interlocks with other triangles, allowing anxiety to flow freely across the entire emotional system. Notice Paul's firm but gentle words to two women in Philippi and to their pastor: "I urge Euodia and I urge Syntyche to be of the same mind in the Lord. Yes, and I ask you also, my loyal companion, help these women" (Phil. 4:2–3). We do not know what the dividing issue was. For Paul, the relationship mattered most.[19] Pastors who are learning to "think systems and watch process" might find creative ways to engage such anxious relationships in the church.

Preaching as a Means of Detriangling

If the basic triangle of God, the pastor, and the people is a given in congregational life, how might the pastor work at detriangling in the work of proclamation? BFST observes that during periods of relative calm in an emotional system, the triangles that form its molecular structure may be stable and quiet. People may be "getting along" with God and one another quite well. What happens, however, when anxiety rises in the life of the congregation or the life of the pastor? Does that primary triangle begin to light up? Do people begin to depend more on the pastor for their theology, their beliefs about ethical issues, their sense of guidance individually or corporately? Do they demand that the pastor address certain issues or hot political topics?[20] Does the pastor sometimes become anxious about matters of church attendance or finances and try to pull God onto the preacher's side to address the issue from the pulpit, rather than encouraging congregants to take the matter up with God themselves?

Preaching itself might become the means for a pastor to work at detriangling, finding ways to stay in touch with the people while pushing them back toward taking responsibility for their relationship to God and Scripture to formulate their beliefs, practice their faith, and discern God's guidance. Jesus turned an inquiring scholar back to Scripture to form his own opinions about the interpretation of the word "neighbor" in Leviticus 19:18 by telling him the story of the good Samaritan. Likewise, thoughtful preaching might find a way to help people hear from God and respond to God with a pastor-coach working alongside them rather than with a pastor-mediator taking on the task for them. We might approach preaching with a key question: How do I stay in touch with these people and with God, while encouraging them to work out the issues between them? We need to be clear about whether our goal is to tell people what to think, believe, and do, or whether it is to place truth before them in such a way that they must come to terms with God, not with us. James Lamkin observed that the preacher "is present to what is happening between God and the listener, *but the preacher is not responsible for that relationship.*" On occasion, when preaching a challenging text, Lamkin says something like this: "I, as a preacher, don't know what to make of this difficult text either. But it is *my* job to remind *you* that it is in *our* Bibles. *Each of us* is responsible for *our* response to *God*."[21] This is detriangling at work from the pulpit.

Preaching and Differentiation of Self

Murray Bowen's definition of a family leader easily transfers to other leadership roles in emotional systems: "Operationally, the ideal family treatment begins when one can find a family leader with the courage to define self, who is as invested in the welfare of the family as in self, who is neither angry nor dogmatic, whose energy goes into changing self rather than telling others what they should do, who can know and respect the multiple opinions of others, who can modify self in response to the strengths of the group and who is not influenced by the irresponsible opinions of others."[22] The well-defined family leader Bowen describes possesses qualities that, if used to describe a pastor, would powerfully shape the task of preaching.

How might work on differentiating a self come to affect the work of proclamation? How might preaching look if done by one whose level of emotional maturity were toward the lower end of the scale? What about someone whose level of differentiation were higher up the scale? The descriptions that follow represent a continuum—showing up one way on the lower end and differently on the higher end. Rather than trying to locate yourself at an exact place, ask, "Which qualities or characteristics would our congregation say I most embody on a regular basis? What about when anxiety is higher in the world, the church, or my own life?"

Preaching at Lower Levels of Differentiation

At lower levels of differentiation, the pastor is less sure of self and more dependent on the approval of others. Galindo argues, "When a pastor of a congregation stands before the flock with messages that communicate 'I will take care of you,' 'I need you to validate my worth and ministry,' 'You need me, and would be lost without me,' 'I bear your burden,' or 'I know it all, I'm the expert,' he or she reflects not only a lack of differentiation but also reveals a neurotic pastor-congregation relationship."[23]

With less emotional maturity to work from, preaching can take on a variety of traits that over time will not serve the pastor or the congregation well. More anxious preachers will generate or accelerate anxiety in the congregation with their preaching, rather than reduce it. When pastors feed the polarization of our society with sermons about some group or person "out there" who is threatening our lives or lifestyle, our values, or our beliefs, they are probably expressing their own anxiety. Preachers who function anxiously in the congregation's space only generate and accelerate the anxiety their hearers likely have brought with them to the preaching moment. People then leave worship more anxious than when they arrived, more reactive, less able to think for themselves, and more likely to act based on feeling.

When anxiety rises, less emotionally mature pastors will be more likely to encourage the congregation to depend on them for thinking, for theology, for ethical decision making. This is a form of overfunctioning that encourages an underfunctioning congregation. Such behavior can also be a form of the triangling mentioned earlier, in which the pastor steps between God and the congregation. Pastor and congregation play reciprocal parts in this dance, in which the congregation tacitly agrees to let the pastor think for them or, in some cases, expects the pastor to do so.

Less emotionally mature pastors will be more likely to take sides in congregational disputes, even from the pulpit. A leader's stepping into these congregational triangles will inevitably increase the congregation's anxiety, yielding the predictable symptoms of increased disagreement, the departure of some of the flock, irresponsible behavior on the parts of church members who become dependent on the pastor to settle matters, and plenty of blame and finger-pointing.

The less well-differentiated the preachers are, the more difficult they will find it to address issues that are critical to the congregation's spiritual and moral formation, such as matters of social justice. They will carefully avoid addressing certain topics to avoid conflict or to ease their own or others' anxiety. They may present this as an attempt to preserve harmony or achieve unity or fellowship in the church, when in reality it is an underfunctioning response that refuses to be responsible with the gospel of Christ and the people of Christ.

Less-well-differentiated preaching may focus on topics more "intellectually," keeping the congregation from relating to either God or the preacher. The sermon may sound more like an academic lecture. Even when the pastor preaches with passion, the subject matter is unrelated to the real lives of the people in the room (the furnishings of heaven, the temperature of hell, or what became of the Hittites?).[24] This is a distancing response in the pulpit.

Out of fear and financial dependence on the congregation (or the congregation's financial dependence on certain families), less-well-differentiated preaching attends most often to "spiritual" matters (prayer, doctrine, comfort). It refuses to address issues of people's real lives or to help them think through issues facing their culture from a biblical perspective, such as greed, racism, privilege, sexism, creation care, or immigration. The dependence involved makes the risk too great.

Preachers who are less sure of themselves may insist on attaining agreement around issues on which mature people often disagree. They may confidently insist that their view is the biblical one against all others. To disagree with the preacher is to disagree with God. This focus on purity of doctrine or practice regarding a peripheral issue may well be an expression of the togetherness force at work in anxious times.

Although preachers have certainly practiced plagiarism for many years, access to sermon manuscripts, audio, and video on the internet has made the option more available than ever.[25] When pastors rely on the writings or sermons of others for content, they may be demonstrating a lack of basic confidence in their own thoughts or beliefs. Alternatively, the issue could be a lack of capacity to organize their time according to what is most important. They may have difficulty saying "no" because they want to please others, or because they have simply not thought through their own values and priorities. Instead, under pressure to preach well and receive others' approval, they simply borrow other preachers' thoughts or words to replace their own thinking. This would be a mark of someone at a lower level of differentiation.

Preaching Farther Up the Scale

At higher levels of functioning, we can expect the pastor's emotional maturity to shape the qualities of the preaching. More emotionally mature pastors, for example, would focus more on the task of bringing the congregation to attention before God rather than on impressing congregants, winning approval, attacking them, or telling them what to think. Out of their own well-defined understanding of what preaching entails, they would keep themselves better focused on what they believe about the purpose of preaching.

These more emotionally mature preachers would be able to express their own thoughts, beliefs, and questions clearly, without demanding that others think or believe the same. They would be able to distinguish between those beliefs and principles they hold at the core of their being and those that they are still working to clarify. They are comfortable when, after the sermon, another well-differentiated person says, "Pastor, if I heard you correctly today, I'm not sure that we see eye-to-eye on that question." They can say "I believe this" without having to say "You must believe this as well."

The better differentiated a pastor is, the more able the pastor will be to manage personal anxiety about issues in the larger world and the denominational family, as well as challenges facing the congregation and relationships within the congregation. When the pastor's own emotional reactivity to such issues is less in play, the pastor is better able to address those matters with the congregation without stirring their reactivity further. To the degree this is possible, congregants will be better able to think through and formulate their own responses.

"Prophetic preaching" is not necessarily a courageous act of differentiation. Boldly addressing controversial ethical issues may be a symptom of anxious overfunctioning, telling the congregation what to think. It can represent a kind of enforced togetherness in which everyone knows the acceptable "Christian" response to an issue. Such preaching discourages people from thinking through issues for themselves or entering dialogue with others who think differently. The preacher may point the prophetic finger at "those people" outside the congregation to blame for the world's ills rather than call the church to responsible action.

More-differentiated prophetic proclamation shows itself in terms of an "I" statement: "This is what I have come to think or believe about this matter for these reasons." Such preaching does not attack others or define those outside the congregation to condemn them. Such preachers approach controversial issues fairly and with acknowledgment and consideration for those who have come to think differently about the matter.[26] Margaret Marcuson offers three pieces of advice to those who would preach about controversial issues: (1) define yourself, not others; (2) prepare yourself: don't get reactive to the reactivity; and (3) stay connected to the people who disagree with you.[27] The ability to approach issues in this way is a function of our own differentiation as pastors.

Better-differentiated preachers can serve as spokespersons for prophetic texts, confronting the congregation with difficult truths, while simultaneously taking the posture of a humble listener to the text. Such preaching will focus less on "you" or "they" as the addressee and more on "we." This participation as one under the authority of the text, acknowledging the same guilt and complicity as one's listeners, makes authentic prophetic preaching a possibility.

As the preacher works from a more differentiated position, over time it might become possible for a more open emotional system to develop, in which the congregation may increasingly trust the pastor to address any necessary issue freely and in which congregational members will listen and form their own opinions.[28]

Finally, with the necessary work on differentiation, pastors should be able to maintain relationships outside the pulpit in such a way that the content or focus of their preaching cannot be affected by congregants who have power or money.

Conclusion

Preaching is a relational domain that does not occur in a vacuum. One brings to the task both the reality of the congregation as an emotional system and the reality of one's own level of basic self. Our own level of differentiation establishes limits for our approach to preaching, even when we are not aware of it, and we cannot escape it. However, work on differentiation of self inevitably contributes to a more authentic and effective ministry of proclamation. Over time, the work one does on self brings a different and more mature person to the task of proclamation, allowing the preacher to function at a better level relationally. That work on self, as a leader in a system, will have influence on the entire system. A more emotionally mature pastor will preach in a way that is more likely to develop the emotional and spiritual maturity of the congregation. Although a congregation may demand a mediator to go to God on their behalf, they will find themselves expected to take responsibility to develop an individual relationship with God. Although they may clamor for someone to do their theology for them, think for them, and tell them how to behave, they will need to face up to biblical truth and make their faith their own, so that they are not merely conforming to what the pastor says is so. This way, they are increasingly living out of what they deeply believe to be right themselves. If the pastor can maintain relationships with the congregants while pulling out of the fusion that has developed from the congregation's dependence on its leader (and vice versa), both pastor and congregation can grow emotionally, relationally, and spiritually.

The task of developing a sermon—listening to a text, to the Holy Spirit, and to the congregation, thinking through one's own principles and beliefs, attempting to stand before the congregation and call the people and oneself to attention before God—can form the pastor as well as the congregation. The work of sermon preparation does not occur in isolation. The emotional pressures and togetherness demands of a congregation are right there in the office as the pastor carefully studies biblical texts, deliberately constructs sentences, and wisely chooses illustrations. Being an "I" in the face of those pressures and stepping into the pulpit with a message so prepared is a weekly exercise in differentiation of self.[29]

●— Questions for Reflection ─────────────────────

1. In what ways are you aware of the "presence" of the congregation in your study as you prepare to preach? Whose opinion of the sermon concerns you most?

2. Which characteristics of preaching at lower levels of differentiation have you experienced? Which have you overcome? How have you done so? Which elements of the relational dimension of preaching still challenge you?

3. Can you think of examples of ways in which your preaching has had an influence on the way that you offer pastoral care to your congregation? How has your preaching played a part in your efforts to lead the church? How have the pastoral needs of your congregation had an impact on your preaching?

6

Pastoral Care

Helping without Hurting

There is a great deal of unmapped country within us which would have to be taken into account in an explanation of our gusts and storms.

—George Eliot, *Daniel Deronda*

Pastoral care is the third of three interlocking domains of pastoral ministry. Like the other two, leadership and proclamation, clergy carry it out in the context of the interrelated emotional systems in which every pastor participates: the pastor's own family, the families *of* the congregation, and the family that *is* the congregation. These interrelated systems play a significant role in the work of pastoral care. A conversation with one person about that individual's life with God could have far-reaching results. A visit to Mrs. Smith at the local nursing home on Monday morning becomes common knowledge among the congregation's senior adults by Wednesday night, and they may perceive a greater sense of the pastor's affection for them and of God's care for them as well.

In pastoral care, as in preaching and leadership, pastors bring their entire selves to their work. Because these three domains of ministry interlock, work done in pastoral care both affects and is affected by the pastor's preaching and leadership. Competent care compassionately and authentically offered to a family during an experience of bereavement, for example, affects the way that family hears the pastor's sermons and perhaps the way they can collaborate with the pastor in discerning the congregation's future. Preaching itself is one of the ways that pastors offer care, as they address the issues of life with which their people struggle. The tasks interlock. Like preaching and leadership, pastoral care is intensely relational. Consequently, Bowen Family Systems Theory (BFST) can help a pastor negotiate this territory of relationships more confidently.[1]

The Task of Christian Pastoral Care

If pastors are not always clear on their theology of preaching, it is no surprise that the functions of pastoral care can be confusing. Clergy often come to this aspect of their work with less training and experience than they do for proclamation. Preachers can hone the discipline of preparing and delivering sermons over the years in the privacy of their study, often with time to consult multiple resources. Pastoral care crises more often appear suddenly, demand a response immediately, and differ from each other like snowflakes. Being theologically thoughtful is challenging.

Secular culture does not offer much help. Willimon cites the observation of his own teacher of pastoral care, James Dittes of Yale, that the last socially acceptable paradigm for pastoral ministry is "pastor as therapist."[2] Willimon suggests that one of the causes of ministerial exhaustion is that people often enter the ministry with no higher calling than "to meet people's needs."[3] They too easily become "a combination minister and masseur," as Flannery O'Conner once described a Protestant pastor in Atlanta.[4]

But pastors are not therapists. Unless we have a license, we are not "counselors." Although the secular therapeutic professions can be helpful and necessary, pastoral care is something distinctively different.

We distinguish pastoral care from counseling and therapy theologically. First, the pastor, as opposed to the therapist, offers pastoral care "in the name of Jesus." That is, the pastor is not representing himself or herself individually, with appropriate educational credentials or professional certification. Willimon writes: "It is not our vocation to 'care for people.' Pastors care for people in the Name of Jesus. The shepherd is responsible not only to the flock, but also to God for the flock. We worry not only about the health and happiness of our people, but about their salvation as well. And that makes all the difference."[5]

Pastors function very much like priests when we walk into experiences of human suffering as representatives of Jesus Christ. We do not step into an intensive care unit simply as ourselves but as persons authorized to represent Christ to the suffering individual and attendant family members. Pastors are not present to find solutions, necessarily, but to remind those who are suffering of God's love and presence with them.

Second, Christ's call upon the pastor's life authorizes pastoral care. A secular counselor or therapist has no business knocking on the door of a client and asking how they are doing with the issues discussed in last Thursday's session. They cannot encounter a client in a grocery store aisle and pick up the conversation about the client's marriage. A licensed counselor cannot phone a person they suspect to be struggling and invite them for coffee and conversation. Pastors can. As long as they are working within the boundaries of their own flock, pastors can take initiative in extending care in ways their secular counterparts cannot ethically do.[6] Pastors engage this work as a part of their legitimate pastoral authority to "tend the flock of God" that is in their charge (1 Pet. 5:2).

Additionally, pastors come to moments of human suffering as representatives not only of Christ but of the church as well. When pastors extend care and compassion to the hurting, we do so on behalf of the congregations we serve. In pastoral care, we offer the body of Christ not only by sharing bread and cup but also by offering the care of the church itself. David K. Switzer contends that caring is *pastoral* "when it is not merely one person's caring for another . . . but when such caring is *an expression of the whole life and purpose of the Christian community.*"[7] Pastoral care has a context, and that context is the church. Professional counselors may be Christians, but they do not deliver care as representatives of the church in the way that pastors do.

Pastoral care consists in thinking with people about their lives in the light of the gospel so that they are better able to connect the ordinariness of life, particularly the experience of suffering, with the work of God in their lives. Willimon encourages pastors to think of pastoral care as "our clerical attempt to help the congregation worship the true and living God in every aspect of their lives."[8] Pastoral care is a way of saying "God" to people during their most difficult situations. Eugene Peterson defines pastoral care as that part of Christian ministry that "specializes in the ordinary."[9] Peterson regards it as a mistake for pastors to see people and their struggles as problems to deal with or solve. Instead, he calls pastors to the task of "directing worship in the traffic, discovering the presence of the cross in the paradoxes and chaos between Sundays, calling attention to the 'splendor in the ordinary,' and, most of all, teaching a life of prayer to our friends and companions in the pilgrimage."[10]

Wayne Menking offers this definition of pastoral care: "The vocation of pastoral care, its 'office' if you will, is to care for others in the moment of their need.

Caregivers seek to embody and extend God's love to those who suffer hurt, pain, disease or any other malady that disrupts life. More specifically, pastoral caregivers seek to strengthen and empower the faith of the hurting and disrupted in order that they may be sustained through their circumstance, and ultimately prevail against the powers that seek to wrest their life away."[11] Becoming clear theologically about the nature of pastoral care is the pastor's first step in being able to offer such care with integrity. Otherwise the pastor will likely succumb to the demands and expectations of a culture that simply wants its needs met.

Relational Vulnerability of the Caregiver

Because pastoral care is essentially relational, it leaves the pastor vulnerable to the togetherness force in situations where anxiety is high. During crises in the lives of people, particularly those to whom the pastor is closely connected, the anxiety will nearly always be intense. The relational challenge for pastors is to manage personal anxiety and maintain a degree of objectivity, so that we are in a better position to help. Switzer observes that the anxiety can be overwhelming and that our reactivity can easily get the best of us in such situations. "A lot of us," he writes, "can faint, so to speak, at the sight and sound of various kinds of emotional 'blood.'"[12]

Our connection to and affection for those in our flock leaves us vulnerable to offering a reactive kind of "care" that does not help. We can, for example, easily get snared in a web of emotional triangles as we step into a family in crisis. We may be tempted to "take sides" as we listen to someone berate a spouse who is not there to offer their side of the story. We can jump to conclusions, forfeiting the more solid ground of our neutrality. We can lose necessary emotional boundaries with the other and surrender our effectiveness. We can join the depressed one in sadness or the fearful one in fear. We can overfunction, stepping in to do for the other what they could do on their own. We can slip mindlessly into a role we have occupied for years in our own family, perhaps as the "responsible eldest," who takes on the task of fixing relationships, attempting to calm others down, solving problems for everyone, thinking for others, or treating others as incompetent to deal with their problems. The list of possible ways to be snagged by the emotionality of pastoral care seems endless.

Can Helping Really Hurt?

Steve Corbett and Brian Fikkert's book *When Helping Hurts: How to Alleviate Poverty without Hurting the Poor . . . and Yourself*, widely read by social work practitioners, applies equally well to pastoral care.[13] If the pastor does not possess a clear sense of self, of responsibilities and of boundaries, pastoral care can be an invasive act of overfunctioning in another's life, reinforcing their helplessness. When the long-term goal of pastoral care is not clear, anxious pastors can move too quickly to alleviate pain. Consequently, work on differentiation is one of the most important pursuits for a pastor who desires genuinely to help a congregation, corporately and individually, to grow in their relationship with God through ordinary events, including confusion and suffering.[14]

When Bill died of a massive heart attack in his early fifties, shock waves moved through both his family and his church. He was a leader in both systems, admired and trusted. His wife, Joan, had depended on Bill for so many things. He had been the breadwinner, had managed the family finances, and had seen that the house and automobiles remained in good repair. Bill had also assumed this responsible posture in the congregation, where he served as a deacon, led various key committees over the years, and served as the chair on a successful capital campaign for a new worship center. The pastor's own father had died only a few years earlier, leaving his mom to struggle with so many practical things in her life. Her children quickly took on many roles their father had previously filled. When Bill died, the pastor felt the togetherness force tangibly pushing him to move in and care for Joan, perhaps by finding someone who could help with financial decisions or home maintenance. Fortunately, before taking any action, the pastor considered the assumption behind such a move: that Joan was incapable of either doing for herself or finding help on her own, although there was no evidence of her "helplessness." Rather than yielding to that initial inclination to "help," the pastor chose instead to remain in contact with her as a pastor, to stay focused on the question of how she was experiencing God during these days of loss and recovery, while affirming a confidence that she could find her way through this wilderness with God's presence and God's people. Despite the difficulties she found herself in, Joan did remarkably well in adjusting to life on her own during the year following Bill's death. A thoughtful response on the part of the pastor had made it more likely that pastoral care would help instead of hurt.

Pastoral Care and Differentiation of Self

BFST can serve as a map to help pastors navigate the waters of pastoral care, which forms such a large part of our vocation and occupies a good portion of our time. BFST does not simply provide new techniques or add a few strategies to the pastor's toolbox. Sometimes the theory seems to come across to clergy in that way. Rather, BFST offers pastors a way to think about ourselves and our relationships that can guide us when the emotional waves are running high. Our own level of differentiation will profoundly affect our effectiveness, especially in times of intense anxiety.

As we did with preaching, let us consider what pastoral care might look like on the continuum of differentiation. To the degree that a pastor is functioning lower on the scale of differentiation, pastoral care will reflect one set of character traits more, especially in times of intense anxiety. As one's level of emotional maturity moves up the scale, another set of traits will increasingly prevail.

Pastoral Care at the Lower End of the Scale

A critical component of emotional maturity is the capacity to define one's own beliefs and principles and to act in accord with them. The alternative is to let others define our roles and then conform to their expectations. At lower levels of differentiation, we would expect to find pastors who have not done the work of thinking theologically and practically about the nature of pastoral care. Defining their role is then easily co-opted by a demanding and dependent church member, or an entire congregation. Willimon calls such an approach to pastoral care a "promiscuous ministry." It is ministry with "no internal, critical judgment about what care is worth giving," in which the pastor becomes the victim of "a culture of insatiable need."[15]

Farther down the scale of differentiation, pastors are more susceptible to being overwhelmed by the emotionality of those they attempt to help. Pastors may "weep with those who weep" (Rom. 12:15) in a way that diminishes the capacity of both pastor and parishioner to think. Pastors risk tossing their objectivity overboard amid a storm of sympathy. Friedman challenges the concept of "empathy," identifying it as an emotionally reactive response that is often unhelpful. In a chapter titled "The Fallacy of Empathy" in his book on leadership, *A Failure of Nerve*, he argues: "As lofty and noble as the concept of empathy may sound, and as well-intentioned as those may be who make it the linchpin idea of their theories of healing, education, or management, societal regression has too often perverted the use of empathy into a disguise for anxiety, a rationalization for the failure to define a position, and a power tool in the hands of the 'sensitive.'"[16]

Wayne Menking distinguishes between empathy (feeling *with*) and sympathy (feeling *for*).[17] He asserts that sympathy is the culprit that contributes to "stuckness" in pastoral ministry. That, rather than empathy, he argues, is what Friedman was addressing.[18]

Sympathy focuses on the feelings of others in a way that may interfere with pastoral care. Sympathetic pastors may seek quick fixes to alleviate the pain of the moment because of their own emotional squeamishness, rather than attempting to lead sufferers to a more solid place. Less emotionally mature pastors may hesitate to say what they are thinking in emotionally intense situations. Palliative sympathy is the togetherness force at work. Empathy, properly understood, can be an expression of individuality, an intellectual function in which we intentionally attempt to understand both the facts of the other's circumstances and that person's emotional reactions to those facts.

Clergy at lower levels of emotional maturity are more likely to attempt to ease their own discomfort in the face of anxiety by comforting others. The hug offered to a grieving widower may be entirely appropriate when offered from a thoughtful posture of what he most needs. But when the purpose is to calm the *caregiver's* anxiety with the other's grief, it fails to express authentic care.

More reactive pastors may have difficulty separating their own emotional needs from those of the people they serve. A pastor's own unresolved emotional attachment to a parent could easily interfere with ministry to a family struggling with a teenager who is acting out. Issues in a pastor's marriage may sabotage attempts to help a couple struggling to modify their conflictual relationship. Walking into a hospital room where a woman the age of the pastor's mother is dying of bone cancer, as the pastor's mother did, may stir up emotions that neutralize attempts to care for this family. Such pastors may assume, out of sympathy rather than empathy, that what the family is experiencing is the same as what they experienced. They fail to understand the uniqueness of this family's relationships and needs and to respond thoughtfully.

Pastors working with less sense of self can easily define pastoral care as "helping people feel better," offering a knockoff version of what pastoral care ought to be. This approach confuses authentically "caring for" with sympathetically "taking care of."[19] Such pastors may see pastoral care as assuaging other people's discomfort, without realizing their own need for others to be calm so that they can be calmer themselves. This quick-fix approach may circumvent the role that suffering often plays in shaping human character. The goal of pastoral care that grows out of the narrative of the cross would be less likely to move too quickly toward such a remedy.

While some reactive pastors may overfunction, others may move toward underfunctioning, becoming paralyzed in the face of certain needs. Pastors who are "allergic" to nursing homes, for example, may find ways to avoid visiting isolated and lonely church members out of their own reactivity.

Stanley Hauerwas once accused the contemporary pastor of being "a quivering mass of availability."[20] Reactive pastors may indiscriminately respond to congregational expectations for help as if the pastor were indispensable. Such a response places the congregation and other staff members in an increasingly helpless position and leaves less time for pastors to engage the other tasks that are theirs to do. The senior pastor need not make every hospital visit. Congregants who learn from reactive pastors to expect their presence at every "crisis," no matter how minor, become less capable of doing the work of caring for one another and accepting care by others as an expression of the church's care. Meanwhile the pastor can spend enormous amounts of time operating in an emergency mode. Family vacations, the pastor's needed time for spiritual or intellectual renewal, work on this week's sermon, providing needed leadership to the church's life, and other events are often interrupted by congregational crises that the pastor responds to like a dog to a whistle.

Pastoral Care at the Higher End of the Scale

As emotional maturity increases on the scale, we could expect to find pastors who have thought through more clearly the nature of Christian pastoral care and of their responsibilities in that domain. They can articulate what they believe about this work, what the congregation can expect of them, and what appropriate boundaries might be. They have considered their theology, gifts, resources, and the congregation's needs. These pastors can live congruently with these positions even when the level of anxiety in their lives or the congregation's experiences rises. It would be worthwhile for pastors working on differentiation to attempt to articulate their beliefs and positions in writing to gain greater clarity on the matter.

Pastors with greater levels of differentiation are less likely to see their congregants as helpless. Instead, they will work from an assumption that with the appropriate kind of care during crises, people can move forward with their lives. The pastor will not assume responsibility for solving the problems of confused or suffering people but will responsibly be with them, remind them of Christ's presence, and think with them about the struggles they are facing. When tempted to "do for" people what they are perfectly capable of doing for themselves, the more mature pastor will refrain from anxiously overfunctioning.

What mature pastors bring to pastoral care situations, however, is formidable. They will assume that people will do better in finding solutions to their problems during times of increased anxiety if someone is willing to think with them, while staying out of the anxious focus they have on the problem. Such listening and managing of one's own reactivity is a form of caring. Pastors become useless when they take sides in a family issue or merely sympathize with others in their pain. I sometimes ask ministry students—who often have learned from the culture to adopt maudlin sympathy as a definition of caring—if they were stuck in quicksand and sinking fast, would they rather someone jump in it with them (sympathy) or understand their situation and remain outside on solid ground, where they could be of most help. At higher levels of differentiation, we should expect to find pastors who work from the assumption that an objective outside position is more helpful.

Admittedly, pastors step into moments of human pain and suffering that are overwhelming, both to the sufferer and to the caregiver. The losses or crises of people we hold in deep affection make maintaining appropriate objectivity a challenge. We can easily become absorbed in the same emotional soup as those we want to help. Willimon acknowledges: "One of the great challenges of our pastoral care is to be present with people in their need and not be overwhelmed by their need, to be available to our people as their pastor without being captured exclusively by them, to take their pain seriously and at the same time to take seriously our task to proclaim Jesus Christ and him crucified and resurrected."[21]

No pastor is so well differentiated as to remain unaffected all the time. Nevertheless, more emotionally mature pastors work to modify their own reactivity and thus are able to offer a bit of objectivity. They then can retain the capacity to serve as a resource to think with sufferers about God's presence and to help them find a way forward. The higher the level of differentiation of self, the greater that capacity.

The farther up the scale of differentiation we move, the more likely we are to find pastors with a sufficiently high threshold for the pain of others that they can be with suffering people without having to alleviate their own anxiety. Managing their own reactivity allows them to be present to others in a caring way, neither distancing themselves from the pain nor irresponsibly ignoring those who suffer. Such maturity allows pastors to respect the pain of others without needing to have "the right words" or to apply a benign theological bandage to congregants' wounds to make themselves feel better.

More emotionally mature pastors understand that listening to people does not require agreeing with them about the issues involved. It is possible to listen carefully and to observe the emotional process, while working to maintain objectivity about the content of their struggle. Such a posture allows a pastor to maintain an outside position that does not take sides with one or another of the people involved, which would effectively remove the pastor from a helpful position in the triangle. The emotionality of another's situation can easily snare us. Keeping out of that trap requires a level of emotional maturity and work on paying attention to one's own reactivity.

Pastors working on differentiation will grow increasingly comfortable with not having answers to all questions, solutions to every problem, or knowing exactly what others should think or do in every situation. Rather, these maturing pastors will work on keeping a sense of "what is mine to do" and will do that responsibly. They will be comfortable with mystery regarding the meaning of human suffering, with ambiguity in matters of theology, with openness to multiple possible solutions to problems, and with the recognition that other capable people also bring resources. Bowen referred to family leaders who "can modify self in response to the strengths of the group."[22] These maturing pastors recognize that they are not the sole repository of answers and solutions to everyone else's problems.

Those pastors who function at a higher level of differentiation will take full and appropriate responsibility for delivering pastoral care to their congregations. Not only will they think through what they believe about Christian pastoral care but they will also develop means to assure that their congregations have access to such care. They will be personally involved in that work but, especially in larger congregational contexts, will ensure that systems are in place among other staff members and lay leaders so that pastoral care needs do not fall through the cracks. Consider the decision of the Jerusalem apostles to devise a structure to meet the needs of the Greek-speaking widows in the church. Although they could not take responsibility for delivering food to these women in need themselves, they could organize others to do so (Acts 6:1–7).

Better-differentiated pastors will pay attention to their own emotional needs so that they can be more fully available as a resource to others during crises.[23] Part of the work on differentiation of self is coming to a fuller, more objective understanding of the emotional processes in our own families that have formed us. The self-understanding coming from such family work helps us to identify our automatic emotional responses to the needs of those we serve. Switzer argues: "To the extent that we can become increasingly aware of what's actually taking place inside of us and can recognize that our behavior is beginning to be particularly influenced by our inner drives, the more capable we become in relating to others in terms of *their* needs which they are now expressing to us rather than in behaviors (including words) which are subtly (and sometimes not so subtly) expressing *our own* needs."[24] Knowing ourselves and our families can be a big step toward being able to care for others more effectively.

More emotionally mature pastors can discern an appropriate role in pastoral care crises, not treating every situation and demand as having a comparable claim on their time and energy. Rather than automatically reacting to every need, thoughtful pastors working with more differentiation will be able to move deliberately into those situations where their presence, expertise, or experience is most required and will be most helpful. This discernment allows them to address their tasks and responsibilities in other pastoral domains.

Conclusion

Pastoral care is inherently relational, bringing the pastor face-to-face with people whose very future may be endangered. These people may have become dear to the pastor over time, or they may have been something of a thorn in the pastor's flesh. Alternatively, they may be relative strangers, whose pastoral care needs have arisen early in a pastor's tenure. In either case, as pastors we bring all of our relational vulnerability to the task. We bring that level of emotional maturity that is ours, and no more. To the degree that we are emotionally immature, we are likely to respond less helpfully to those in crisis, although we do the best we can. Our efforts will usually be of some help. But following the map provided by BFST offers the possibility of growing a greater capacity to care for the flock of God.

Although pastors can develop pastoral care skills, such as active listening, the most effective way forward requires more than techniques or tools. Working on differentiation of self will contribute to a more authentic and effective ministry of pastoral care. This capacity to remain connected to others in times of increased anxiety, while maintaining our principles and managing our own automatic responses, does not develop overnight. Such work on differentiation is a lifelong process, but each increment of growth will powerfully affect our ability to deliver effective pastoral care. We can be more fully present and accounted for without so easily succumbing to the anxiety inherent in the pain and suffering of those under our care. We can remain more thoughtful in difficult situations while others are caving in to the anxiety swirling around them.

Conversely, a thoughtful approach to pastoral care will offer the caregiver an opportunity to work on differentiation of self. Each pastoral conversation, hospital call, bereavement visit, or moment of crisis is an opportunity to attend to our own functioning and reactivity, thereby becoming aware of togetherness pressures generated by the anxiety of the moment. Paying attention to our automatic reactions and working to manage them is work on differentiation. Clues we pick up from our reactions during the crises of others may point us toward working on our own unresolved attachments in our families of origin. Noticing the emotional triangles that light up during a crisis and our own role in them can aid work on detriangling. We can meet our urges to take over, to provide the answers, or to overfunction with an intentional effort to calm ourselves, to look for the resources that others bring, and to examine our assumptions about the capabilities of those we serve. Observing the way that the sudden appearance of an anxious person requesting help diminishes our own ability to think clearly can teach us to turn to practices we have learned to use to calm down and think, such as prayer. We learn to attend to how feeling sorry for a sufferer pushes us to make them feel better so that we will feel better. We learn to let emotional reactions pass, for the good of the other. In so many ways, the work of pastoral care provides the opportunity to serve Christ by addressing the needs of others in Jesus's name, yet also brings occasions for growing in maturity as a pastor.

●— **Questions for Reflection** ———————————————————

1. How do you see the pastoral domains of proclamation, pastoral care, and leadership intersecting and overlapping? What would be an example from your own ministry where action in one of the domains affected outcomes in another?

2. How would you define "pastoral care" to a member of your congregation who asked?

3. What was your most difficult experience in offering pastoral care? Can you recall what emotional reactions you experienced as you heard about the need, encountered the person in need, and responded to their situation? How did those reactions affect the way in which you offered care? Would you do the same thing in the same way if you had opportunity to respond today?

7

Spiritual Formation

Growing in Christlikeness

Knowledge is an island in a sea of mystery. The metaphor takes its power from a firmly held fact: We live in a universe that is infinite, or effectively so. Our brains are finite, a mere 100 billion nerve cells. Our mental maps of the world are therefore necessarily finite. As time passes, the scale and detail of our maps increase, but they no more exhaust the worldscape they describe than a map of the Grand Canyon depletes the power of that natural chasm to astonish and surprise.

—Chet Raymo, *Skeptics and True Believers*

The work of Christian spiritual formation—both our own and that of those we serve—is one of our important tasks as pastoral theologians. Formation is not optional in the life of a pastor. Our spiritual practices affect our capacity to think theologically. Howard W. Stone and James O. Duke claim that work on spiritual formation is vital for all Christians to bridge the space between our day-to-day experiences and theological reflection. They write, "Food for a mature faith, including elements for theological reflection, can be provided by the church's guidance in spiritual disciplines—whether under the leadership of spiritual directors, in sharing groups, or in educational settings."[1] Our own ongoing experience of relationship with God grounds our theological reflection on our practices and experiences.

The task of pastors, then, is twofold: to enter personally into practices that contribute to our own formation in Christ and to equip those we serve to do the same. What do we mean by "spiritual formation"? Is it related in any significant way to the process of differentiation of self? What could Bowen Family Systems Theory (BFST) offer to help us understand and engage the process of spiritual formation? These are a few of the questions we take up as we think about this significant aspect of our ministries.

Dallas Willard on Spiritual Formation

The late Dallas Willard, professor of philosophy at the University of Southern California, led the way in thoughtful exploration and description of the experience of Christian spiritual formation among Protestants in the latter half of the twentieth century.[2] Willard's extensive thinking provides a foundation for considering what BFST might contribute to understanding and practicing spiritual formation. This chapter will attempt a conversation between Willard and Bowen around personal transformation, which Willard calls "renovation of the heart" and Bowen names "differentiation of self." As with any good conversation, we can anticipate exchange back and forth. How might working on differentiation contribute to efforts at spiritual formation? And how might spiritual practices aid the effort to differentiate a self in one's family?

Willard contends that *everyone* is formed spiritually.[3] We all undergo a process by which our "human spirit" or "will" takes on a definite character. Each of us becomes a certain kind of person in the depths of our being. This is spiritual formation. *Christian* spiritual formation, then, is a specific kind of experience. Willard describes it as "the Spirit-driven process of forming the inner world of the human self in such a way that it becomes like the inner being of Christ himself."[4] He asserts the seeming paradox of two important principles: on the one hand, Christians must make an effort for formation to take place, and on the other hand, no amount of effort alone can produce a Christlike character. That Christian spiritual formation is "Spirit-driven" means that it is God's work, not our own. It is grace, not merit, that produces such changes in us. Nevertheless, human intention and effort are involved. "Grace," he declares, "is opposed to earning, not to effort."[5]

Willard introduced "The Golden Triangle of Spiritual Growth" as a mental model for spiritual formation.[6] At the top of the triangle he placed "The Action of the Holy Spirit" (John 3:5; Rom. 8:10–13; Gal. 5:22–26). On the lower left corner he identified "The Ordinary Events of Life" (trials and temptations), and on the lower right corner "Planned Discipline to Put on a New

Heart." Willard labeled the center of the triangle "Centered in the Mind of Christ" (Rom. 13:14; Phil. 2:12–15). He understood the intervention of the Holy Spirit to be an absolute necessity. Otherwise, trials and temptations may only embitter us, instead of shaping us to reflect the character of Christ (Rom. 5:1–5; James 1:2–4). Without the aid of the Holy Spirit, the practice of spiritual disciplines will devolve into legalism instead of forming Christ in us (Col. 3:12–17; 2 Pet. 1:5–10). The top angle of the triangle, then, is vitally connected to the other two.

The crucial aspect of Willard's model is planned discipline. Trials and temptations will come and go; we need not seek them. Scripture encourages us to endure those experiences faithfully by dependence on God, allowing the Holy Spirit to use them to further form us (Rom. 5:3–5; 8:28–29). Spiritual disciplines are activities we intentionally engage.[7] Willard sorts the classical spiritual practices into two groups: (1) disciplines of abstinence, in which we deliberately give up something we would normally engage in for a time in order to attend to God (solitude, silence, fasting, frugality, chastity, secrecy, sacrifice, watching), and (2) disciplines of engagement, in which for a time we intentionally take on something that we do not ordinarily practice (study, worship, celebration, service, prayer, fellowship, confession, submission). He suggests that the disciplines of abstinence function to weaken or break the power of things that may interfere with our involvement with the kingdom of God. Disciplines of engagement immerse us more deeply in that kingdom.[8] We do these things not to earn God's favor or to get God's attention; rather, we practice them to give our attention to God.

According to a legend of one of the ancient desert monks, a disciple approached an elder and asked, "Holy One, is there anything I can do to make myself enlightened?"

The teacher replied, "As little as you can do to make the sun rise in the morning."

The surprised disciple asked, "Then of what use are the spiritual exercises you prescribe?"

"To make sure," said the teacher, "that you are not asleep when the sun begins to rise."[9]

Willard observes that Christians who desire to be Christlike often ask the wrong question.[10] We may sincerely ask, "What would Jesus do?" and then attempt to imitate his behavior in intense situations. We might as well ask, "What would Beethoven do?" and then attempt to play the piano. The better question is, "What did Jesus do *before* intense situations arose?" The Gospels show him practicing such classical disciplines as solitude, silence, prayer, retreat, corporate worship, and Scripture reading and meditation.

These practices shaped him, as they would shape us if we properly and consistently engaged them (Luke 2:52).

Willard teaches a process of personal transformation built around the acronym VIM, which stands for vision, intention, and means.[11] This, he argues, is how we begin to make any real changes in our lives, from learning a language to achieving sobriety. We begin with a *vision* of what is possible—in this case, what it would be like to live more fully in the kingdom of God, reflecting the character of Christ. Second comes *intention*, in the literal sense of deliberately setting one's mind on a matter. It refers to a concrete decision to move forward in obedience to Christ. We intend to obey Christ, and we decide to do so. Finally, with a clear vision and solid intentions, we seek out and apply appropriate *means* to learn to follow Jesus. For spiritual formation, the means will include practicing the "holy habits" that Christians have found useful over the centuries.

Spiritual Formation and Differentiation of Self

The goal of the personal transformation that Willard describes is an increasing conformity to the character of Christ. As we shall see in chapter 11, Jesus demonstrated the capacity to remain connected to others and yet to teach and live by deeply held principles, even when the anxiety and relationship pressure grew intense. This ability is what Murray Bowen labeled "differentiation of self." How might these two concepts—Willard's idea of transformation into greater Christlikeness and Bowen's understanding of differentiating a self—mutually interpret each other?[12]

Let us begin with the problem each is attempting to address. Willard is clear that the obstacle we are up against in being able to live the Christian life is the power of sin that is hardwired into our bodies. He says, for example, "Doing what he [Jesus] said and did increasingly becomes a part of who we are. But for this to happen *our body* must increasingly be poised to do what is good and to refrain from what is evil. *The inclinations to wrongdoing that literally inhabit its parts must be eliminated.* The body must come to serve us as an ally in Christlikeness."[13] The body's capacity to respond to others in destructive ways is automatic. It is done without thinking. "Such attitudes make me ready to harm others or to see them suffer, and these attitudes quickly settle into my body. There they become more or less overt tendencies to act without thinking in ways that harm others or even myself."[14]

The struggle between what we think, believe, or profess and how we behave is real. Willard writes: "But while the human being is to be identified with his or her body, within the embodied self there are diverse and powerful forces that turn the individual personality into a battlefield. Sometimes, as it did for Simon Peter, it often appears as if the body has a life of its own, capable of action to some degree independent of, or in conflict with, our conscious thoughts and intentions."[15] The struggle against un-Christlike behavior and the effort to replicate responses like those of Jesus necessarily connect to the life we live in our physical bodies.

Willard does not regard the body as inherently evil, however. In fact, he explicitly rejects that notion.[16] Instead, he understands the process of spiritual formation to be a bodily process in which the body increasingly becomes a resource for spiritual life. Every spiritual discipline is something one does with the body. Every encounter with God implicitly involves the body in one way or another.[17] Yet Willard recognizes that the power of sin also connects with our bodies—hence the need for retraining them to comply with God's will and purposes. Willard believes that in the quest for deep personal transformation, we are up against the indwelling power of sin in our bodies, to which temptation easily appeals. Under pressure, we easily compromise our principles, our relationships, and our commitments.

Bowen's thinking does not contain a category for sin. Science does not evaluate human behavior theologically. What Bowen sees at the heart of the human problem is the automatic emotional reactivity hardwired into brain and body over many millennia of evolution. This reactivity is what we must bring under control if we are to function at higher levels of differentiation. Our instinctual response to threats, real or perceived, generates the anxiety that is a constant part of our lives and of the emotional systems of which we are part. As anxiety increases, so does our reactivity, especially at lower levels of differentiation of self.[18] These automatic emotional responses are seldom helpful, however. With enough anxiety, and lacking the capacity to manage our reactivity, we will produce the common symptoms of the emotional process: conflict, distance, overfunctioning/underfunctioning, and projection. These reactions will often only intensify the anxiety and reactivity as the emotional system spirals downward.

What, then, is the pathway to change? For Willard, the power of God's Spirit is necessary. Renovation of the heart does not occur by human effort alone. Yet neither does such transformation take place apart from our involvement. Willard calls for believers who have a vision for such change and who have decisively set their minds on obedience to Christ to engage the spiritual disciplines. These disciplines—all of which involve the body submitted to the Holy Spirit—are means of "putting to death" all that is "earthly," evil habits of the old way of life before Christ (cf. Col. 3:5–11). The regular practice of spiritual disciplines under the guidance of and in dependence on the Spirit of God produces change over time.[19]

Bowen describes the work of change as "differentiating a self." This he sees as entirely an effort by an individual human being, apart from any outside grace or power. Bowen believed that even with effort over time, only minor change in the level of differentiation of self was possible, but that those small changes produced "a new world of a different lifestyle."[20] However, he described the effort required for change as a "monumental life task" and suggested that some would consider the rigor required not worth the effort.[21] The goal of the differentiating process is to develop the capacity to notice and manage one's reactivity in the presence of intense emotionality. Bowen describes concretely how the results might appear: "When any key member of an emotional system can control his own emotional reactiveness and accurately observe the functioning of the system and his part in it, and he can avoid counterattacking when he is provoked, and when he can maintain an active relationship with the other key members without withdrawing or becoming silent, the entire system will change in a series of predictable steps."[22] Although the process of achieving a greater level of differentiation may be considerably more complicated than suggested here, this description helps to make clear what the outcome could look like.

Bowen does not offer simple step-by-step instructions for differentiation, since the process is not simple. He does describe how the effort took shape in his own life and how he directs others to proceed in therapy.[23] Bowen encourages those working on differentiation to seek out the help of a "coach" to supervise the effort.[24] He suggests that individuals seek to develop a "person-to-person" relationship with each living person in their extended family.[25] He encourages those working on differentiation to become better observers of themselves and of their family and to learn to see and manage their own emotional reactiveness.[26] He teaches them to detriangle themselves from emotional situations.[27] Bowen encourages people pursuing this work to avoid the emotional reactiveness that pushes one to automatically become "part of the group" when returning to visit family. Instead, one can try to work separately with each parent; engage grandparents and other extended family members; return home frequently, particularly during times of high anxiety such as marriage, death, or serious illness; learn the language of BFST in order to take greater responsibility for thinking about one's family; avoid blame and confrontation; and develop a multigenerational knowledge of one's family.[28]

Clearly Willard and Bowen come to the problem of change in human life and relationships from distinctive perspectives. Yet the symptoms they address and the means they employ are not so different. Bowen hoped to see clients develop the capacity to distinguish between their intellectual and emotional functioning. This capacity, he believed, marks a critical stage in differentiation.[29] In the same way, Willard challenges the "modern" condition in which "feeling will come to exercise almost total mastery over the individual."[30] "In people without rock-solid character," he says, "feeling is a deadly enemy of self-control and will always subvert it. The mongoose of a disciplined will under God and good is the only match for the cobra of feeling."[31] Both see human life as inherently biological, whether one is addressing a person's relationships, emotional health, or spiritual maturity. Both advocate for a regimen of practices over the course of a lifetime, not a quick fix of pop psychology or religious self-help.

Several practitioners of BFST have tried to connect spirituality and differentiation of self, as have scientists.[32] Louise Rauseo, who for years directed a Bowen-based program in El Paso, Texas, found connections between the lives of Christian mystics and high levels of differentiation.[33] Doug Hester, who has long engaged in training clergy in BFST, also sees a direct connection between differentiation and spirituality.

> It seems to me that to say differentiation of self is a spiritual journey does not simply mean that there are parallels to be drawn here, but that they are one and the same path. It is a wholistic effort to become more of a self, to become more of who God created me to be. Rather than trying to force a connection between differentiation of self and spirituality, I believe it is a natural outgrowth. It is a connection that I see going all the way back to the early chapters of Genesis. Even as the cells of our body differentiate into various organs and tissues, there is a relationship to all of creation. It is when we try to separate ourselves from creation that we have the most difficulty seeing differentiation of self as a spiritual journey. Perhaps it is when we, as human beings, begin to see ourselves as unique that differentiation of self is no longer a spiritual journey. The capacity to become oneself is not about uniqueness, it is about relationship.[34]

Differentiation of self and spiritual formation are the same for Hester.

Although I am not ready to identify the two processes, I believe they belong in the same category of human spiritual development and that they may be mutually supportive rather than exclusive processes. Persons with no Christian faith or practice at all—that is, those not spiritually formed in Christ—might have a high level of differentiation because of the emotional processes in their own extended families over multiple generations. We might better ask the question of the relationship of the two processes from the other direction: How does one's work on spiritual formation contribute to one's level of differentiation? This formulation of the issue is more in line with Bowen's ninth concept, which sees the supernatural as a functional fact in human life.

Spiritual Disciplines and Differentiation of Self

Can the practice of classical spiritual disciplines, such as prayer, fasting, meditation, and solitude, enhance our capacity to overcome the pressure of togetherness forces, to be able to be *with* others without having our thinking and reacting determined by the relationship? That is, can the practices involved in Christian spiritual formation contribute to a better-differentiated life?

In *The Spirit of the Disciplines*, Willard makes a case for the importance of the body in spirituality. The function of the classical spiritual disciplines, he argues, is to provide a means to align the body with the pursuit of a life dedicated to God. Meditation, prayer, fasting, study, serving, solitude, silence, and other disciplines are bodily activities for "spiritual ends."[35] Willard argues,

> The conflict between flesh and spirit is the experience of all who begin the spiritual life by the influx of God's life-giving word. Sometimes the conflict is long, sometimes short. This is where the spiritual disciplines come in. The disciplines for the spiritual life, rightly understood, are time-tested activities consciously undertaken by us as new men or women to allow our spirit ever-increasing sway over our embodied selves. They help by assisting the ways of God's Kingdom to take the place of the habits of sin embedded in our bodies.[36]

If the struggle with the body is largely a struggle to deal with the reality of emotional reactivity, then how do these disciplines help? Does the practice of various disciplines provide means to manage dimensions of reactivity, with the result that practitioners are better able to live in relationship with others without being so frequently caught up in each other's anxiety? In other words, is there reason to believe that the practice of classical disciplines in pursuit of Christian spiritual formation may also increase one's ability to function at a higher level of differentiation?

Willard, like Bowen, recognizes that all people struggle with anxiety, and for good reason. The world is often a threatening place, and we instinctively respond. He writes,

> Of course, everyone is at peace about *some* things, one hopes, but few have peace in general, and fewer still have peace that reaches their body and its automatic responses to such a depth that it does not live in a covert state of alarm. Most people carry heavy burdens of care, and usually about the things that are most

important in life: what will happen to their loved ones, their finances, health, death, their physical appearance or what others think of them, the future of society, their standing before God and their eternal destiny.[37]

Anxiety is a part of ordinary human life.

Bowen notes the way in which anxiety becomes chronic in a relationship system, like a family or congregation, and spreads rapidly. Managing one's reactivity or being a less anxious presence—being at peace, in Willard's terms—requires work on differentiation so that we can remain connected to others without taking on their reactive stance.[38] The practices Willard recommends as a part of learning to trust God amid an anxious life contribute to the experience of this peace with God, circumstances, self, and others.[39]

But is the converse true as well? Could intentional work on differentiation of self also contribute in any way to one's being spiritually formed in a Christian sense?[40] Reflection on this question only makes sense theologically if we assume that the effort is placed, along with other practices, on the lower right-hand corner of Willard's "Golden Triangle," in which one is pursuing a life of Christlike character, not just better functioning in relationships. Otherwise the effort at differentiation becomes merely a human attempt to improve one's life in some way. Self-improvement is not necessarily a bad thing, but evangelical Christian theology does not have a place for salvation by good works. It understands both God's forgiveness and the experience of spiritual growth to be gifts of grace.

Could the work on differentiation as Bowen described it, engaging with our families and other intense relationships in a different and more intentional way, become for us a spiritual practice? What if we submitted the process to God prayerfully, with the desire to become more Christlike—better able to genuinely love others and better able to reflect Christ's character even when the pressure to walk away from our principles is strong? Reading the Gospel accounts of Jesus's life from the perspective of the concept of differentiation certainly implies a connection between the pursuit of Christlikeness and the pursuit of a better-differentiated life in all our relationships (see chap. 11 below). Paul's account of our inner struggles against "the flesh" (Rom. 7), of the nature of Christian love (1 Cor. 13), and of authentic Christian community (Rom. 12) implies a connection between the capacity to live the Christian life more faithfully and the ability to be less reactive in the face of anxiety (see chap. 12 below).

The correlation of Bowen's concept of differentiation and the Christian notion of spiritual formation raises a significant question: How much growth in differentiation is possible? Although Bowen himself was not optimistic that great progress is possible, even with great effort, Louise Rauseo notes that Christian mystics seemed to have experienced a significant leap forward in differentiation, making a major change in their functioning, usually because of some intense, conversion-like experience. She says,

> These people seem to have had a "crash course" in differentiation of self. It always took place in the context of their search for the real and for a life connected to God's love in the greatest possible way. Something in each life, early or late, changed their lives completely. It was often described as an immediate encounter with God. From that time on, their earlier struggles changed and they then lived their lives with a new integrity, steadily in one direction. In the process, the ability to live by principles, to recognize the limits of human togetherness, and to move toward greater individual integrity never changed.[41]

Although this acceleration in differentiation seems to have grown out of a singular experience, these saints often devoted themselves to prayer and other practices, both before and after their decisive encounter with God. Paul himself would fit into that category.

Conclusion

Both BFST and classical Christian spirituality hold out the possibility of personal transformation. Bowen called this change "differentiation of self," a relational and biological reality. Christian spirituality understands it as renovation of the heart, a rewiring of the human will (heart, spirit) so that it reflects more Christlike thought and behavior. BFST can help us understand the accounts of Jesus's life and of Paul's teaching from a perspective that considers the insights of systems thinking, such as the impact of differentiation, reactivity, and anxiety on spiritual life and character development. Furthermore, Christian spirituality offers classical, time-tested practices that seem to have had the effect of producing people who demonstrate higher-level functioning because of their lifelong engagement with these disciplines.

These mutual connections offer several practical implications for those involved in the work of spiritual formation themselves or with others in their congregations. First, we ought to be able to mark spiritual progress by increased evidence of the capacity to remain connected to others without participating in their reactivity, especially when anxiety is high. This characteristic of Jesus himself is one that we would expect to see in the life of a person who is pursuing Christlikeness.

Second, the proper practice of classical spiritual disciplines ought to contribute to our ability to make our way through life with less anxiety, becoming less reactive to both people and circumstances. In other words, the pursuit of formation that includes spiritual practices may also contribute to our emotional maturity.

Third, as Bowen and Willard agree, such changes as differentiation and spiritual formation do not take place in isolation from other people. They are inherently relational experiences. Bowen is explicit that we pursue differentiation only in relationships, and the more intense ones are the most important. Willard, likewise, urges that formation take place in the set of relationships that compose the church. How, for example, do we learn to forgive like Christ without someone around to offend us occasionally? How do we love like Christ if we live in isolation?

Fourth, even as the practice of spiritual disciplines might contribute to our emotional maturity over time, deliberate effort to differentiate a self in the important relationships of our nuclear and extended families might itself become a spiritual practice. Developing a family diagram through family research might prove as helpful as the practice of journaling, for instance. Intentional visits to our parents or other family members might be as useful in our formation as solitude at times. Learning to relate as a person to the others in our families might do as much to shape our hearts toward the *agapē* of 1 Corinthians 13 as a fast. Willard defines the practice of spiritual disciplines as intentionally doing something we *can* do now in order to be able eventually to do something we now *cannot*.[42] These and other practices related to differentiating a self might easily become spiritual disciplines for pastors and for those they direct in the process of spiritual formation.

Fifth, we accomplish neither the work of differentiation nor the work of Christian spiritual formation well on our own. Even as a spiritual director proves to be a useful companion in the work of formation, a BFST-trained coach enhances the likelihood of a successful effort at differentiation. The work involved in this process is such that reading a book and having a brown-bag gathering of pastors will not produce the desired results. A person engaging a disciplined program of reading in theory, available training opportunities, and the insight and outside perspective offered by a coach will more likely succeed in progress toward a higher level of emotional maturity.

Sixth, pastors who begin the work on learning and practicing BFST in their own lives frequently want to evangelize others with their new learning and insights by offering courses, reading books together with others on the church staff, inviting outside speakers in to present, or attempting to coach others. (Let him who is without sin cast the first stone.) Although such enthusiasm over new and helpful ideas is understandable, this pathway can be fraught with complications. If we are to be offering coaching or spiritual direction, we ought ourselves to be in an ongoing, disciplined program of learning, not staying just one step ahead of those we are teaching. Pastors endeavoring to learn and practice theory might consider simply giving ourselves to that work for a time, without announcing it or attempting to spread the good news, until the ideas of the theory begin to gel in our own lives a bit.

Theological reflection on this practical aspect of ministry invites us to seek an understanding of exactly what is transpiring when we undergo formation. How do the various practices we have learned to employ work? BFST provides some insight into the way that our instinctive bodily reactions progressively come under the control of our renovated "hearts," as we increasingly differentiate our automatic emotional reactivity and our intellectual capacities. The theory also offers some possibilities for including differentiating practices in our repertoire of spiritual disciplines.

●—Questions for Reflection —————————————————

1. Which spiritual practices have you found to be most effective in helping you to break the power of things that interfere with your participation in the life of the kingdom of God? Which practices have helped to immerse you more fully in that kingdom?

2. Which practices have been most challenging or difficult for you to sustain? What do you think makes them so for you?

3. What practices related to differentiating yourself or working on your family relationships are you planning to attempt? What do you think the challenges will be around that practice? Who might you talk to about the effort before attempting it?

8

Christian Community

Journeying with Others

Believable fairy-stories must be intensely practical. You must have
a map, no matter how rough. Otherwise you wander all over the
place. In *The Lord of the Rings* I never made anyone go farther than
he could on a given day.

—J. R. R. Tolkien, interview with *Telegraph* magazine

Christian life is inherently about relationships. The Jesus Creed is simple: LOVE GOD AND LOVE NEIGHBOR.[1] At no time in Jesus's ministry did he have only one disciple. He came into the *community* of the people of God, and he expanded that community beyond Israel. He taught about relationships—loving enemies, forgiving offenders, and serving others. Nothing in his teaching or practices suggests that Christian life is something that can be experienced fully in the absence of other people.[2] Withdrawing into what Henri Nouwen calls the furnace of solitude may sometimes be necessary for our spiritual formation;[3] however, it is only in the furnace of relationships that we can fully obey most of Jesus's instructions. Relationships become the place where our obedience is most deeply challenged. Relationship systems, whether family or church, consistently challenge our spiritual and emotional maturity. In so doing, they shape our character. Consequently, having a map to navigate the territory of relationships can help us lead and serve congregations, who, despite their faith and commitment to Christ, remain very human. As do we.

Assumptions about Life in the Christian Community

The local church was a wonderful place for me to grow up and then to invest my life and ministry for more than forty years as an adult. The joy and grief shared among people, the important and formative friendships, the hours spent in corporate worship, prayer, study, and service—these have meant everything to me. The New Testament vision of the Church with a capital C speaks to me: the Body of Christ, the Bride of Christ, the New Israel, and the People of God. But I have learned to view church with a lowercase *c* with a kind of stereoscopic vision, keeping in mind both this ideal perspective and a more realistic one. Both are part of my theology.

Most of us who serve congregations have at one time or another abandoned any pure idealism about the nature of Christian communities. Clyde Fant, one of my seminary professors, observed, "In order to be disillusioned, you first have to be illusioned." If our own experience in churches did not open our eyes to the reality that church members are merely people, with all that implies, reading the New Testament ought to do the job. The Gospel stories of Jesus's disciples—their arguments, competition, and frequent misunderstandings of Jesus—indicate the material Christ chose as the foundation of this edifice, the Church (Eph. 2:19–20). The book of Acts shows us *churches*, the gathering of disciples in Jerusalem, Antioch, Corinth, Philippi, and other places. The stories deal with greedy disciples, grumbling factions, and prejudice and discrimination. Being God's redeemed people does not imply being God's perfect people. Paul would never have written most of his letters, at least not in their current form, if churches were not communities in which people sometimes behave like ordinary human beings. The letters to the seven churches in the Apocalypse offer the same evidence (Rev. 2–3). When people say they would like to be part of a true New Testament church, I wonder, "Which one? Corinth? Galatia? Laodicea?" In many respects those ancient congregations differ little from the church down the street.

As we prepare to think about how Bowen Family Systems Theory (BFST) can offer a perspective on our relationships with those we serve and their relationships with each other, I will acknowledge a few assumptions I hold about human beings and congregational life together.

First, we learn to relate to others in the context of a nuclear and extended family and its distinctive emotional processes. We learn there how to focus our anxiety when it becomes overwhelming, whether primarily by becoming conflictual, withdrawing, taking over, giving up, or finding someone to worry about or blame. We learn to be more or less open about our thinking, to be more or less open to the thinking of others, and what we will do when those around us grow anxious. We learn how to relate to people with more power than we hold and to people of the same or opposite gender. We learn means of getting our way. We absorb attitudes about a variety of issues, including money, sex, power, faith, food, religion, disease, and death. The list could go on. We are all formed in distinctive ways by our family settings.

Second, we carry this learning into all other intense relationships, including congregational life. We do not choose to do this. We take the person we have become with us into all relationships, including those in a congregation. If we intentionally work on a project like differentiation or spiritual formation, we are likely to become conscious of these automatic processes we have absorbed. Every church member brings emotional processes into church life. This is why family systems theory has something to say to churches. Congregations are not families, but human behavior is human behavior. In intense relationships, our automatic reactivity will inevitably come into play.

These people in this place—with their experiences together, their distinctive levels of maturity, their practiced ways of doing things—form a local congregation. The shared life and ministry of these people assures that they are also forming an emotional system in which they learn to relate to one another in patterned and familiar ways. A newly arriving pastor can be naively unaware that the church's ways are not the pastor's ways and that the church's thoughts are not the pastor's thoughts. This congregation is not the previous congregation that the pastor served. This new pastor is not the previous pastor, either. The two partners in ministry can be as distant as heaven and earth in their automatic emotional processes. The differences show up most often in ordinary things: how they make decisions, how upset people become over issues such as finances (and who becomes upset over which issue), how they handle personnel matters, how much secrecy operates among those with power, which ministries get the most attention and which get the most affection—the list goes on and is unique to each congregation. The emotional processes of conflict, distance, overfunctioning/underfunctioning, and projection will be at work as distinctively in a congregation as they are in a family. Observing the way these processes operate and having a way to understand them will serve a pastor well.

Third, congregational life ought to be an intense set of relationships. This assumption might not be true for someone who understands church as simply attending worship occasionally. We might wonder, though, what emotional processes keep people from engaging other followers of Christ more personally. The New Testament uses family language to describe the early church (mother, brothers, sisters, household of God), implying a degree of intimacy that might not be common in other associations. As Jesus, Paul, Peter, and others in the New Testament address Christian life in the community, they often call for mutuality in relationships (see, for example, the "one another" commandments in the New Testament).[4] Paul describes this life together in ways many contemporary Christians would have difficulty imagining fully (Rom. 12:9–13:10). In addition, the apostle directs a good bit of ethical instruction to issues of relationships in general: church, home, work, outsiders (Eph. 4:1–6:7; Col. 3:1–4:6).

Instruction about the importance of mutual forgiveness recurs with great frequency.[5] Jesus and the apostles exhort Christians to forgive one another and to seek forgiveness from one another, maintaining peace in relationships. We easily overlook the implication of this instruction: we should expect relationships within the church to be intense enough that serious offense sometimes occurs. This aspect of relationships in the Christian community is worth examining under the lens of BFST, since it holds such a prominent place in New Testament teaching.

Forgiveness and the Church

"Forgiveness" is a strong word: it requires a significant wound before it is either necessary or possible. We do not need to ask for forgiveness for accidentally bumping into one another in the hallway. "Excuse me" will do. We need forgiveness for injury done to another through our own selfish behavior. Forgiveness connects to wrongdoing, hurt, pain, disappointment, and injury.

Forgiveness is inherently social. It always involves both the offended and the offender. Miroslav Volf observes that "forgiveness is a social affair. We forgive to take care of a wrongdoing, but a wrongdoing always happens between people, not just in the thoughts or actions of an individual."[6] The Christian practice of forgiveness is social in another way: it is intended to bind up the wound that sin inflicts on Christian community. Contemporary notions of forgiveness are often merely *interpersonal*, a transaction between one person and another, without regard for the impact of either sin or reconciliation on the life of the congregation. Further, modern focus on the autonomous individual can turn the act of forgiveness into an *intrapersonal* transaction, something therapeutic that occurs in the head of the offended and relieves them of their own anger or resentment, without regard for a restoration of the offender to the community.[7]

Since BFST is not a theology but a scientific theory of human behavior, it does not have a place for the notion of "sin." That concept, however, is integral to how Christian theology understands human nature. We are people created for one kind of life (love for God and for neighbor), but we are flawed. Left to ourselves, we pinch, wound, injure, and even destroy one another (Gal. 5:13–15). In Christian theology, these behaviors are more than evolutionary survival instincts or emotional reactions for which we bear no moral responsibility. We are responsible before God for our behavior. We fall short of what God has created us to experience in relationship with each other. We commit "sin" (Rom. 3:23). We are "sinners" (Rom. 5:8; 1 Tim. 1:15).

Christian theology declares that the way out of this kind of destructive behavior is available in the salvation offered in Jesus Christ, which includes a restored relationship with God (John 17:1–3) and a reconciling relationship with others. Jesus's death is intimately and mysteriously part of God's forgiveness of human sin. The early Christians proclaimed: "Christ died for our sins" (1 Cor. 15:3).

We experience God's grace and forgiveness by faith in Christ, and we enter a new relationship with God in which we learn to grow, mature, and live human life in love, as God intended for us.[8] The life of Jesus exemplifies human life lived as God hoped it would be. God's forgiveness of our debt of sin puts us under obligation to forgive "our debtors" (Matt. 6:12, 15; 18:21–35). Forgiveness becomes a way of life for Christians living in community with other forgiven sinners as well as among their enemies. L. Gregory Jones writes: "For Christians, forgiveness is not simply an action, an emotional judgment, or a declarative utterance—though Christian forgiveness includes all those dimensions. Rather, forgiveness is a habit that must be practiced over time within the disciplines of the Christian community. This is because . . . in the face of sin and evil God's love moves toward reconciliation by means of forgiveness."[9]

Christian life in community is not marginal or optional in New Testament teaching. Knowing God's grace and forgiveness while being in community with others who have experienced that same grace is the essential state of the Christian. Offering the gift of forgiveness to others and receiving their forgiveness allow that community to sustain the relationships that it comprises.

Since forgiveness is a response to sin in Christian theology and practice, BFST does not address the topic. The practice is necessary in Christian thought, however, to deal with both the relationship between a human being and God and the relationships between human beings. Forgiveness is a necessary intervention if broken relationships are to function again.

What Is Forgiveness?

From a biblical perspective, forgiveness is an act of the will. Both Jesus and the apostles command it. We are to forgive as God forgave us (Matt. 6:15; Eph. 4:2). New Testament writers never describe forgiveness as a feeling or an instinctual action. It is rather something one must decide to do, an action one must intend to take. Jones considers it even more than that. It is, he says, a set of practices that Christians engage in, including baptism, Eucharist, confession, prayer, and healing.[10] Volf assesses forgiveness as an act "embedded in a way of life that is committed to overcoming evil by doing good."[11]

The New Testament verb *aphiēmi*, translated "forgive," means "to loosen, let go, or send away."[12] When we forgive, we release the obstacles that stand between human beings; we let go of both the offense and its consequences. Those offering forgiveness forgo seeking either revenge or retributive justice. Volf writes: "Because in Christ God overcame our sin and reestablished communion with us by forgiving sin, we do as God did. We forgive because 'recalling' the offenders from sin matters more to us than 'avenging' wrongs we have suffered. We forgive because 'saving' our enemies and making friends out of them matters more to us than punishing them."[13]

The act of forgiving is not merely overlooking offense; rather, it is first a condemnation of the behavior. We must name the wrongdoing. This is what Volf calls "the negative presupposition of forgiveness."[14] Following the condemnation of the act is the positive gift of not counting the wrongdoing against the offender. We could describe forgiveness as the willingness on the part of the one offended to absorb the injury inflicted so that the relationship may continue and so that the community's wound may heal. In Jesus's parable, the king who forgives the debt of ten thousand talents owed by one of his servants does not magically make the debt disappear (Matt. 18:27). He absorbs it. In effect, he pays the debt. It stands no more. Wherever forgiveness occurs, someone has had to pay a price. The failure to forgive keeps the debt on the books within the relationship, holding it over the head of the offender, maintaining the breech in the community's life.

Richard Foster defines forgiveness as an act of grace "whereby the offense no longer separates. The power of love that holds us together is greater than the power of the offense that separates us. In forgiveness, we release our offenders so that they are no longer bound to us."[15] From the perspective of BFST we might describe forgiveness as *an act of differentiation whereby we determine to apply a deeply held value/principle of grace to a relationship in which we have been injured by another.* Forgiveness is more about who we are and what we value than what the other has done to us.

Bowen Family Systems Theory and Forgiveness in the Church

A systems approach to congregational life understands that nothing occurs in a vacuum. The offensive behavior of one individual correlates to the level of chronic (or acute) anxiety in the emotional systems of which the person is a part, including the extended family, the nuclear family, the work system, the congregation, and even society at large. These systems form interlocking triangles that affect and are affected by each other. This fact does not absolve the offender, however. No one forces a person to behave offensively. Nevertheless, when anxiety rises, offenses more likely will occur. We become more vulnerable to wounding and being wounded.

For example, Bowen observed that when anxiety increases in the family emotional process, it sometimes expresses itself in conflictual relationships. With increasing anxiety comes more all-or-nothing thinking. Anxious people can develop tunnel vision and become incapable of focusing on anything but the one threatening them or their escape route. People take things personally and make things personal. The togetherness force increases. People confuse their feelings with opinions and beliefs. They equate dissent with disloyalty. The likelihood of conflict increases, and with it the likelihood of interpersonal offenses.

The anxiety may also find expression in people withdrawing from relationships and becoming more distant. Relationships can become cold and superficial. The congregation may begin to overlook the needs of church members. People at lower levels of differentiation or higher levels of chronic anxiety may feel mistreated, shunned, or ignored. They take this personally, and the distance may increase. Or they may finally explode in anger, if that is their backup behavior.

Others will react to increased anxiety by overfunctioning or underfunctioning. Some take on responsibilities that rightfully belong to others, and those others may feel pushed aside in the process. Overfunctioners may resent underfunctioners as unwilling or incapable of doing their jobs or even thinking for themselves. Underfunctioners may resent overfunctioners for being bossy know-it-alls or bullies.

Additionally, as anxiety increases, the focus of the congregation may shift to one person or group in the system as deserving of blame for the problems they face, or as someone they agree to worry over. The "one person" may often be the pastor. Fingers point. Gossip increases. Rumors fly. Resentment grows.

As we learn to think about systems and watch the emotional process, we can become more aware of the nature of anxiety in the system and its effect on human behavior. Such insight alone might allow us (on good days) to take less offense and to remain more objective about people's poor behavior. This is an act of grace. Forgiveness becomes necessary less often because offense is less often taken. Resentment flu does not spread like an epidemic in the congregation.

A systems perspective can also allow one to seek forgiveness more easily when the realization dawns that we have behaved badly. We can see the anxiety in the system and notice our reaction to it. Thus we can own our part in a problem and seek to make things right. We can see our tendencies toward conflict, distance, overfunctioning, underfunctioning, projection, and blame. We can claim our part in the situation and seek to find grace from those we have wounded.

The less well-differentiated we are, the more our relationships shape or determine our behavior. The lower our level of emotional maturity, the more the behavior of others and their reactivity will affect the choices we make, the words we speak, the reactions we have, and the behavior we engage in. The better differentiated we are, the more we can experience the reactive behavior of others without taking deep offense or reacting in a way that causes deep offense.

Differentiation of Self and Forgiveness

Forgiveness has two sides: giving and receiving. Levels of differentiation affect how both operate in a system. The more differentiated we are, the less reactive we are to others and the lower our need for "togetherness." With an increase in differentiation also comes a greater capacity to manage ourselves in the face of anxiety—the less likely we are to "take things personally." We can be more objective in our relationships, giving grace rather than taking offense when others react under the pressure of rising anxiety.

The more emotionally mature we are, the freer we may be to extend forgiveness to others for their offenses, rather than to harbor resentment, live at a distance, retaliate, form triangles, cut off, overfunction, or underfunction. Well-differentiated persons are more able to be responsible for self and only for self, keeping the focus off others' behavior and more on their own. Theoretically, we can perform the repair work of forgiveness more easily as we become more emotionally mature. Depending less on the approval of others, we can offer forgiveness out of more mature motives, rather than to win the approval of others. Our own principle of seeking to be obedient to Christ or of imitating Christ can more consistently override our reactive desire for revenge or retributive justice.

Elisabeth Elliot—whose first husband, Jim, along with four other missionaries, died as a martyr at the hands of a tribe of Auca Indians in 1956—knows something about the practice of forgiveness. She writes: "Forgiveness is re-linquishment. It is a laying down. No one can take it from us, any more than anyone could take the life of Jesus if He had not laid it down of His own will. But we can do as He did. We can offer it up, writing off whatever loss it may entail, in the sure knowledge that the man who loses his life or his reputation or 'face' or anything else for the sake of Christ will save it."[16] This willing-ness to let go of the desire for revenge, to set the offender free, and to love the other cannot proceed out of an anxious reactivity but only from a self that is coming to terms with its own principles, beliefs, and values. The words or actions of the other do not determine the act of forgiveness.

On the other hand, a more differentiated person, having wronged another, ought to find it easier to seek forgiveness and reconciliation, which exempli-fies taking responsibility for one's own behavior and emotional reactivity. A less differentiated response would be to become defensive, grow distant, form triangles, or cut off from the offended party. The more emotionally mature we are, the more capable we are of remaining neutral, and the freer we are to take responsibility for our own reactivity. We can see our part in the problem and say, "I was wrong. Forgive me."

If 1 Corinthians 13 describes a well-differentiated life, then it is accurate to say that a well-differentiated person can choose responses in relationships, including "not keeping a record of wrongs" (cf. 1 Cor. 13:5 NIV). This capac-ity to zero out accounts is not an emotional response to the anxiety of such experiences. People who pull off this feat commonly testify to how difficult it was. It does not happen automatically, but over time and with thoughtfulness and focused effort.

Projection (Triangles) and Forgiveness

When people react to heightened anxiety by projecting blame or worry on one member or part of the system, their behavior may not express the love that Scripture instructs us to have for one another. Judgment, condemnation, gossip, rumor, and blame violate the clear teachings of Jesus (Matt. 7:1–12). When we identify such behavior in ourselves, we can accept responsibility for it, seek forgiveness, and work to change our anxious response. We can learn to notice the reactivity that sends us automatically reeling and strive prayerfully to manage our own anxiety so that we do not participate in this process as quickly or as often. We can choose to make amends in relationships we have damaged. We can also learn, from our own vulnerability in such situations, to offer grace to those who behave reactively toward us as part of their own emotional immaturity.

Distance, Cutoff, and Forgiveness

Cutoff is distancing taken to an extreme. Bowen used the term particularly to describe how, in response to intense anxiety in the family, children separate themselves from the previous generation to "start over."[17] In congregations, emotional cutoff between individuals, family units, or larger factions is also common.

Those who work with Bowen theory in clinical practice sometimes speak of clients' "bridging" the cutoff in their families as part of their work on differentiation of self.[18] This usually includes increasing the frequency of contact with family members, including relatives in branches of the family tree that over time have become separated from the family.[19] To be clear, Bowen does not have "forgiveness" or "reconciliation" in mind, at least not in the way Christian theology frames those concepts. He is interested in the way an individual overcomes cutoff in the family and moves toward establishing relationships with those from whom one is cut off. The purpose of this effort is differentiating a self and lowering the level of anxiety in the family, not a biblical reconciliation or forgiveness.

Emotional cutoff can show up in congregations, as it does in families. An interesting research question might be whether people who cut themselves off from their families contribute to fostering or participating in cutoff in their other emotional systems. People in congregations may move beyond the distance of superficial relationships to church splits, often following a period of intense emotional conflict. Sometimes, with or without conflict, anxiety in the congregation drives members to leave and join other churches or simply to drop out of participation in any church. Schisms and factions form, separating church members from one another. These behaviors offer evidence of our emotional immaturity, fusion in our relationships, and our need for growth. At times the cutoff is sufficiently severe that a church splits, with a significant number of members leaving to form a new congregation or join an existing one. Such divisions have hit most extended denominational families as well.

In a church where a schism has occurred one or more generations ago, resulting in another congregation's being formed in the community, the gulf between these two "sisters" may remain unreconciled. Current members of each congregation may have no personal memory of the split or knowledge of the "issues" that provoked it. The emotional system, however, is not dependent on those memories or that knowledge. These two have learned to live without a relationship with each other, and the cutoff remains. Overcoming the cutoff would require intentional effort from one side or the other. Some of the moves that Peter Titelman recommends for individuals working on bridging cutoff in their families might be helpful. The pastors, staff members, or key lay leaders of the two congregations might begin to work on establishing person-to-person relationships.[20] They might learn the history of the division and discuss it. Leaders could attend significant events in the life of each other's congregation. The two sisters might find common work to do together. Ultimately, mutual forgiveness will be a necessary factor in any successful reconciliation.

Multigenerational Transmission Process and Christian Community

Bowen's concept of the multigenerational transmission process explains how a given family (congregation) may have members who are at various levels of maturity. Over time a family will produce people at both higher and lower levels of differentiation, based on the way the family projects its anxiety onto one or more of the children. The members who compose a congregation will not likely all be at the same place in the scale of differentiation of self either. We might wonder, given Bowen's assertion that people tend to seek out spouses who are at the same level of differentiation, whether our level of differentiation also affects our friendships and other associations, such as the churches we join. Do we seek out people whose level is close enough to our own that we feel comfortable? Would the level of emotional maturity in each congregation tend to lie within a rather narrow range? Experience seems to indicate that within a congregation we will find at least some degree of variability.

During times of increased anxiety, either in their own lives and families, in the church, or in the world, members who are less well-differentiated will likely become more reactive, raising the potential for bruised or wounded relationships. Given enough anxiety in the system, even more mature people will join in the reactivity and participate in potentially relationship-damaging behavior. With awareness of their own capacity for such behavior, those who are "more mature" in the congregation might show grace to the "less mature," who more easily become reactive. Just as Paul called the "strong" in faith to bear with the "weak," so the more mature ought to consider how to live with grace and forgiveness toward those whose sensitivity to the anxiety is greater than their own, rather than joining in the reactivity by blaming or projecting a worried focus (Rom. 14:1–15:4).

Societal Process and Forgiveness

The church of Jesus Christ will find itself in various cultures, times, and social conditions that represent a regressed state. During times of greater regression, anxiety will be higher across the board, both in the culture and in the church, and offenses of one sort or another may be more frequent between members in a congregation. In congregations that react to the anxiety with distance, love may grow cold (Matt. 24:12). Political polarization in American culture, for example, may send a fault line through the middle of many congregations, just as it does through many families. People in some congregations may line up on opposite sides of hot-button issues. Some members may fight. Others, allergic to conflict, will remain distantly silent, resulting in a superficial harmony. In either case, the potential is great for times of increased societal regression to affect congregational relationships.

During contentious times, leaders who are working on differentiation of self can serve their congregations well by thoughtfully defining themselves on issues where necessary without insisting on agreement from others or separating from those who disagree. When anxiety in the culture and the church is intense, this is a challenging project. Keeping unnecessary offenses to a minimum and being able to seek and offer forgiveness when relationships are damaged are marks of greater emotional maturity.

Conclusion

Congregations that move toward the life of the new community envisioned in the New Testament will necessarily be relationally and emotionally intense. Paul's description of life in the church stirs the imagination for what is possible (Rom. 12:1–13:10). People in a congregation gather around beliefs and issues that often grow out of their own family history. They deal with some of the most important questions in their lives: the will of God, eternal hope, mission and purpose in life, right living, death and dying. For some, the congregation may be the most intense relational system they know outside of their own families. The church building often emotionally anchors family history and experiences as well. This all makes possible a life in Christian community that, as in a family, can be rich and supportive but also potentially disappointing and damaging.

Congregational life may rise toward our best hopes when leaders are working on differentiation, learning to see relationships from a systems perspective, taking responsibility for their own part in the system, and focusing on themselves rather than others. Pastoral leaders will inevitably work with bruised or broken relationships, engaging the reparative functions of the body of Christ, including dealing with church discipline, division, and reconciliation. Leaders who can observe the emotional process, maintain a degree of objectivity, manage themselves in the inevitable triangles, and develop person-to-person relationships with people around various issues will enrich congregational life. This is not an easy project for a congregational leader to undertake, and it will not always succeed. We will need to tend our relationships in the church by the giving and receiving of grace expressed in the Christian act of forgiveness.

We could describe forgiveness as grace applied to the system. A systems perspective can contribute to the capacity to resist the automatic tendency to blame others, take offense easily at the reactive behavior of others, and diagnose an individual as "the problem." Instead, we can see that we each have a part to play in the chronic issues our congregation experiences. We can understand that people come into the congregational system with all the anxiety of their own family and of the regressive world outside the church doors. We come to see some destructive behavior in congregations as the result of people overwhelmed by the anxiety in their own lives. Although that does not excuse damaging actions or words, such understanding can help the leader to be less reactive, to extend grace, and to do the Christian work of forgiveness when needed.

Forgiveness can be an act of differentiation. When we forgive, we go beyond our instinctive reactions that might demand revenge or justice. Forgiveness is a way of choosing to do the right thing, to act according to principle, regardless of what others are doing to us. Jesus's instructions and example take precedence as principles in our lives that can override the automatic emotional reactivity so deeply ingrained within us. Forgiveness both requires and enhances work on differentiating a self. By it we learn to stay in relationship with others without their anxiety ensnaring us in emotional triangles or stirring up our own reactivity. Both offering and receiving forgiveness are steps toward taking on what Elisabeth Elliot calls "the clear-eyed and cool-headed acceptance of the burden of responsibility."[21]

●—Questions for Reflection ────────────────────

1. Can you think of a recent experience in your congregational life in which increased anxiety resulted in behavior on the part of some members that others found offensive? Are you able to see the role that emotional process played in the event?
2. How might a pastoral leader who is working on differentiation of self affect the practice of forgiveness between Christians in a congregation?

3. What steps could you take to bridge cutoff between two congregations in a community that emerged through separation? How might
   warring factions within a denomination move toward reconciliation? What would the situation require of pastoral leaders for this to
   succeed?

PART THREE

A Map for
Reading Scripture

Bowen Family Systems Theory and Biblical Interpretation

The Rules of the Game

It is not down on any map; true places never are.

—Herman Melville, *Moby-Dick*

Reading the Bible, understanding its meaning, and connecting that meaning to the life of the congregation in preaching, teaching, and conversation—all this is a core pastoral task. "Hermeneutics" is the term we use for that interpretive work. Despite the simplistic claims of some ("God said it. I believe it. That settles it."), biblical interpretation is a complex task requiring both art and science. When we read Scripture, we attempt, from the platform of our modern world, to find meaning in ancient texts, written in ancient languages, addressed to people in ancient Near Eastern cultures. To build a bridge of meaning between the two worlds, we must be thoughtful.

Asking Questions of the Bible

The Bible contains a wide spectrum of literary genres, including fictional and nonfictional narrative, poetry, prophetic oracle, personal correspondence, apocalyptic visions, and historical records. Understanding this literature

117

requires us to wield an adequate interpretive, or *hermeneutical*, approach. We might understand biblical hermeneutics as a set of questions that interpreters take to texts. The answers we get from a text depend largely on the questions we ask. A sound interpretive approach tries to ask *appropriate* questions of the biblical texts, questions that the text can answer. We hope to come away with *valid* responses that we can attribute to the texts themselves.

Biblical texts do not answer all our human questions. Interrogating Scripture for answers to questions a text does not address may torture that text's meaning. For example, asking scientific questions of a nonscientific text can twist the text to accommodate the interpreter's assumptions.

In the last fifty years, scholars have begun to transcend traditional categories of interpretation by asking new questions of texts, whether biblical or modern. Recognizing that most biblical interpreters historically have been Euro-American men, interpreters have developed such approaches as African American, Afrocentric, liberation, and feminist hermeneutics. Scholars have also found that rhetorical, sociological, and literary analyses open new horizons on ancient texts.[1] Each approach brings fresh questions to the Bible to discover or understand something that other approaches have missed or ignored.

Bowen Family Systems Theory and Hermeneutics

Since the Bible contains accounts of human behavior, it is appropriate for interpreters to bring questions from the fields of sociology, anthropology, and psychology as well. Although social science interpreters have attempted a variety of psychological approaches, they have largely left untapped a hermeneutic of natural systems, based on the family systems theory developed by Murray Bowen.[2]

Bowen set out to formulate a comprehensive scientific theory of *human behavior*, arguing that his eight interlocking concepts could account for human behavior all along the continuum of human functioning. Could his theory be helpful in interpreting aspects of biblical texts that describe human behavior or that are themselves expressions of it? How would a biblical hermeneutic of natural systems broaden our understanding of these ancient writings? What assumptions must we acknowledge as we apply such a hermeneutical filter to our reading of the Bible? Given the scientific nature of Bowen Family Systems Theory (BFST), what qualifications must we establish before moving between a scientific theory and literary texts we regard as sacred Scripture?

A hermeneutic based on natural systems can bring questions and concepts to narrative texts in which we might better understand human behavior by thinking through the presence of anxiety, the fusion between characters, the togetherness force, and such family emotional processes as conflict, distance, overfunctioning/underfunctioning, and triangles. Bowen's concepts of differentiation of self or emotional cutoff might provide insight into the words and actions of characters.

Additionally, stories implicitly underlie texts that are not themselves narratives, such as laws, letters, prayers, and psalms. These writings may both describe human behaviors and be examples of them, making it possible for interpreters to read the texts through the lens of natural systems as well.

Interpretive Principles for Using Bowen Family Systems Theory

Kamila Blessing has done creative, groundbreaking work in bringing Bowen theory to bear on biblical texts.[3] Blessing has brought theory into conversation with such texts as the creation narratives, the patriarchal accounts, the story of Samuel's birth, New Testament birth narratives, the Johannine account of the wedding in Cana, selected parables of Jesus, and Paul's conflict with Peter as described in Galatians. Her studies of the prodigal son (Luke 15) and of Galatians 1–2, as well as her application of the theory to various biblical family stories, are among the few published scholarly attempts to use natural systems theory as a basis for reading biblical texts. In addition, Blessing is the only scholar to put into writing an attempt to think intentionally about the implications of using the theory in biblical interpretation. She boils her interpretive "rules" down to two statements:

1. The Bible often does not contain emotional information per se; yet from the actions of the people it is valid to infer the existence of the eight family systems characteristics.
2. It is absolutely insupportable to infer actions or emotions that cannot be found or supported in the text. Very close attention to what it actually says is the first and most important step.[4]

The first rule affirms a key assumption behind the use of Bowen theory as an interpretive tool. Bowen believed that his eight concepts described "human" behavior, something that transcends cultures, ethnicity, language, and history. Applying Bowen theory to reading ancient texts requires this assumption.[5]

In addition, the first rule affirms Bowen's assumption that the important data are factual, not speculative. Human behavior is what matters. Actions that can be observed are functional facts, and from them we can understand the workings of particular systems. As a hermeneutical tool, Bowen theory does not require us to psychoanalyze biblical characters. We need only attend to their actions, asking the questions we would normally ask in thinking through any life situation: What? When? Who? Where? How?[6]

Blessing's second rule is important in all hermeneutics but especially when using a psychological approach. She affirms that the interpreter needs to stick closely to the text, not inferring actions or emotions the text does not explicitly supply. Otherwise we engage in mere speculation, not interpretation. Walter Brueggemann writes: "There is a danger, in the eclectic enterprise of psychological criticism, to impose a psychological theory on the text in a way that overrides the specificity of the text itself and that distorts the text in order to serve the theory that an interpreter may advocate."[7]

Although both rules are valid and necessary, those of us who try to bring biblical texts into conversation with other disciplines ought to acknowledge and adhere closely to at least one additional interpretive principle. Just as Blessing's second rule insists that we treat the biblical text fairly, a sound approach in building on her work requires us to treat the psychological theory with integrity as well. That is, we ought not to reinterpret the theory to fit the text any more than we reinterpret the text to fit the theory. We must treat both partners in the conversation, the Bible and the theory, with the utmost respect.

We should attempt to bring as much of the theory as possible to bear on the text, rather than borrowing a few terms or concepts. Our work should include the key ideas that underlie Bowen's thinking, such as the role of anxiety, the togetherness and individuality forces, the various responses to anxiety in the family emotional process (conflict, distance, overfunctioning/underfunctioning, projection), as well as the eight concepts that make up the theory. Bowen was explicit that his concepts interlocked. We can understand none of them as though independent of the others.

Representing theory comprehensively puts a burden on the interpreter to employ the theory's terms, concepts, and definitions as accurately as possible. Innovation with theoretical terminology risks that one is using the named theory no longer as a hermeneutical tool but rather as a synthesis of concepts gathered from a variety of sources.

Blessing's application of Bowen theory sometimes takes liberties both with Bowen's terms and with the theory itself. For example, she uses and applies Bowen's concept of the emotional triangle in a way he did not. Bowen specified that a triangle is a three-*person* system that operates in specific, identifiable ways. To apply the concept of triangle as Blessing does at times (for example, the narrator, reader, and text; or the blind man in John 9, Jesus, and the man's sight) goes beyond Bowen theory.[8] Expanding Bowen's terms to include something other than persons in a triangle changes the way one understands triangles and how one behaves within them. Her use of the terminology "stretching the triangle" to describe what happens in emotional cutoff incorporates an understanding that does not appear in Bowen's theory.

Blessing also employs the term "fugue" as a synonym for Bowen's term "emotional cutoff." Use of this term is particularly problematic since in other psychological contexts it refers to the temporary amnesia and loss of identity of a "fugue state."[9] This has implications completely unrelated to Bowen's concept of cutoff and may add to confusion rather than offer clarity.

In chapter 5 of *Families of the Bible*, titled "Thy Brother's and Sister's Keeper: Siblings in the Family of God," Blessing focuses on stories of "sibling rivalry" in the biblical narrative. This chapter appears to be based on Bowen's sixth concept, which he called "sibling position." Here is the one concept that Bowen borrowed in its entirety from the research of Walter Toman. In *Family Constellation* (1961), Toman focuses on how one's position as a sibling in the family affects such things as the way one relates to people of the same or opposite gender and how one relates within a marriage and in other social settings. Neither Toman nor Bowen used the term "sibling rivalry," a concept that apparently originated out of Freudian theory. They are interested in sibling *position*. Marriage partners may find their own sibling positions (two firstborns, for example) predisposing them to conflict when anxiety rises. However, we should probably understand conflict *between siblings* by using the concept of the nuclear family's emotional process, where conflict is one of the instinctive reactions to anxiety, not a function of one's relationship to a sibling. Sibling rivalry often takes place in the triangle between the siblings and one of the parents, who also plays a part in the conflict. Blessing's chapter does not deal with sibling position at all.[10]

This attention to terminology and usage is not about being a "Bowen fundamentalist," who insists that everyone say things just right.[11] Accurately representing a theory should apply with any psychological approach brought to a text. We must allow both the text and the theory to speak for themselves. To revise terminology can easily lead to speaking of Bowen theory but applying an amalgam assembled by the interpreter. The way forward in building on the work that Blessing has initiated is to attend as closely to BFST as one does to the biblical text so that the conversation between the two may be authentic.

Six Assumptions

With these three interpretive rules in place, let me acknowledge six foundational assumptions necessary for reading biblical texts through the lens of Bowen's theory.

First, the questions raised by BFST regarding human behavior are normally asked in the context of living, accessible families or individuals. To raise those questions of families and individuals that are accessible only in the words of a text lays an additional layer of interpretation on the conclusions one draws. Although a BFST practitioner working with an actual family may also impose interpretation on that family system prematurely, at least that family is available for further questions or investigation to clarify whether the interpretation is factual. However, when we try to understand a family or individual accessible only within a text, limited information hampers us. The family or individual is not available to allow us to clarify our conclusions. Consequently, we must acknowledge that working with texts and not people requires more interpretation. We must be careful in assuming that a text alone is adequate for such interpretation.

Second, we must assume that terms in one realm or field of study (such as BFST) do not automatically equate with terms in another (for example, in biblical texts or Christian theology). Words and concepts in BFST may both denote and connote different meanings when they, or terms like them, appear in Scripture. Examples are terms like "self," concepts of marriage as "one flesh" vis-à-vis the concept of "fusion" in BFST, and Bowen's understanding of "togetherness" versus the biblical concept of "fellowship" or "unity." If we use the terms as though they were equivalent, we misunderstand and misuse them. Part of the interpreter's task is to help the biblical text and the theory come to terms with each other. Appendix B, "Bowen Theory and Theological Language," might assist with this task.

On the other hand, understanding human behavior from a natural systems perspective may lead us to read and understand biblical concepts differently. For example, while we might ordinarily read admonitions in passages such as Romans 12:9–21 in the theological category of church unity, we might instead read them from the perspective of Bowen's concept of differentiation.

Third, we assume that BFST can supply questions and concepts for us to bring to bear on texts in which we may better understand human behavior by thinking through the presence of anxiety, the fusion between characters, the togetherness force, and the family emotional processes such as conflict, distance, overfunctioning/underfunctioning, and triangles. Concepts such as differentiation of self or emotional cutoff might provide insight into the words and actions of characters.

Fourth, we assume that we can apply BFST principles to a variety of biblical literary forms, not just stories. Biblical texts clearly come in genres other than narrative. We can read some texts, such as passages in Paul's letters that describe human behavior, rather easily through a natural systems lens. Other genres, such as the poetry of the Psalms, prophetic oracles, or apocalyptic visions, stand farther away from the more factual descriptions of narrative or of discursive literature. These, however, also have a story implicit in them (Who produced this text? For what purpose?) and are themselves a functional fact (demonstrating the things a particular writer believed about God or humanity). We assume that a hermeneutics of natural systems can necessarily encompass the variety of genres we encounter in Scripture.

Fifth, we assume that interpreters, in making the move between the scientific description of human behavior found in BFST and the theological/religious account of human behavior found in Christian Scriptures, must proceed deliberately and slowly. Interpreters must take care that they have clearly understood the concepts of each so that they do not too quickly equate the two. For example, Paul's description of indwelling sin in Romans 7 sounds in many ways like descriptions of emotional reactivity in BFST. If an interpreter makes the claim that these concepts are two attempts to describe the same human experience, one in scientific terms and one in theological terms, the burden of proof must lie with the one who would argue for their connection and attempt to make the case.

Sixth, we assume that BFST and biblical theology understand the human dilemma differently. Bowen sees our problem as facing reactivity and anxiety, with some limited amount of emotional maturity (differentiation). He sees humans struggling in relationships because of instinctual, emotional processes—products of our evolutionary past. A biblical theology expresses our condition in a different way. Biblical writers describe our condition as the result of sin, a broken relationship with our Creator (however God may have accomplished that creation). We cannot redeem ourselves; we need God's salvation to find wholeness. The worldview of the two perspectives is different (naturalistic versus theistic). The assumptions are different (for example, the degree to which our own efforts can help remedy our problems or the degree to which our behaviors have any moral implications). However, just as we learn to bring science and faith into dialogue in other aspects of theology and practice, we can allow these two perspectives to interact in a way that contributes to our understanding of human behavior and our response as ministers to human needs.

In the next three chapters, I will attempt to map some biblical texts with the tool of BFST: the stories of the patriarchs in Genesis, the example of Jesus in the Gospels, and the teachings of Paul in his letters. David's story is also taken up in appendix A. You may judge the effectiveness of that effort. I hope that these examples will stir your imagination into ways of bringing the concepts of BFST to the ministry task of Bible reading, interpretation, and proclamation.

●— **Questions for Reflection** ————————————————

1. What are the dangers and challenges of using a psychological theory to help interpret an ancient biblical text?
2. How would you justify the attempt to use a theory like BFST as an aid in biblical interpretation?
3. What biblical texts or stories come to mind that you might fruitfully explore by using BFST as a map?

10

Mapping the Family of Abraham

Family Systems, 2000 BC

The past informs the present. Memory makes the map we carry, no matter how hard we try to erase it.

—Cara Black, *Murder in the Bastille*

The stories of the Hebrew patriarchs found in Genesis, from the closing paragraph of chapter 11 through the end of the book, provide the most extensive family material in the Bible. Covering at least six generations, they begin with Nahor, Abraham's grandfather, and end with the story of Joseph and his siblings, Abraham's great-grandchildren. Since we are interested in ways that Bowen Family Systems Theory (BFST) can provide insight into biblical texts, we will read these stories with questions derived from the concepts of Bowen theory.[1] I recommend that readers open a Bible to encounter the stories for themselves as they make their way through this analysis, even if the accounts are familiar.

The Anxious World of Abraham

Abraham and his descendants lived in an anxious world.[2] Families like his faced external threats to survival: natural disasters, such as famine (Gen.

12:10; 26:1; 41:1–57; 47:13); scarcity of resources (13:1–7); and threats of terrorism and violence (12:12; 14:1–12; 20:11; 26:7; 32:11). Additionally, they dealt with anxiety and its impact within the family: significant deaths and grief (11:28, 32; 23:2; 24:67; 25:8; 35:19), conflict between brothers (27:41–42; 32:11; 37:17–35), and struggles with in-laws (26:34–35; 27:46; 29:21–30; 31:1–55). BFST would predict that as anxiety rises in a family emotional system, that system eventually will become symptomatic. Family emotional processes will take over. Conflict will increase, or some will become distant (or in extreme cases cut off relationships from others). Other members might demonstrate physical, emotional, or social dysfunctions. Or the system might conspire unconsciously to identify one member as the problem. We can expect one or more of these symptomatic responses in an emotional system facing the stresses of the external world, coupled with the chronic anxiety and emotional attachment passed on from previous generations. Consequently, we would anticipate discovering evidence of such reactivity in the stories of Abraham and his family, testimony that they too functioned as a human emotional system. They did the best they could with the resources they had in themselves, in one another, and in their faith.

Emotional Triangles and the Patriarchs

Bowen believed that emotional triangles, the smallest stable human relationship, were the molecules of emotional systems. A two-person relationship, he observed, was notoriously unstable. If either one of the two members grows anxious in some way, the relationship will become unsettled. When such imbalance occurs, human beings instinctively reach out to a third person to help manage the anxiety between them. Under less anxious circumstances, two people will get along with each other just fine. But when anxiety rises, the two-person relationship becomes unstable and adds a third.

The patriarchal stories offer many accounts of emotional triangles. The triangle of Abraham, Sarah, and Hagar is prominent. Abraham and Sarah were unable to conceive a child. Such childlessness may very well have been a symptom of their anxious lives.[3] This condition certainly contributed to the anxiety in their relationship, since the narrator mentions it frequently (11:30; 15:2; 17:17; 18:13).[4] God's promising Abraham that he would have descendants (12:1–3; 15:1–21; 17:1–16; 18:9–15) complicated this tension.

At one point, Sarah concedes to a cultural practice and offers Abraham her Egyptian slave girl, Hagar, as a wife, so that they might be able to bear children (16:1–3). In terms of BFST, Abraham and Sarah manage the anxiety between them by triangling Hagar into the relationship. Abraham agrees with the plan, and Hagar soon conceives. Her pregnancy intensifies the emotional triangle. Hagar, when she became aware of her conception, "looked with contempt on her mistress" (v. 4). Now the anxiety in the triangle shifts away from Abraham and Sarah and settles on Sarah and Hagar. Sarah turns to Abraham: "May the wrong done to me be on you! I gave my slave-girl to your embrace, and when she saw that she had conceived, she looked on me with contempt. May the LORD judge between you and me!" (v. 5). Abraham yields to Sarah's anxiety and allows her to dismiss Hagar, even though she is bearing his son, Ishmael (vv. 6, 15).

Bowen observed that the number of triangles in an emotional system can increase and interlock as anxiety rises.[5] An example of such interlocking triangles shows up in the stories of Abraham's grandsons, Jacob and Esau, twins born to Isaac, Abraham's son, and his wife, Rebekah. The narrator posits tension in the relationship even at birth: "The first came out red, all his body like a hairy mantle; so they named him Esau. Afterward his brother came out, with his hand gripping Esau's heel; so he was named Jacob" (25:25–26). Jacob's name carries the meaning "supplanter," one who grabs the heel or trips others up.

This foreshadowing at birth unfolds in the lives of the two boys. Esau grows up living in the outdoors, a skillful hunter, the pride of his father. Jacob was his mother's delight. The parental favoritism (25:28) sets in place a series of interlocking triangles that come into play at significant moments. Triangles now exist between Isaac, Esau, and Rebekah; Isaac, Esau, and Jacob; and Rebekah, Jacob, and Esau. BFST suggests that such a favored focus by each of these parents toward a son would be one way the couple was managing the anxiety in the marriage.

The tension that grows in the competition and conflict between Esau and Jacob lights up the interlocking triangles. Jacob bargains for Esau's right as firstborn to inherit both the larger legacy (twice as much as any other sibling, so in this case two-thirds of his father's property [Deut. 21:17]) and the patriarchal promise given by God to Abraham and reaffirmed to Isaac. When the time comes for Isaac to bestow those blessings on Esau, the triangles ignite. Rebekah overhears the plan and conspires with Jacob to deceive Isaac and steal from Esau. The plan is "successful," but the triangles remain operative. Suspecting Esau's plan to wait for Isaac's death and then kill Jacob, Rebekah manipulates Isaac into sending Jacob off to her family in Haran to seek a wife. Esau's two Hittite wives trouble Rebekah and Isaac (26:34–35; 27:46). Esau, still trying to please his father, marries a third wife, a distant relative (28:8–9).

Even after their parents die, the anxiety between the twins, fueled by the favored focus projected on each, continues. When Jacob, fleeing from his father-in-law, Laban, determines to return to Canaan, he knows he must face Esau. They manage, however, to reconcile, allowing the anxiety that had driven their relationship for so long to diminish (32:1–33:17).

Jacob replicates the behavior of his parents, focusing his favored attention on two sons, Joseph and Benjamin, born to him by Rachel, the favorite of his two wives (37:3–4; 42:4, 36). The anxiety contained in the resulting interlocking triangles repeats in Jacob's generation as the conflict and competition for Jacob's affection plays out between the sisters, Leah and Rachel, and their servant girls, Zilpah and Bilhah. The favored focus that Jacob directs toward Joseph only serves to activate additional triangles between him and his brothers, who seek to destroy him.

Accounts of Jacob's relationships with his extended family in Haran (Laban and his daughters) and relationships between Jacob and his sons are examples of many other emotional triangles at work in Abraham's family.

Emotional Process in Abraham's Family

Unsurprisingly, stories of the patriarchal family demonstrate the same kinds of reactivity that we experience in our own families when anxiety exceeds the system's capacity to contain it. Family emotional process, whether in the form of conflict, distance, reciprocal functioning (overfunctioning and underfunctioning), or projection, was as much a reality for Abraham's family as for any other natural system.

Conflict

Conflict, a frequent symptom of rising anxiety in an emotional system, runs as a common theme throughout the narratives. Notice the strife between Abraham and Lot (13:5–7), Abraham and Sarah (16:4–6), Sarah and Hagar (16:6; 21:8–11), Jacob and Esau (25:19–26; 27:41), Jacob and Laban (29:15–30; 30:25–55), Rachel and Leah (29:15–30; 30:1–24), and Joseph and his brothers (37:1–36).

Sometimes these conflicts resolve themselves in the story. Abraham and Lot work out a way to separate so that they can maintain their relationship (13:8–11). Abraham even comes to his nephew's rescue when the kings of Canaan raid his camp (14:1–16). Ishmael returns to join his half brother, Isaac, in burying their father (25:9). That Sarah had preceded Abraham in death may have made this bridging of the tense relationship possible. Despite the tension between Jacob and Esau, which escalated to the point where fratricide seemed likely (27:41), and the cutoff that existed for years, the two reconcile peaceably (33:1–17). Like Ishmael and Isaac before them, Jacob and Esau appear together at the cave of Machpelah to bury their father (25:9; 35:28–29). Jacob and Laban manage to part ways on relatively amicable terms (31:43–55), although Laban's blessing on his son-in-law may have had an edge to it: "'See this heap and see the pillar, which I have set between you and me. This heap is a witness, and the pillar is a witness, that I will not pass beyond this heap to you, and you will not pass beyond this heap and this pillar to me, for harm. May the God of Abraham and the God of Nahor'—the God of their father—'judge between us'" (31:51–53).

The reconciliation between Joseph and his brothers is one of the more powerful family stories in the Bible (42:1–45:28; 50:15–21). That this family's conflict can have a tide-like rise and fall helps us see it as a symptom of the family's struggle with the intensifying anxiety in their lives.

Distance

Increased anxiety can also take the form of distancing from others rather than engaging them. Abraham and Lot separate (13:5–11), perhaps for practical reasons, such as managing scarce resources like grazing land and water for their herds. On some level, however, their decision may also have been an automatic response to manage the anxiety that had produced conflict. Sarah twice manages the anxiety that she focuses on Hagar by insisting that Abraham send the young woman and her child away. Jacob flees Esau, at his mother's insistence, and travels across the country to Haran. When things become intense in Haran, he flees his uncle Laban and returns to Canaan. Joseph's brothers handle their intensely anxious focus on him and their father by attempting to rid the family of this favored son, selling him into slavery in Egypt.

One of the more intriguing episodes in the patriarchal narrative is the account of Abraham's attempt to offer his son Isaac as a sacrifice to God (22:1–19). The text does not answer all our questions about the relationship between Abraham and Isaac. We are left to wonder about the relationship between father and son from this point forward (and between the father and the child's mother!). How much accumulated emotional distance between father and son can we read into the later statement about Isaac's rather intense attachment to his mother, Sarah (24:67)?

Reciprocal Functioning

Overfunctioning and underfunctioning are also emotional reactions in an anxious system. The behavior of Rebekah, wife of Isaac and mother of Jacob and Esau, might be an example of overfunctioning. Even back home in Haran, her father, Bethuel, and brother Laban appear to defer to her in the decision regarding marriage to Isaac, an action that seems out of place in a patriarchal culture in which women held few rights (24:57–61). She agrees to return with Abraham's servant Eliezar to marry Isaac.

In these family stories, Isaac consistently demonstrates a kind of passivity or underfunctioning. He submits to his father's attempt to sacrifice him on the mountain. His emotional attachment to his mother results in deep grief upon her death that only his marriage to Rebekah finally assuages (24:66–67). He is the only patriarch to have just one wife and not to father children with a concubine. He repeats his father's ploy of lying about his relationship to his wife to preserve his own life (26:6–11; cf. 12:10–20; 20:1–18). He excavates the wells his father has previously dug and gives them the same names (26:17–18). When the herders of Gerar quarrel with Isaac's herders over water rights, he abandons the wells (26:19–22). He allows Jacob to deceive him, so that he gives the patriarchal blessing to the younger son instead of to Esau (27:1–40). He yields to Rebekah's demands to send Jacob away to find a wife (27:46). He and Rebekah demonstrate a kind of reciprocal functioning in their life together.

Projection

The fourth expression of anxiety, projection, is a form of the emotional triangles discussed earlier. In projection, a triangle takes the form of an intense focus on one or more children in the family. The focus on Isaac, the child of promise born to Abraham and Sarah in their old age, is understandable, making Abraham's apparent unquestioning willingness to sacrifice him even more remarkable. Abraham hears God's call to offer "your son, your only son Isaac, whom you love" (22:2). In the next generation, Isaac projects an intense positive focus on his oldest son, Esau, while his wife, Rebekah, directs a positive focus toward Jacob (25:27–28). Likewise, Jacob projects a positive focus on his youngest sons: Joseph (the elder son of his favorite wife, Rachel; 37:3–4) and, to some degree, Benjamin (Rachel's second son; 35:18–20; 42:4, 36; 44:20–31). This anxious focus, although positive, consistently accompanies other behavior in the family, such as cutoff and even attempts at fratricide.

Multigenerational Transmission Process

The functioning of multiple generations of Abraham's extended family and his descendants is not so well documented, as the narrative focuses theologically on family members who are bearers of the covenant promises to Abraham

(12:1–3; 15:4–6; 17:1–8, 15–19), and continued through Isaac (26:1–5) and Jacob (28:13–17; 35:9–15). Other branches of the family appear in the story mostly as they come into contact with these three central characters.

Nevertheless, readers can observe certain emotional processes recurring from one generation to the next. Predominantly, Abraham's faith in the God who called him continues to find expression in the lives of his son Isaac, his grandson Jacob, and his great-grandson Joseph. Although these figures display different personalities, each identifies with Abraham's faith. The relationship between God and these first three becomes a part of God's identity for Israel as the "God of Abraham, Isaac, and Jacob."[6]

The theme of the dominance of the younger brother over the older runs through these stories for four generations.[7] Additionally, one generation after another faces the issue of infertility: Abraham and Sarah (11:30), Isaac and Rebekah (25:21), Jacob and Rachel (29:31), and Jacob and Leah (30:9). Incest shows up over the generations as well: Lot and his daughters (19:30–38), Reuben and Bilhah (35:22), and Judah and Tamar (38:12–30).

Family Projection Process

We can see the interlocking nature of the eight concepts of Bowen's theory as the analysis of one aspect of the family's life and behavior also illustrates other concepts in action.[8] The family projection process is a good example. The anxious focus of parents on a child, which is the core idea of this concept, is also an example of emotional triangles at work and at the same time an example of family emotional process. Because of its capacity to help us understand the way in which one child emerges from the family of origin with a significantly different level of emotional maturity, however, Bowen treated the family projection process as a separate concept.

The concept of the projection process also helps us read more completely the patriarchal stories. The anxiety in Abraham's family finds its focus on the only son born to his wife, Sarah. When Sarah bears Isaac in her old age, her jealousy toward Hagar returns. She pressures Abraham to send Hagar and her son away (21:10–14). The cutoff resulting between Ishmael (the legendary progenitor of the Arab people; 17:20; 25:13–16) and Isaac (the father of the people of Israel), bridged briefly at Abraham's burial, plays out in history and remains in the present.

Does the projection process impair Isaac in any way? Does it result in his living with more dependence in his relationships than he might have otherwise? As described earlier, the stories portray Isaac as much more passive than either his father or his son Jacob. His wife, Rebekah, appears much more dominant in the marriage. We might understand this greater level of dependence on Isaac's part as the projection process playing out in Abraham's family.

The projection process continues in the generations that follow. Isaac and Rebekah each appear to manage the anxiety in their relationship by focusing on one of their sons. The emotional immaturity of these two off-spring may have left them with fewer resources to manage their own anxiety. Esau turns to plans for violent conflict. Jacob takes the route of extreme distancing.

Jacob will carry his emotional immaturity into his relationships with his father-in-law, Laban; with his wives, Leah and Rachel; and with his own children (29:1–31:55). It is not clear what happens in Esau's life so that when Jacob returns, anxious over his brother's anger and desire for revenge, Esau seeks a peaceful reconciliation. Jacob does not seem to have changed much. He organizes a parade of gifts meant to bribe his brother and arranges for a caravan of his wives and children to meet Esau, with his favorite wife and favorite son at the back of the line, and himself even farther back—apparently ready to lead the retreat if necessary (32:1–8, 13–21; 33:1–3). He appears genuinely surprised by Esau's softened approach (33:4–17).

In the next generation, the projection process continues as Jacob focuses his favor and attention on Joseph, his eleventh son, born to his favorite wife, Rachel (30:22–23). Rachel eventually dies while bearing him a twelfth son, Benjamin, who receives a similar kind of focus from his father (35:16–21). The nature of the births of these boys helps us understand how their parents singled them out for intense focus. Many years of childlessness for Rachel had ended with Joseph's birth, and for a time he was the youngest in the family. When she gave birth to Benjamin, she lost her life in the process. These facts, accompanied by Jacob's already intense focus on their mother (29:18, 20, 30), made them especially susceptible to receiving their father's attention. Such projection on a child is not benign. It is a way of binding the anxiety in the family, usually in the marriage.

That Jacob's marriages are anxious is not surprising. He married two sisters who are jealous of each other and who vie for Jacob's favor, attention, and offspring (29:30–30:24). The consequences of this focus for Joseph are nearly disastrous. His conflict with his brothers and their jealousy toward him find expression in their plan to take his life (as Esau had planned to take the life of his own brother, Jacob, their father). Like Jacob and Esau before them, the brothers find a surprising reconciliation after years of cutoff. Joseph has managed to emerge from his trials with magnanimity, although his broth-ers fear he will seek revenge once their father has died. They unnecessarily attempt to manipulate him to be generous and merciful to them (50:15–21). In one generation after another, the projection process appears with powerful consequences.

Sibling Position

One of the distinctive themes in the patriarchal accounts appears to contradict Bowen's concept of sibling position. Sibling position attempts to understand the automatic behavior of human beings as a function of their location in the "family constellation." Issues of rank (oldest, middle, youngest, only) and gender relationships (brother of brothers, brother of sisters, sister of sisters, sister of brothers) emerge from engagement with siblings in the emotional system of the nuclear family.

Oldest children often develop as leaders among their siblings, dominating relationships. However, the recurrent theme of younger siblings becoming preeminent in their families marks the story of the patriarchs. Isaac, the younger of Abraham's two sons, becomes the heir of the patriarchal promise. Jacob, the younger twin, barters for his brother's birthright and steals his father's blessing. Rachel, the younger daughter of Laban, is the beloved wife of Jacob, not her older sister. Joseph, the second-youngest son, lives into his dreams of ruling over his brothers and becomes second in authority in Egypt. When Joseph takes his two sons, Manasseh and Ephraim, to aged Jacob for a blessing, the old man crosses his hands and blesses the younger over the older (48:1–22).

This may be more a theological theme than an expression of family emotional process.[9] Perhaps the unexpected dominance of younger over older hints that God's sovereignty overrules the ordinary and is expected to accomplish his purposes. The choice of the younger over the older continues in other biblical stories, such as that of King David.

We may, however, observe the emotional process of sibling position at work even in the patriarchal accounts. The dominance of the younger, especially in the cases of Jacob, Rachel, and Joseph, evokes a strong emotional reaction of conflict in the family. Perhaps this is reactivity connected to the sense that an upstart younger sibling is disrupting ordinary relationships.

On the other hand, the patriarchal accounts contain at least one story in which usual patterns of sibling position come into play. When Shechem sexually assaults Dinah, Jacob's daughter by Leah, her older brothers, Simeon and Levi, seek revenge for the act (34:1–31). On an emotional level, we may see the protective nature of older brothers of sisters.

Emotional Cutoff

Emotional cutoff is an intense expression of the emotional reaction called distancing. It particularly applies to the way people manage their unresolved emotional attachment to their parents. The notion of cutoff helps explain the way people separate themselves from the previous generation to make a new start. Bowen describes this concept as a process of "separation, isolation, withdrawal, running away, or denying the importance of the parental family."[10]

Cutoff can occur through establishing geographical distance from the family, or it may be present in a simple cold withdrawal that denies the importance of a relationship with the parental generation. When cutoff has become an established means of managing the anxiety of this primary relationship, it can show up in a capacity to walk away easily from other important relationships in life.

The Abrahamic family has its share of behaviors that might suggest the experience of cutoff. Could the migration from Haran to Canaan that began with Terah (11:31) and continued with his son Abraham and his grandson Lot (12:4) be an expression of cutoff from the family? That emotional reality would not preclude its being the experience in which Abraham encountered a call from God and placed faith in God's promises.

Abraham and Lot are not in Canaan long before they establish a cutoff relationship (13:1–13) that is only temporarily bridged when Abraham learns of Lot's capture by some tribal kings and comes to his rescue (14:1–16). Lot's descendants, the people of Moab and Ammon, prove to be enemies of Abraham's family when Israel returns to settle in the land of Canaan (19:36–38).

The slave girl Hagar's final dismissal with Ishmael from Abraham's home results in a cutoff between father and son that lasts the rest of the old man's life. Ishmael returns to bury his father but has lived many years without a relationship with him (25:9). The cutoff that is present in this family continues to show up in broken relationships down the generations to the present ongoing struggle between Jews and Arabs in the Middle East.

Rebekah leaves her family to marry Isaac. Esau isolates himself from his parents and violently threatens his brother, resulting in alienation for many years. Isaac and Jacob part ways as father and son when Jacob returns to his mother's family, seeking a wife. Rachel and Leah leave their father to return with Jacob and their children to Canaan. Even when Esau ceases threatening to kill Jacob, the brothers depart from each other and do not reunite until their father's burial (35:29). Esau's descendants, the Edomites (36:1, 8), and Jacob's seed, the Israelites, although neighbors in Canaan, are warring enemies throughout their history. Joseph finds himself separated from his father and brothers for many years before taking steps to bridge that cutoff relationship.

To describe these various relationships as cutoff is to say more than that people experienced conflict or that they grew distant from each other. In case after case, they learned to live without a relationship to people who by all reckoning ought to have been important to their lives. The process of cutoff, established in a family, can intensify through the generations.

Societal Emotional Process

The final theoretical concept Bowen added to his theory in the early 1970s, societal emotional process, observes that human society itself reacts symptomatically to increased anxiety as a nuclear family does. The same emotional processes play out in both—conflict, distance, reciprocal functioning, and projection. Increased anxiety in society brings additional pressure to bear on the functioning of families as well.

Speculating about societal emotional process is a bit more difficult in the patriarchal narratives, since societal data is not readily available. The stories themselves bear witness to serious societal challenges, such as migration, violent tribal conflicts, and struggle over scarce supplies of water and food. The presence of such threats testifies that Abraham and his descendants were trying to survive in a relatively hostile environment, which would surely have meant that these families faced a higher level of acute anxiety. Such threats posed a challenge to survival and likely persisted over a significant stretch of time. Did that ancient society also experience a high level of chronic anxiety that was not based in reality, which would have had an impact on Abraham's family? I am not sure we can answer that question with confidence. We would expect the symptoms of the family described earlier—intense conflicts, cutoff, and projection—to be more prevalent in such an anxious setting as Abraham and his family endured.

Conclusion

To be clear, the effort to read these narratives through the lens of BFST is speculative and experimental. Israel did not preserve these stories to provide data about family functioning; however, they represent authentic human behavior, which is what Bowen was attempting to describe and understand. The theoretical tools of BFST can be a useful way to mine the stories for truth about human behavior that other interpretive approaches would miss.

What difference does all this make in reading and interpreting these accounts? Abraham's family story makes clear that human behavior remains the same through time and across cultures. Fear, anxiety, jealousy, anger, conflict, deceit, family favoritism, violence, love, loyalty, and courage are not recent developments among humans. Four thousand years ago, such reactions were as common as they are now. Although these stories are written in a language most of us cannot read, coming from a culture and time far removed from our own, we can easily identify with them. In these stories we recognize ourselves and our families.

In many ways these are ordinary families. God's promise does not come down to Israel through perfect specimens but through flawed families like ours.[11] Given our own emotional immaturity, the anxious times in which we live sometimes get the better of us. Our automatic responses make relationships more difficult. We, likewise, often struggle to find a thoughtful response. We may see our families and their symptoms as somehow too flawed for God to use. The grace of God that worked through the patriarchs and matriarchs of the faith, despite their emotional reactions and anxiety, can surely work through us as we face the challenges of life in an anxious world.

●— Questions for Reflection

1. How do you see God working in Abraham's family, working with and through the various actions and responses of the individuals, even when reactivity seems to be driving them?

2. How does God's work in Abraham's family influence your thinking about God's work in your own family? Can you look at your own family and identify emotional processes at work in your decision to enter vocational ministry?

3. Which principles of BFST does Abraham's story make clearer to you? How do they do so?

Mapping the Character of Jesus

Differentiation and Christlikeness

Doctrines are not God: they are only a kind of map. But that map is based on the experience of hundreds of people who really were in touch with God—experiences compared with which any thrills or pious feelings you and I are likely to get on our own are very elementary and very confused. And secondly, if you want to get any further, you must use the map. . . . You will not get eternal life by simply feeling the presence of God in flowers or music. Neither will you get anywhere by looking at maps without going to sea. Nor will you be very safe if you go to sea without a map.

—C. S. Lewis, *Mere Christianity*

Jesus and Differentiation of Self

Murray Bowen introduced the concept of differentiation of self to describe human functioning on a continuum from the lowest possible level to the highest. Zero on the scale represents the lowest level of "undifferentiation." The highest theoretical level of differentiation is 100. Bowen says: "When the scale was first devised, the 100 level was reserved for the being who was perfect in all levels of emotional, cellular, and physiological functioning. I expect there might be some unusual figures in history, or possibly some living persons who would fit into the mid-90 range."[1]

We can think of differentiation of self as the ability of people to steer their own course under pressure to be *for* the system and to conform to its values, plans, and ways. Bowen's hypothesis was that a 75 on the scale would demonstrate an extremely high level of functioning and that those above 60 would still represent only a small percentage of the population.

If Bowen reserved the highest level on the scale of differentiation for that being who is "perfect in all levels of emotional, cellular, and physiological functioning," then who might approach that ranking?[2] For two millennia Christian theologians have tried to understand Jesus as both fully human and fully divine. The ancient church councils wrestled with balancing these two ideas that the New Testament holds in tension. Although much attention has focused on understanding what it means to speak of Jesus of Nazareth as the divine one, attempting to grasp the implications of his humanity is equally fascinating.

Luke, Paul, and the author of Hebrews present Jesus as the True Man, the "second man," the new "Adam," the "last Adam" (Luke 3:38; 1 Cor. 15:45–46), the one who fully bears the image of God.[3] They understood Jesus to be what God intended all humans to be. For Paul, Jesus's life provides the standard against which we measure all other lives (Eph. 4:13). The goal of Christian living becomes *conformity to Christ* (Rom. 8:29; Gal. 4:19).

What would we expect to discover about Jesus's human character if we compare his life and teachings to Bowen's description of a highly differentiated self? A comparison of the words and works of Jesus in the New Testament with Bowen's concept of differentiation reveals ways in which Jesus, as a human, functioned at a high level of differentiation in his relationships. This has implications for our own spiritual formation, as discussed in chapter 7. Here we will consider the ways in which Jesus's life illustrates a well-differentiated human being amid an intense emotional system pressuring him to conform in a variety of ways.

A Few Caveats

The four New Testament writings known as Gospels provide the only historical sources for studying the life of Jesus. However, we must issue some disclaimers before using that material for such a study as this.

First, the Gospels are not scientific biographies of the life of Jesus of Nazareth. They are brief, containing only six hours or so of his teaching and accounting for no more than approximately fifty days of his public ministry, which may have extended up to three years. They say little about Jesus's early life but focus instead on his last three years, and particularly on his last week.[4]

Second, the Gospels are not unbiased accounts. They do not pretend to be. Rather, they present a theological interpretation of who Jesus of Nazareth was and what he did, not a psychological profile. The Gospel writers unapologetically tell the story of Jesus in the belief that he was the promised messiah of Israel. In this sense, we may regard these writings as "narrative Christology" (the doctrine of Christ's person and purpose communicated in story form) rather than as historical biography.[5]

Third, the Gospel writers did not intend these accounts of Jesus's words to supply material for the study of Jesus's psychological or relational functioning; to use them in this way is to some degree to misuse them.[6] This is the case with all of our efforts to apply Bowen Family Systems Theory (BFST), or any psychological approach, to a reading of the Bible. We cannot conduct psychological analysis of ancient characters using biblical materials. We can, however, read them with an eye toward the human behavior described and compare that to what Bowen observed about how human beings function in relationships.

With these cautions in mind, we will proceed with a naive approach that will take the Gospels' portrait of Jesus at face value, working with his words and deeds as recorded. Whether we understand these documents to describe the historical Jesus or whether we see Jesus in the Gospels as more of a literary-theological figure, the question of his level of differentiation remains a valid question for investigation.

Jesus and Differentiation of Self in the Synoptics

Jesus's Actions

Our level of differentiation of self is formed in the context of our extended and nuclear families, and these families transmit it through generations. Matthew's Gospel appropriately begins with a genealogy, rooting the story of Jesus in the multigenerational story of the people of Israel, particularly in the family of David (Matt. 1:1–17). Jesus is the "son of David," Israel's long-expected messiah (1:1, 6, 17, 20; 9:27; 12:23; 15:22; 20:30–31; 21:9, 15; 22:42–43).

The New Testament opens with a family story. Betrothal, divorce, pregnancy, marriage, sexual relations, and birth are central components (Matt.

1:18–25). This Gospel presents events from the perspective of Joseph, Jesus's earthly father. That Joseph decides to proceed with betrothal and marriage to Mary, despite what must have been tremendous social pressure to do otherwise, suggests a high level of functioning. Joseph follows his dreams and his inner sense of what is right, rather than what we might assume to be the togetherness forces of his family and society (1:18–2:23).

Luke's account of Jesus's birth reflects Mary's perspective. She knows the supernatural nature of her pregnancy and proceeds through it without shame, identifying herself as the "servant of the Lord" (Luke 1:38). She seeks support from her relative, Elizabeth, who, despite being well past the normal age of childbearing, is also pregnant (1:8–25, 39–40). The two of them share their joy and expectation (Luke 1:41–56). Joseph and Mary each demonstrate the ability to take a firm position when circumstances threaten their reputations, their relationships with their families, and even their lives.[7] Their ability to discern and follow an alternative path provides reason to suppose that Jesus was the eldest son raised by two well-differentiated parents.[8]

Matthew narrates nothing of Jesus's experience between approximately ages 2 and 30. Luke's story, however, hints at the process of maturing during childhood and adolescence (Luke 2:40–52). At age 12, Jesus travels to Jerusalem for the Feast of Passover. He becomes separated from his parents, who do not discover his absence for an entire day. When they miss him, they spend a day traveling back to Jerusalem and then another looking for him among their relatives and friends. Losing a child would be a highly anxious experience for any parent. On the third day they eventually find him in the temple area, sitting among the rabbis, listening and asking questions. Mary asks, "Child, why have you treated us like this? Look, your father and I have been searching for you in *great anxiety*" (emphasis added). The adolescent Jesus replies less anxiously, "Why were you searching for me? Did you not know I must be in my Father's house?" (2:48–49). The young Jesus takes an I-position with his anxious parents, demonstrating an already growing differentiation from them and a growing awareness of the relationship with God and God's purposes that would serve as the organizing principle of his life.[9]

His parents do not understand the meaning of their son's words, however, and Jesus, in obedience, returns with them to Nazareth (Luke 2:50–51). He spends the next eighteen years or so in his parents' home. Luke observes that Mary reflected thoughtfully on all these events (v. 51). Meanwhile, Jesus continued to increase "in wisdom and in years, and in divine and human favor" (v. 52).

At some point during this time, Joseph dies.[10] When Jesus's story picks up at "about thirty years old," Mary continues to appear in the narrative, but Joseph is mentioned only to identify the lineage of Jesus (Matt. 13:55; Luke 3:23; John 1:45; 6:42). Jesus, as eldest son, would have taken up the role of head of household for a time.[11] Consequently, we might understand his leaving home to seek the baptism of John and to pursue his calling as Israel's messiah to be a significant act of differentiation from his family of origin. Togetherness pressure to remain at home and care for his mother would have been intense. This act certainly carried the potential of traumatizing the nuclear family. Their anxious reaction will eventually surface when they seek to retrieve him, fearing he had gone "out of his mind" (Mark 3:21).[12] That Jesus's decision to leave was rooted in differentiation of self, in choosing his own path rather than emotional cutoff, may be evident in Mary's continuing to be a part of Jesus's life and ministry all the way to the cross (John 2:1–11; 19:25–27). Despite having a higher calling than his family's domestic life and refusing to yield to pressure to remain with them, Jesus did not cut off from his mother and siblings.

Matthew picks up the story of the adult Jesus when he seeks out John the Baptizer (a relative) to baptize him, thus identifying with John's message and movement. John initially refuses to baptize Jesus, recognizing a holiness that exceeds his own. But Jesus insists, defining himself and his own sense of obedience to God (Matt. 3:15). Jesus takes this strong I-position with a man widely believed to be in the line of the ancient Hebrew prophets, a man Jesus himself will describe as "more than a prophet" and as the greatest "among those born of women" (Matt. 11:9, 11). Such a stand requires a strong sense of self. After John's death, Jesus takes up the preaching of the kingdom of God that John has begun (Mark 1:14–15) but carves out his own methodology, which contrasts with John's in ways that are apparent even to outsiders (Matt. 9:14–17; 11:16–18). Rather than waiting for the lost to come to him, as John did, Jesus's ministry involves seeking them out (Luke 19:1–10).

For literary and theological purposes, Luke inserts the genealogy of Jesus between two significant acts of differentiation—his baptism and his temptation in the desert (Luke 3:23–38)—rather than at the beginning of the story (Matt. 1:1–17). From the perspective of BFST, the genealogy places these two events in the context of Jesus's multigenerational story. When Jesus determines to leave home and engage a mission he believes is his divine destiny, he acts as part of the story of Israel over generations.

Jesus's temptation in the wilderness provides another example of his well-defined self. All three Synoptic Gospels[13] tie this experience closely to Jesus's baptism, when a voice from heaven announces his call to messiahship: "You are my Son, the Beloved" (Mark 1:11 and parallels, echoing Ps. 2:7, a royal psalm for the coronation of a Davidic king), "With you I am well-pleased" (reflecting Isa. 42:1, a song of the suffering servant of the Lord). Having heard this summons, Jesus retreats to the wilderness to consider prayerfully and thoughtfully its meaning and implications. The scriptural images of the Davidic messiah and the suffering servant of the Lord had not converged in traditional Jewish theology. How will he fulfill the calling of messiahship by means of suffering? In the temptation stories, Jesus struggles with and ultimately rejects the economic, religious, and political pressures to pursue power by becoming the royal messiah that people anticipated. He reformulates that role in a way no one expected by wedding the prophetic image of the son of David with that of Deutero-Isaiah's suffering servant.[14]

The evil one tempts Jesus to reject suffering, to rely on spectacular deeds to gather a following, and to approach the kingdom of God as a material, political entity (Matt. 4:1–11; Mark 1:12–13; Luke 4:1–13). All this runs counter to his calling and the way that Jesus has conceived God's kingdom. Jesus stands on his beliefs.[15]

Murray Bowen distinguished between "basic self" and "pseudo-self." Basic self is that part of us not negotiable in the relationship system. Neither is it changed by coercion, by the pressure to gain approval, or to enhance one's standing with others. Pseudo-self, however, will wilt under such strain. When relationship pressure is less intense, we may appear to be functioning at a higher level than we can sustain when important relationships impinge on us.

Tempted to exchange his "self" for power and comfort, Jesus repeatedly refuses. To carry out his mission, Jesus opts for a radical commitment to what he understands to be God's will for him, rather than another approach. These same temptations surface repeatedly in the story of Jesus's life, and in each instance he refuses to compromise.[16] In other words, he acts out of solid, or basic, self.

Examples of Jesus's well-differentiated self abound in the Sermon on the Mount (Matt. 5:1–7:29; cf. Luke 6:20–49). This classic section deals with inner righteousness versus legalism (Matt. 5:17–48). Rabbinical pedagogy required a teacher to have "a place to stand," grounding his teaching in either the Scriptures or the oral tradition. That is, the rabbi was not his own authority. The crowds who hear Jesus deliver these teachings respond with amazement because "he taught them as one who had authority and not as their scribes" (7:28–29). That authority shows up repeatedly in a series of statements concerning his interpretation of the Mosaic law: "You have heard that it was said to those of ancient times, . . . but I say to you . . ." (5:21–22, 27, 31–32, 33–34, 38–39, 43–44). The "I" in each instance is an emphatic construction in Matthew's original language, emphasizing the contrast between previous teachers and Jesus.

Jesus not only differentiates himself from the other rabbinical teachers by offering his own teaching without "a place to stand," but he also, in Matthew's version, clearly confronts the behavior of those teachers (5:17–20; 6:2–4, 5–15, 16–18). He will do this in detail later (23:1–39).

Sometimes Jesus says "no" to would-be followers (Matt. 8:20–22). Jesus rejects even the request to place burying one's father ahead of loyalty to the kingdom (v. 22). He himself has done the difficult thing of valuing the kingdom of God ahead of family relationships and calls his disciples to be willing to do the same (Matt. 10:34–39; Luke 14:25–27). Jesus allows a rich young man to walk away despite Jesus's concern for him (Mark 10:17–27 and parallels). In each case Jesus acts firmly on principle. He understands the kingdom of God to call for undivided allegiance and refuses to accept half-hearted commitment.

Jesus avoids an anxious response in a variety of situations (Matt. 6:25–34; 8:23–26). Every response he makes, no matter how severe the crisis, appears to be thoughtful. When the religious establishment pressures him to conform to practices that Jesus believes to be contrary to the spirit of God's law, he flatly refuses (9:10–13; 12:1–14). When the crowds demand that he stay with them, he instead acts on his internal sense of mission (Luke 4:43). When John and John's disciples request an answer to a direct question concerning his identity as messiah, Jesus instead turns the question back to John. John must decide for himself what he believes concerning Jesus's role in the story of Israel's redemption (Luke 7:21–23). Jesus soon requires his closest disciples to make the same decision (9:18–21).

Jesus calls those who follow him to differentiate themselves from their own families, a costly decision he modeled in his own life. In one episode, his mother and brothers come to "speak to him" (Matt. 12:46). His decision to step away from the responsibilities placed on him as the eldest son has left his mother in the care of his brothers and sisters, possibly generating significant anxiety among his family members.[17] Mark says they come to "restrain him" because they believe he has "gone out of his mind" (Mark 3:21). When someone tells Jesus they are there, he asks, "Who is my mother, and who are my brothers?" Then, indicating his disciples, he states, "Here are my mother and my brothers! For whoever does the will of my Father in heaven is my brother and sister and mother" (Matt. 12:46–50; Mark 3:31–35; cf. Luke 11:27–28). Jesus maintains his principles in the face of pressure to yield to important others. If his family had had their way, he would have abandoned his call.[18]

Jesus's teaching method often reflects differentiation of self as well. Using a didactic approach of indirection, Jesus frequently refuses to think for others, forcing them to reach conclusions for themselves. An expert in the law tests him with a weighty question: "Teacher, what must I do to inherit eternal life?" Jesus responds, "What is written in the law? What do you read there?" The lawyer returns an answer that Jesus agrees with, that one should love God wholeheartedly and that one should love one's neighbor unselfishly. Jesus commends the answer and tells the man to go and live what he knows to be true. The lawyer presses the issue, asking Jesus for a definition of "neighbor." Jesus replies with the parable of the Good Samaritan, again turning the thinking back into the head of the inquirer by asking, "Which of these three, do you think, was a neighbor to the man who fell into the hands of the robbers?" (Luke 10:25–37). Jesus's heavy reliance on parables as a teaching method may reflect his understanding that ultimately every hearer must make decisions regarding their beliefs and responses to his message (Mark 4:3–34). His methodology forced the issue, requiring a moment of defining self by his listeners.

In addition to parables, Jesus often relies on questions as a didactic tool that preserves self and permits others to think for themselves.[19] He sometimes answers questions with questions (Mark 10:17–18). He pushes his disciples to define themselves more clearly by interrogating them (8:27–30; 9:33). He frustrates his opponents' attempts to define him by means of questions as well (12:35–37).

When Jesus's friend Martha attempts to draw him into a triangle with her sister, Mary, Jesus declines the invitation. He calls attention to Martha's anxiety and leaves Mary to her own choices (Luke 10:38–42). When a man endeavors to recruit Jesus to side with him in a conflict with his brother over an inheritance, Jesus refuses to become part of the triangle and confronts the man with his own greed, forcing him to reexamine his own part in the conflict (12:13–21).

Although it is not difficult to find examples of emotions in the descriptions of Jesus—for example, compassion (Mark 1:41) or anger (3:5)—it is a challenge to find anything in Jesus's story that resembles the kind of anxious reactivity that less-well-differentiated persons regularly experience. Jesus repeatedly responds to emotion with thoughtful, helpful, and appropriate behavior.

As Jesus approaches his final trials, he agonizes in the garden of Gethsemane over "drinking the cup" of suffering and death (Matt. 26:36–46; Mark 14:32–42; Luke 22:39–46). Even here, in the face of an early and painful death, Jesus struggles against the pressures of "togetherness" and chooses a path that will separate him from his family and disciples because it is God's will for him. This decision, like resisting temptations earlier in the wilderness, requires an unusually high level of differentiation on the part of Jesus.

Jesus's Teachings

Jesus's teachings themselves have implications regarding the effort to differentiate a self. First, he calls followers to choose, as he himself has, a commitment to the will of God over pressures to conform to family demands (Matt. 6:24, 33). Jesus says: "Whoever loves father or mother more than me is not worthy of me; and whoever loves son or daughter more than me is not worthy of me; and whoever does not take up the cross and follow me is not worthy of me. Those who find their life will lose it, and those who lose their life for my sake will find it" (10:37–39). Such a commitment would require work on differentiating a self that could choose such goal-oriented behavior in the face of relationship pressure.

Jesus recognizes that the effort to differentiate from one's family of origin by choosing God's will over family demands could have cataclysmic consequences in the family system.

> Everyone therefore who acknowledges me before others, I also will acknowledge before my Father in heaven; but whoever denies me before others, I also will deny before my Father in heaven. Do not think that I have come to bring peace to the earth; I have not come to bring peace, but a sword.
>
> For I have come to set a man against his father,
> and a daughter against her mother,
> and a daughter-in-law against her mother-in-law;
> and one's foes will be members of one's own household. (Matt. 10:32–36, citing Mic. 7:6)

He tells his followers that in the process of proclaiming the kingdom, they are going to meet resistance from their own families, just as he has (Matt. 10:21). Although not advocating emotional cutoff from one's own family, Jesus teaches that the togetherness forces that would pull one away from commitment to the kingdom of God must not have the final say. One must choose to stand with the principles of the kingdom even when pressured to do otherwise by the closest of relationships.

A second aspect of Jesus's teaching that echoes the process of differentiating a self is his admonition to those in his kingdom to work on themselves, rather than on others. He says, for example,

> Do not judge, so that you may not be judged. For with the judgment you make you will be judged, and the measure you give will be the measure you get. Why do you see the speck in your neighbor's eye, but do not notice the log in your own eye? Or how can you say to your neighbor, 'Let me take the speck out of

your eye,' while the log is in your own eye? You hypocrite, first take the log out of your own eye, and then you will see clearly to take the speck out of your neighbor's eye. (Matt. 7:1–5)

Jesus asks his disciples to think about their own reactivity rather than the behavior of others. Such a focus leaves intact the boundaries of a better-defined self.

A third facet of Jesus's teaching that intersects the project of differentiating a self is his instruction to kingdom citizens to live life without anxiety. He teaches his disciples that a less anxious approach is possible through learning to trust their heavenly Father, who knows their needs, responds to their prayers, forgives their failures, and provides for their welfare (Matt. 6:7–15, 19–34). He teaches specific practices, such as generosity, fasting, and prayer, that focus faith and attention on God as a means of dealing with one's anxiety (vv. 1–8). People high on the scale of differentiation live with less anxiety. Jesus is calling his disciples to the same high-level life that he lives through faith in his heavenly Father.

The Fourth Gospel

The differences between the ways the Synoptics and John's Gospel tell the story of Jesus are many and significant.[20] Given those differences, the fact that both traditions describe a well-differentiated life stands out even more.

The Fourth Gospel has no concrete information concerning Jesus's early childhood or adolescence. When the story opens, he is a grown man.[21] Nevertheless, the first account of Jesus's miraculous power involves his family. At a wedding celebration in Cana, Jesus's mother informs him that the supply of wine has been depleted, but she requests nothing of him directly. His response to her, however, is a differentiating one: "Woman, what concern is that to you and to me? My hour has not yet come" (John 2:4).[22] Then, in his own time, Jesus performs the initial sign in this Gospel by transforming water into choice wine (vv. 4–11). John intends the reader to understand that Jesus's decision to transform the water is a response not to maternal pressure but to a sense of divine timing.

Matthew, Mark, and Luke present Jesus's teaching as focused on the kingdom of God,[23] a subject seldom mentioned in the Fourth Gospel (John 3:3, 5; 18:36). Instead, the focus of Jesus's teaching in John is on Jesus himself. The parables of the kingdom, so characteristic of Jesus in Matthew, Mark, and Luke, are noticeably absent. John replaces them with the "I am" (*egō eimi*) sayings of Jesus, which do not appear in the other three Gospels. Many metaphors of the kingdom in the Synoptics have parallels in the "I am" sayings.[24]

These pronouncements are all phrased in emphatic terms: *egō eimi* (I myself am, I and no one else). This is reminiscent of the speech of God in the latter part of Isaiah as it appears in the Septuagint, the ancient Greek translation of the Old Testament.[25] Jesus's very speech serves to define himself to both his disciples and his opponents.

John, like Matthew, Mark, and Luke, presents Jesus as a self-determined leader who will not succumb to pressure from outside. He will not submit to the demands of family, crowds, or opponents. He does not give in to requests for miraculous signs (John 2:4, 18; 4:48; 6:26). He rejects political pressure (6:15). He will not adjust his claims or demands to be more popular (vv. 41, 52, 60–71). He will not let challenges by his own family direct his plans (7:2–9).

Even his death is not something that happens *to* him. He claims that it is his own choice (10:11, 17–18). He intentionally "lays down his life." No one takes it from him. He lives out that claim in his last hours. The narrator prefaces his final evening with his disciples, which involves a dramatic demonstration of humility, with these words:

> Now before the festival of the Passover, Jesus knew that his hour had come to depart from this world and go to the Father. Having loved his own who were in the world, he loved them to the end. The devil had already put it into the heart of Judas son of Simon Iscariot to betray him. And during supper Jesus, knowing that the Father had given all things into his hands, and that he had come from God and was going to God, got up from the table, took off his outer robe, and tied a towel around himself. Then he poured water into a basin and began to wash the disciples' feet and to wipe them with the towel that was tied around him. (13:1–5)

The events of his last hours with his disciples, and of his arrest and trial, make increasingly clear that Jesus is the one in charge, not the police, priests, or procurator (18:1–19:12). Even in death Jesus demonstrates a remarkable control of self as events unfold, placing his mother's life in the care of one of his closest friends (19:26–27).

Jesus does not offer his disciples extensive ethical instruction in John. The Fourth Gospel contains no text even remotely like the Sermon on the Mount. Jesus's teaching throughout the story focuses primarily on his self-identity. The only ethical teaching in the Fourth Gospel is Jesus's "new commandment": "I give you a new commandment, that you love one another. Just as I have loved you, you also should love one another. By this everyone will know that you are my disciples, if you have love for one another" (13:34–35).

Individual disciples must work out this commandment for themselves in each instance. The command is "new" in the sense that the disciples must always be thinking it through and obeying it as circumstances change. Although the commandment focuses one's attention on relationship with others, the model for how to love others is Jesus's own differentiated life.

Conclusion

Jesus, as the four New Testament evangelists present him, reflects well the concept of differentiation of self that Murray Bowen observed and described. Although the writers could not have been intentionally gathering examples of this, their report of Jesus's teachings and actions reflect such a life. They portray Jesus as a person who functions ultimately in relationship to the will of God, as he understands it, and not in response to the togetherness forces of family, friends, or foes that pressure him to do otherwise. The fact that this portrait is consistent among the Gospels indicates that the memory of Jesus's character had embedded itself deep in the earliest church's traditions. We could not make the same claim for other early church leaders, no matter how prominent. The book of Acts does not idealize even Peter or Paul but displays both flaws and virtues.

Murray Bowen's theoretical 100 on the scale of differentiation was reserved for "the being that was perfect at all levels."[26] Although Bowen did not expect to find such a person in the human population, the church has long held a theology that claims for Jesus both full divinity and perfect humanity. As the "second man" or "last Adam," Jesus offers us the clearest picture of what full humanity can be. Jesus's own expression of differentiation enabled him to live fully by his principles, to stay connected to family and friends, and to avoid succumbing to the anxiety of his world.

In his human relationships, Jesus lived a life marked by a high level of differentiation of self. He connected intimately with family and friends. He even managed to maintain significant contact with his opponents. Yet the emotional reactivity of these did not determine his behavior. Commitment to God's will, or to the kingdom of God, which Jesus both lived and taught his followers, functioned for him as a *principle* against which he evaluated all the relational pressures in his life.

For Jesus, however, this was a commitment not to an abstract principle but to a *relationship*. God, as Jesus spoke of him, was not an impersonal spirit but his Holy Father. Jesus lived to do the Father's will. He sought to please the Father. In this sense, Jesus, whose life represents a high level of differentiation of self in his earthly relationships, was *totally determined* by his relationship to God. It was this relationship of dependence and obedience to the Father that gave Jesus the ability to live a well-differentiated life with other people.

Jesus's life demonstrates how relationships are at the heart of what it means to be human. He reduced the entire teaching of the law and prophets to a relationship of wholehearted devotion to God, which results in a relationship of unselfish love toward one's neighbor. That primary relationship to God governs all others. Does surrender of self to God, which Jesus called for, make it possible for one to live among others and surrender less self in relationships? Is it possible that an increasing "fusion" of self in relationship to God is the only legitimate dependency? Is there a relationship that makes it possible to engage all other relationships without surrendering self? The implications of Jesus's life lead in that direction.

●— Questions for Reflection ──────────────────────

1. Can you think of any counterexamples from the life of Jesus that call into question his ability to act in a differentiated manner?
2. Does our goal in spiritual formation toward Christlikeness suggest that formation is in some sense work on becoming better differentiated?
3. How might our living with an increasing sense of dependence on God, surrendering our self to God, make it possible for us to live with others with less fusion and dependence?

Mapping the Teaching of Paul

New Life in Christ and Community

Physicist's models are like maps: never final, never complete until they grow as large and complex as the reality they represent.

—James Gleick, *Genius: The Life and Science of Richard Feynman*

Bowen Family Systems Theory and Paul

Bowen Family Systems Theory (BFST) provides a valuable lens to view the stories of Scripture, particularly their accounts of human behavior and relationships. But how might the theory offer useful ways of listening in a fresh way to more discursive texts, such as the letters of Paul? Might it affect how we understand Paul's theology and perspectives on Christian life? Let us start with the observation that Paul's writing these letters was an act of human behavior. His interaction with his friends in Corinth or Rome or Philippi is behavior and is thus open to interpretation. His descriptions of human interactions, such as his conflict with Cephas (Peter) in Antioch (Gal. 2:1–14), are also examples of human behavior. His relationships with his readers, with his opponents in various places, and with the fellow workers he mentions may be understood in a new light as well. In his instructions about how human beings who are part of the church are to live with each other under various circumstances, he also deals with human behavior. Consequently BFST could provide a helpful interpretive tool for understanding Paul and other New Testament writers.

One challenge in reading the New Testament epistles from a BFST perspective is that they all bear a clearly theological perspective. Paul does not intend to provide a scientific or objective account of his topics. He views everything through the lens of the gospel of Jesus the Christ, who has been crucified for our sins and raised from death by the power of God. Human sin is a reality for Paul. We are up against the forces of sin and death, which are more than flesh and blood (Eph. 6:12). Paul assumes, rather than argues, that life has more than merely natural dimensions.

BFST, on the other hand, offers a scientific perspective on human behavior. It does not entertain categories of right or wrong, good or evil, sin or righteousness. Human beings, as individuals or as emotional systems, may be more or less "functional," but that is an observation, not a judgment. Bowen theory has no category for sin as a power or for human sinfulness or corruption. It sees only indications of levels of differentiation of self in the presence of more or less anxiety.

Consequently, in each passage a reader may contend with at least two levels of interpretation. We will address both the more literal and scientific description and interpretation and the spiritual and theological interpretation. These two do not necessarily stand in opposition to each other. The fact that we can describe a phenomenon scientifically does not rule out truths about it for which science has no categories or capacities to judge. Asked to analyze a Pulitzer Prize–winning novel, one could perform tests accurately on the chemical composition of the ink on a page and the paper on which it was printed. That would hardly constitute an analysis of the narrative, its characters, and the art by which the author presents the story. We may find meaning at more than one level.

How, for example, would BFST help us to understand what Paul describes as the indwelling power of sin in human life? Or the power of the Holy Spirit in the life of the believer? How would BFST understand what Paul sets forth as Christian love? How might Paul's description of Christian life or Christian community fit with Bowen's concept of differentiation of self? Bringing such questions to Pauline texts might help us hear them in a fresh way. Concepts we have understood only theologically might become clearer if we raise different questions about them.

Understanding Human Behavior as Emotional Reactivity

Romans 7 has been a source of controversy in New Testament studies for many centuries. In Romans 7:14–25 Paul writes,

For we know that the law is spiritual; but I am of the flesh, sold into slavery under sin. I do not understand my own actions. For I do not do what I want, but I do the very thing I hate. Now if I do what I do not want, I agree that the law is good. But in fact, it is no longer I that do it, but sin that dwells within me. For I know that nothing good dwells within me, that is, in my flesh. I can will what is right, but I cannot do it. For I do not do the good I want, but the evil I do not want is what I do. Now if I do what I do not want, it is no longer I that do it, but sin that dwells within me.

So, I find it to be a law that when I want to do what is good, evil lies close at hand. For I delight in the law of God in my inmost self, but I see in my members another law at war with the law of my mind, making me captive to the law of sin that dwells in my members. Wretched man that I am! Who will rescue me from this body of death? Thanks be to God through Jesus Christ our Lord! So then, with my mind I am a slave to the law of God, but with my flesh I am a slave to the law of sin.

Disagreement has swirled around just who the "I" is who speaks here. Is Paul writing autobiographically, describing his own experience, or is he speaking simply as a human being, describing something universal? Is the "I" in verses 6–13 the same one as in verses 14–25? Is the speaker a person *before* baptism and without Christ? Or one who has professed faith in Christ and still struggles with temptation? Augustine first espoused the view that Paul is describing someone *before* Christian conversion but later changed his mind. Martin Luther and other Reformers sided with Augustine's later position, thinking that Paul was indeed speaking of himself as a Christian and on behalf of all other believers who struggle to live righteously. Since the work of W. G. Kümmel in 1929, however, most interpreters have concluded that the passage is not autobiographical.[1] More recent understandings propose that Paul, although using first-person pronouns throughout, is describing universal human experience, based on the Genesis 3 story of Adam and his disobedience.[2]

For purposes of this study, the question of the "I" is not determinative. One way or another, Paul is describing human experience, whether his own or that of Adam and all humans after him. Rather than attempting to psychoanalyze Paul, we can focus on the way he describes human behavior and the experience of moral struggle and failure.[3] What he describes is indeed universal.[4] Other than people on the extremes of human functioning who exhibit symptoms of psychopathic or sociopathic behavior, on occasion we humans find ourselves acting in conflict with principles or values we profess. At times we fail to live up to our own standards, much less those of God.

In this passage, Paul describes the internal struggle to do right as a war waged between what he calls "the law [or principle] of sin" and the "law [or principle] of [the] mind." He locates the law of sin as working in "the members" of the body. In this struggle, the human, held prisoner by the law of sin, regularly loses. Human beings experience that struggle as an internal civil war.

The Pauline description of human behavior is subjectively accurate: we human beings experience the phenomenon of wanting to do better or differently in some aspect of life but find ourselves incapable of making or sustaining the change under pressure.

When Paul describes his experiences with "the flesh," he writes of his struggle against an ingrained power. He distinguishes this "flesh" (*sarx*) from the "I" (*egō*) that wrestles with it. He identifies the desire to do good with the "I" and the evil action over which we seem to have no control with the "flesh." He rests the discussion with this conclusion: "So then, with my mind I am a slave to the law of God, but with my flesh I am a slave to the law of sin" (Rom. 7:25).[5]

Paul's word "flesh" is a theological term, showing up ninety-one times in his letters, twenty-six times in Romans alone. It carries a variety of meanings, from a literal reference to our bodily, earthly physical existence (1 Cor. 7:28; 2 Cor. 4:11) to a metaphorical reference to our human condition corrupted by living apart from God (Gal. 5:17, 24).[6] As he uses the term in Romans 7, the flesh is that part of us to which the power of sin can appeal. Were it not for this aspect of our being, we presumably would find sin unappealing. James Dunn says, "The problem with the flesh is not that it is sinful per se but that it is vulnerable to the enticements of sin—flesh, we might say, is 'the desiring I' (7.7–12). It is the all too human/fleshly need to satisfy appetites which leaves the individual exposed to the wiles of sin (7.8) and indeed, or so it would seem, impotent before the power of sin at work within the 'I' (7.23)."[7]

Paul's analysis of this struggle is an example of phenomenological language, which describes an experience from the observer's point of view in subjective language. Referring to the sun's "rising" or to "the four corners of the earth" is using phenomenological language. In using this common manner of speaking about experience, the speaker does not intend the words as an objective statement about reality. The experience Paul presents *feels* like an internal struggle between powers from the perspective of the subject. But what is the reality behind that subjective language? At this point, traditional historical hermeneutical principles must surrender to the speculation and theology of the interpreter. This is also the point at which a hermeneutic of natural systems could prove helpful.

Emotional Reactivity and "the Flesh"

Bowen described an organism's response to its environment as "emotional re-activity."[8] The word "emotional" is central to understanding the term. Bowen is speaking of the aspect of behavior that human beings share with all other forms of life. It is a response/reaction at an instinctive level, an automatic reflex below the level of consciousness. "Emotional" does not merely equate with "feelings." Bowen writes: "There are emotional mechanisms as automatic as a reflex and that occur as predictably as the force that causes the sunflower to keep its face toward the sun. I believe that the laws that govern man's emotional functioning are as orderly as those that govern other natural systems and that the difficulty in understanding the system is governed more by man's reasoning that denies its existence than by the complexity of the system."[9]

According to Bowen, the automatic responses of the human emotional system govern far more of behavior than the intellectual system does. He says, "According to my theory, a high percentage of human relationship behavior is directed more by automatic instinctual emotional forces than by intellect. Much intellectual activity goes to explain away and justify behavior being directed by the instinctual-emotional-feeling complex."[10]

This "automatic" aspect of human behavior in Bowen's theory, described from a scientific perspective, begins to shed light on the struggle that Paul describes. Bowen uses the term "reflex" to describe the process.

> What is "emotional reactiveness" and how does it operate? I have used the term *emotional reflex* which is accurate and which makes it a little more synonymous with biology. . . . The term *reflex* is accurate in that it occurs automatically and out of awareness, but like a reflex it can be brought within limited observation and under limited conscious control just as one can control a knee jerk with specific energy. The reflexes operate with antennae-like extensions of all sensory modalities, but a high percentage operate from visual and auditory stimuli. For example, one spouse may return from work with a higher than average tension level, reflected in a glum "look," which raises tension in the other and which is reflected in an octave or two increase in the verbal response. . . . Systems therapy directed at helping spouses discover the reflexes can give each a bit of control over the automatic emotional reactiveness.[11]

Bowen sees this automatic reflex as something wired not so much into the indi-vidual (though it certainly must show up as neuronal pathways in the brain) as into relationships. These relational reactions are part of the stimulus-response mechanisms in human biology. Bowen says: "Some responses are unpleasant. Examples are feelings of revulsion in response to habits and mannerisms in the other, reactions in which one's flesh crawls, and jarring emotional responses to sensory stimuli. An equal number of responses range from mildly to hurtfully pleasurable. For example, a wife felt a strong sexual attraction at a look of helplessness on her husband's face. The stimuli may involve any one of the five senses. There surely must be responses in which one kills in response to the stimulus."[12]

These automatic reactions of human beings to each other in relationship can change only with great effort over time.[13] Roberta Gilbert writes: "Although the functioning of basic emotional/instinctual behaviors may become impaired as the result of anxiety or illness, their hard-wiring and insistent quality make it difficult to access them for change voluntarily. They can sometimes be so strong they seem to carry with them life and death urgencies."[14] The theoretical understanding of emotional reactivity as used in BFST may provide a scientific perspective on the realities Paul reports in Romans 7.

Bowen described several relationship postures people assume when anxiety rises. Conflict, distance, cutoff, overfunctioning/underfunctioning, a symptomatic spouse, and projection are all instinctual attempts to "solve" the problem of chronic anxiety in relationships.[15] While these may have their roots in human adaptation and survival, in systems characterized by high chronic anxiety, they often become counterproductive and even destructive. They occur without thought. One can be aware of what is happening and yet feel powerless to do anything about it.

A hermeneutic of natural systems raises the question of whether Paul and Bowen might be describing the same human phenomenon. Does the term "emotional reactivity" help a reader understand Paul's internal war between "the law of the mind" that sides with God and God's ways, and "the law of sin" that, under pressure or stress, leads him into behavior of which he himself disapproves? Is the struggle that Paul describes related to the strain experienced by someone who intentionally makes an effort to overcome the automatic responses of emotional reactivity and to differentiate a self in relationship to others? When brought to Paul's description of this human struggle, a hermeneutic of natural systems can raise such questions.

As a scientific theory, BFST lacks a category for "sin."[16] It judges human reactivity, however destructive it might be to individuals or to relationships, only as higher or lower functioning, not as wrong. Christian theology, in contrast, evaluates human behavior against God's revelation in Jesus Christ. That theology judges as sin any words or actions not in line with the principle of loving God wholeheartedly and one's neighbor unselfishly (Matt. 22:34–40). It understands sin to be destructive of human life, a precursor to death (Rom. 6:23).

Paul understands sin as more than simply acts of bad behavior. It is a power that resides within human beings over which we are powerless on our own (Rom. 7:14, 20, 24). Sin is an automatic reaction, and it "dwells within me," "in my flesh" (Rom. 7:17, 18, 20). Theologically, this inherent tendency is the product of our being "in Adam" (Rom. 5:14; 1 Cor. 15:22), an expression of the reality that we are fallen human beings.[17] BFST portrays emotional reactivity in a similar way, as deeply embedded in the brain and body. Survival instincts that were useful in our ancient past have become destructive behaviors that tend to emerge despite our best efforts to manage them.

Theologian and philosopher Dallas Willard describes sin as hardwired into our reactions, using language that sounds like Bowen's description of emotional reactivity: "These various tendencies actually present in our bodily parts can move our body into action independently of our overall intentions to the contrary—often quite genuine—and of our conscious thoughts. Thus, we act or speak 'before we think.' The part of our character that lives in our body carries us away."[18] Using the example of Simon Peter's denial of Jesus despite his earlier promises of faithfulness, Willard says that Peter was unable to withstand the "*automatic tendencies ingrained in his flesh* and activated by the circumstances."[19]

1 Corinthians 13: Christian Love and Differentiation of Self

The concept of indwelling sin in Romans 6 and 7 belongs to Paul's theology of "the old man," the person outside of Jesus Christ. The other side of his message, his gospel, focuses on the new life in Jesus Christ lived out in the church, a new community of God's people, by the power of the indwelling Spirit (Rom. 8; 12). The nature of this new life is conformity to the character of Jesus Christ himself (Rom. 8:29; Gal. 4:19; 5:16–25). Its defining characteristic is love (*agapē*).[20]

First Corinthians 13 describes in detail the nature of this Christian love. Reading the passage through the lens of natural systems theory provides a way to contrast this presentation of "love" with the sentimental view often expressed in our culture.[21] The "love" described here is not mere sentiment. It is not simply feelings or subjectivity. Rather, this poetic description personifies love, which serves as the subject of a series of verbs describing how love *behaves*, what love *does*. Paul portrays love in terms of conscious, deliberate choices made by the one who lives a Christlike life in the context of the new community.

The acts of love described here are not determined by the behavior of *the one being loved*; rather, they are the consequence of the character of *the one who loves*. This divine kind of love is not based on the worthiness of the beloved but flows out of its own character. To act in this way, one must have the capacity to overrule the automatic reflex to act defensively, vengefully, or destructively. Love requires an act of the will, not simply a feeling. Love will often call for actions contrary to our ingrained tendencies. The power of the indwelling Spirit must counter the power of indwelling sin.

Love is not reactive to the other in relationship but acts out of its own will. It behaves with patience and kindness. It is not jealous or proud. The alternatives (impatience, unkindness, pride, and jealousy) are reactive stances. The same is true of rudeness, self-seeking, touchiness, and resentfulness. Love desires truth. There is an objectivity about authentic love that is dissatisfied with anything less than reality. It neither pretends nor finds satisfaction in mere subjectivity. Contrary to common wisdom, this love is not blind.

Paul describes the movement into a life of love as akin to growing into maturity. In maturity one abandons "childish ways" (1 Cor. 13:11). Love is the capacity to see both God and one's neighbor with clarity, not "through a glass, darkly" (1 Cor. 13:12 KJV). These qualities describe how a well-differentiated person lives. Such persons choose their reactions to those they love out of deeply held principles and values. Such love is a differentiating move. It allows one to remain connected to others without succumbing to their anxiety or being emotionally snared by their behavior.

The early Christians chose the Greek word *agapē* to express this kind of love. Other words were available in the Greek language (*philia, eros*), but the church chose *agapē*, a word Ethelbert Stauffer describes as "colorless"—that is, relatively meaningless in the ancient world.[22] Taking up this "colorless" word, they transformed it by using the sacrifice of Jesus to define it (John 3:16; Rom. 5:8; 1 John 4:9–10). Such love then became the standard by which followers of Jesus were to relate to one another (John 13:34–35; Eph. 5:1; 1 John 4:11–12). In this way, *agapē* became a word with distinctively Christian content.

For Paul, the way we deal with others in concrete human relationships marks our spirituality. He describes the "fruit" produced by "the Spirit" as "love," followed by eight other relational qualities (Gal. 5:22–23). Life in the Spirit is not mystical or ecstatic. It is not the withdrawn life of a desert monk. It is love lived out in the quotidian experiences of the Christian community, where the requirements for sustained relationships include patience, kindness, forgiveness, and trust. In the new community, Christlike love displaces such relationship killers as jealousy, boastfulness, arrogance, rudeness, and selfishness—all products of anxious, reactive human beings (Gal. 5:19–21; cf. 1 Cor. 13:4–7).[23]

Living in this manner requires, on the one hand, the indwelling power of the Spirit. It is not something we can do by gritting our teeth and clenching our fists. It comes from a changed heart. To speak of this kind of life is to speak theologically. We learn to trust our own needs to God in Christ so that jealousy, boastfulness, arrogance, rudeness, and selfishness are no longer necessary. Less and less do we feel the need to defend ourselves or to push ourselves forward. Love for the other begins to dominate our relationships. We learn to accept God's appraisal of both our own life and the lives of others so that our behavior increasingly flows from our character, not from our feelings. We become willing to deal with the obstacles that inevitably arise in intense relationships. Such qualities as patience, forbearance, endurance, and forgiveness make that challenge something we can face.

On the other hand, from the perspective of differentiation of self, the more we emotionally fuse in relationship to others, the less we can love them in the way of Christ. The less well-differentiated we are, the more reactive we are to the behavior of others, and the less we can act toward them based on principles. In such relationships, we tend to define love as a feeling and tend likewise to "love" those whose behavior toward us engenders that feeling. Nothing about these feelings allows us to do the hard work of loving those who seem, at least in the moment, unlovable. The better differentiated we become, the less the other's behavior determines our own, and the more our choices grow out of our own principles and commitments.

Romans 12 and Life in the New Community

Bowen described two forces that operate in any emotional system: the togetherness force (the pressure to be "we") and the individuality force (the pressure to be "me"). He observed that in times of increased anxiety, the togetherness force increases in its pressure, calling for conformity in thinking and behavior. This raises the question of what Christian community might ideally look like from the perspective of BFST.

In Acts, the earliest Christian community came into existence in the intensity of persecution and threat. Christians moved toward each other for the sake of survival in a time of acute anxiety. An experience of unity characterized this early church (Acts 2:1, 42–47; 4:32–35). The same anxiety also generated other less desirable symptoms, such as jealousy and division (5:1–11). These narratives show the new community of faith in action.

In Romans 12 Paul presents a vision of Christian community, laying out principles of behavior for relationships. He describes a community of people living with one another on distinctively Christian terms. All community members are to present themselves to God first, with their bodies (lives) becoming "a living sacrifice" (12:1). Out of this submission of life to God, believers live with each other in a new way, characterized principally by the love defined by Jesus's own life of sacrifice (5:8; 12:9–10; 13:8–10). This community exhibits a mature interdependence in which each one takes responsibility for making a unique contribution to the life of the whole (12:3–13). Life together flows from a mutuality that transcends social classes (v. 16), in contradiction to the pressures of the surrounding culture. In the face of opposition and persecution, members of this community choose responses reflective of Christ's teaching and example rather than reactive acts of vengeance and retaliation (vv. 14, 17–21; cf. Matt. 5:11–12, 38–48).

Bowen outlines characteristics of well-differentiated individuals, but he does not describe what a *community* of such emotionally mature people would look like.[24] His profile of highly differentiated people (75–100 on his scale), however, describes how he imagines such people would interact together.

> They can hear and evaluate the viewpoints of others and discard old beliefs in favor of new. They are sufficiently secure within themselves that functioning is not affected by either praise or criticism from others. They can respect the self and the identity of another without becoming critical or becoming emotionally involved in trying to modify the life course of another. They assume total responsibility for self and are sure of their responsibility for family and society. They are realistically aware of their dependence on their fellow man. With the ability to keep emotional functioning contained within the boundaries of self, they are free to move about in any relationship system and engage in a whole spectrum of intense relationships without a "need" for the other that can impair functioning. The "other" in such a relationship does not feel "used."[25]

Of course, Bowen's vision of such a person is as much an act of imagination as Paul's is in Romans 12. Bowen says that people in the upper quarter of the scale are those "I have never seen in my clinical work and that I rarely meet in social and professional relationships."[26] The visions of the new community in Christ and of the highly differentiated life are both imaginative acts that provide a direction in which to strive.

Conclusion

Reading biblical stories and attending to the ways that those ancient accounts reflect Bowen's description of human behavior is straightforward.

Taking the concepts of BFST to more theological texts, however, is more challenging. Theology works from a perspective for which science does not have tools. Bowen's so-called ninth concept, sometimes termed "the supernatural," however, is a place to start the conversation between these two disciplines. Bowen viewed theological beliefs as "functional facts." That God demonstrated his love for us through the sacrifice of his son (Rom. 5:8) is not a scientifically verifiable fact. That people believe this affirmation about God, however, is a fact, and we can study that fact. This recognition makes it possible to bring BFST into conversation with theology. Paul's theological ideas and his theologically grounded practices and instructions are amenable to such investigations.

Paul's theological language describes the experience to which Christians have testified over the centuries. We can analyze this experience and belief in terms of Bowen's theory of human behavior. Two of his ideas are especially helpful in this quest: the notion of emotional reactivity, which helps us understand something about our experience of sin as a "power" we are not able to overcome on our own, and the concept of differentiation of self or emotional maturity, which can help us imagine dimensions of the new life of love and community to which God has called us in Christ.

This is not to say that Bowen's ideas comprehend Paul's, or vice versa. The conversation between the two is somewhat akin to the analysis of the Pulitzer-winning novel described earlier. Although BFST can help us analyze some dimensions of our lives and relationships, theology works in a dimension that science, by its own definition, cannot penetrate. For Paul to say that "sin dwells in me" may leave me wondering just how this is possible. When Bowen describes emotional reactivity as wired into our brains and bodies at an instinctual level, I can begin to understand the process in a different way. Bowen's argument for the ways in which one's quality of life is deeply affected by one's level of differentiation of self may be appealing but abstract. When Paul describes the life of Christian love in the new community in similar terms, we can imagine such emotional maturity more clearly.

The map that BFST provides for reading Scripture is useful in a variety of ways, from opening windows of meaning on the lengthy narratives of the patriarchs, to seeing Jesus's own actions in a fresh light, to pondering some of the more esoteric aspects of Paul's theology. These studies are merely suggestive; many others would be possible. The pastor whose hermeneutical toolbox includes a working familiarity with BFST can think, teach, and preach the biblical texts with an additional layer of understanding.

● — **Questions for Reflection** ————————————————

1. What other concepts of Paul might yield fresh insights if viewed through the lens of BFST? How would you think, for example, about his teachings on family relationships in Colossians 3–4 or Ephesians 5–6?

2. How might we use BFST to think through the background of some of Paul's letters, such as the conflicts in the church at Corinth (1 Cor. 1)?

3. What events from Paul's life might we also usefully examine through the lens of BFST? How would you use the theory to understand his conflict with Cephas (Peter) in Galatians 1–2?

Mapping the Family of David

Family Systems, 1000 BC

Other than the stories of Abraham and his family in Genesis 11–50, nothing in the Bible offers the quantity of family information available in the stories of David. If we count the unfolding of the Davidic dynasty through the centuries, then these stories outstrip even those of the patriarchs. The Davidic narratives offer a rich source of family emotional material, and Bowen's perspective provides insight into their workings. These accounts of David and his world in 1 Samuel 16 through 1 Kings 1 are full of drama, intrigue, sex, and violence. Readers can more fully understand and identify with David and his family, his friends, and his enemies through the lens of Bowen Family Systems Theory (BFST). Reading the stories as we think about them from this perspective will enrich the experience.

David's Anxious World

The world of Israel during the Late Bronze Age and into the Iron Age—from the period of the Judges (ca. 1200 BC), to the rise of the monarchy under Saul (ca. 1020 BC), to the Babylonian captivity (587 BC)—was an intensely anxious place. Stories in the Old Testament books of Judges, 1 and 2 Samuel, and 1 and 2 Kings make that fact clear. The book of Judges closes with this ominous observation: "In those days there was no king in Israel; all the people did what was right in their own eyes" (21:25).

The people of Israel, anxious for a quick fix and ascendency over their enemies, began to lobby the prophet/judge Samuel for a king: "We are determined to have a king over us, so that we also may be like other nations, and that our king may govern us and go out before us and fight our battles" (1 Sam. 8:5, 19–20).

Samuel vehemently opposed their request but eventually granted it at the Lord's instruction, however reluctantly. Nevertheless, he warned them of the ways of kings. A nation easily places a sovereign on a throne, but they do not so easily remove them from power. Those given such power will, in fact, inevitably abuse it. He said:

> These will be the ways of the king who will reign over you: he will take your sons and appoint them to his chariots and to be his horsemen, and to run before his chariots; and he will appoint for himself commanders of thousands and commanders of fifties, and some to plow his ground and to reap his harvest, and to make his implements of war and the equipment of his chariots. He will take your daughters to be perfumers and cooks and bakers. He will take the best of your fields and vineyards and olive orchards and give them to his courtiers. He will take one-tenth of your grain and of your vineyards and give it to his officers and his courtiers. He will take your male and female slaves, and the best of your cattle and donkeys, and put them to his work. He will take one-tenth of your flocks, and you shall be his slaves. And in that day you will cry out because of your king, whom you have chosen for yourselves; but the LORD will not answer you in that day. (1 Sam. 8:11–22)

As the monarchy took root in the soil of the nation, Samuel's words proved true. The first king, Saul, was everything they desired. He was tall, handsome, and powerful. He led the armies of Israel against one foe after another. But morally and spiritually, Saul proved to be a weak leader. In time his paranoia overcame him, and his dynasty did not extend beyond his own reign.

At the close of Saul's regency another figure gradually arose who would follow as king and whose dynasty would never end, according to the divine promise (2 Sam. 7:16). David, the shepherd, arises to shepherd God's people Israel. He is "a man after [God's] own heart" (1 Sam. 13:14). Where Saul was unfaithful to the Lord, David was faithful. But David's life was not perfect. His family is marked by dysfunction, violence, and rebellion. The emotional processes within King David's family operated just as they do in our families. And given the stressful days in which he lived, the anxiety in the family sometimes ran high.

Saul came to power at a time when Israel's enemies were threatening on all sides. The Philistines were a consistent danger. He faced off successfully against a variety of Israel's enemies who surrounded them: the Ammonites, Amalekites, and the Philistines. Along the way, however, he managed to alienate the prophet Samuel, who was never keen on the idea of a king anyway. The threat of external enemies and the paranoia that produced fear of enemies from within eventually became Saul's undoing. His mental state deteriorated, and he fearfully opposed David, who nevertheless remained loyal to King Saul until his death in a battle against the Philistines at Mount Gilboa (1 Sam. 31).

In the narrative, David joins the royal court as a servant of Saul and eventually joins Saul's family by marriage, amid a stew of anxiety found both in society and in Saul's own household. David functions as something of a calming presence to both the king and the nation, yet eventually his own family faces significant turmoil as well. Reading David's story with the eight concepts of BFST provides access to the emotional-systems side of this period of Israel's history.

Emotional Triangles in the Stories of David

Emotional triangles abound in the stories of David. The earliest one is apparent when the prophet Samuel comes to Bethlehem to anoint young David as king, even though Saul remains on the throne (1 Sam. 16:1–10). The Lord instructs Samuel to anoint the youngest of Jesse's sons as Saul's successor (16:11–13). The relationship between Samuel and Saul had been intense and troubled almost from the first day Saul assumed the crown (13:8–15; 15:10–23). Eventually David becomes the third person in this triangle with Samuel, as the prophet announces Saul's rejection as king and chooses David over Saul. In time, David finds himself in several triangles in which Saul is the outsider, including relationships with two of Saul's children. Theologically, one might even see a triangle among Saul, David, and the Lord in which Saul is the uncomfortable outsider (16:13–14; 18:12).

Soon after his anointing in Bethlehem, David enters the service of the king as his armor-bearer and court music therapist (1 Sam. 16:21–23). When he becomes part of Saul's court, David befriends the king's son Jonathan (18:1–4) and eventually takes the king's daughter Michal as his wife (vv. 20–27). David engages two significant triangles that place Saul on the outside: he wins the hearts of both Michal and Jonathan (v. 29). As the conflict between David and Saul intensifies, the closer David becomes in his relationships with Saul's children, who act against their father and protect David's life (19:1–18; 20:1–42).

Emotional triangles become a significant factor in David's own family when he fails to act justly in response to the rape of his daughter. Amnon,

David's firstborn by Ahinoam (2 Sam. 3:2), assaulted Tamar, his half sister, David's daughter by Maacah (v. 3). Absalom, Tamar's full brother (v. 3; 13:1), incensed by their father's lack of response, kills Amnon and leads a coup against his father (13:1–18:33). The triangles—among David, Absalom, and Tamar; among David, Absalom, and Amnon; and among Absalom, Amnon, and Tamar—all become active and begin to spread to the point that a triangle develops among Absalom, David, and the nation (15:1–18).

The story of David's relationship with Bathsheba represents another powerful emotional triangle (2 Sam. 11:1–12:25), involving David, Bathsheba, and her husband, Uriah the Hittite; as well as David, Bathsheba, and the prophet Nathan. At the end of David's life, the emotional triangles light up during the period of anxiety created by the king's imminent death. David is caught in this network of triangles formed on the one hand by the attempt of his son Adonijah to secure the throne through his connections with Joab, David's nephew and former general, and Abiathar the priest (1 Kings 1:5–10); and on the other hand those triangles formed by the plotting of Bathsheba, mother of Solomon, to obtain the throne for him, supported by Zadok the priest and Nathan the prophet (1:11–40).

The concept of emotional triangles becomes a helpful concept to bring to David's story, observing how the anxiety in the nation and in the families of Saul and David moves about in key relationships, sometimes igniting intense violence and even death. That the triangles are so intense may be evidence of the level of anxiety faced by these leaders and family members.

Scale of Differentiation

Bowen proposed a scale of differentiation of self to describe what he observed in human behavior: some people manage the anxiety and crises of their lives better than others. Some function more thoughtfully in the face of anxiety than others. Some people, in the face of rising stress and anxiety, are less emotionally reactive and can retain access to their intellectual system.

It is impossible to measure accurately and specifically where a person shows up on Bowen's theoretical scale. In the Davidic stories, we might look for evidence of an individual's ability to maintain principles despite pressure to do otherwise. David's high functioning might appear in his refusal to take Saul's life or harm him even when the opportunity arose (1 Sam. 24:1–22). Saul's jealousy and fear of David and his relentless pursuit of him provide evidence of a lower level of differentiation on the part of Saul. David's use of power in taking Bathsheba and ordering the death of Uriah (2 Sam. 11) and his behavior around Absalom's rebellion (2 Sam. 13–19) might provide evidence of lower functioning during that period of his life. We would require a significant amount of life information to speak definitively about the level of differentiation in a life. The stories about David provide some evidence of this scale of human functioning, but it is not possible to definitively argue for locating David on some specific spot on the scale. As anxiety rises and falls, so does David's functioning as Israel's king and leader. Saul's story, however, seems to offer little evidence of higher functioning. Saul is often done in by the anxiety swirling around him and does not demonstrate the capacity to act on principle when stressed. We know little about the families of origin of either of these kings, but we can observe them side by side as leaders and notice the difference in functioning under pressure.

Family Emotional Process

Bowen described the nuclear family's emotional process in terms of a repertoire of instinctive, automatic behaviors that anxious human beings display: conflict, distancing, overfunctioning or underfunctioning, or projection onto a third person.[1] Although this behavior expresses the anxiety, the behaviors themselves contribute to the system's reactivity, and a vicious regressive cycle begins to spiral downward.

Conflict

These reactions to the anxiety of both society and the family system emerge in the stories of the king. Early in his relationship to David, Saul experiences internal conflict. On the one hand, David is Saul's loyal supporter, armor-bearer, and comforter (1 Sam. 16:17–23). On the other hand, the people of Israel find the young man David attractive and admirable (18:6–9), as do Saul's own children Jonathan and Michal (vv. 1–3, 16, 20, 28), raising Saul's anxiety and presenting what he perceives as a threat to himself and to his kingdom (v. 29). Saul's automatic response is violent. He attempts to kill David on several occasions (vv. 10–11) or to have him killed in battle (vv. 12–17, 20–25), but his efforts fail.

David's own family experiences its share of conflict as a symptom of the chronic anxiety they face. He himself turned to violence and abused his power by taking Bathsheba, the wife of Uriah. In the anxiety that followed the news of Bathsheba's pregnancy, David orders Joab, his nephew and henchman, to see that Uriah dies in battle (2 Sam. 11:14–25). The conflict within the family is evident also in the violent rape of Tamar by Amnon, in Absalom's murderous reaction to this half brother, and in the armed rebellion against David that followed (13:1–18:33). David's reign endured warfare and conflict with his enemies as well (8:1–8).

Distance

Saul's own children distance themselves from him in their anxious response to their father's fear of David. Siding with David, they offer him protection against Saul's threats on a variety of occasions (1 Sam. 19:1–18; 20:1–42). David responds to Saul's threats by fleeing to the wilderness, living in the caves and countryside of the Judean wilderness and in the land of the Philistines (21:1–28:2; 29). In Saul's case, his violent attempts on the life of David were reactions to the chronic anxiety of the emotional system. David posed no threat to Saul or his kingdom. The threat Saul perceived existed primarily in his own mind. In David's case, Saul's threat of violence and death were real. Distancing himself from Saul rather than attempting to respond violently was a response to the acute anxiety stirred by the attempts on his life.[2]

Amnon's sexual assault of his half sister Tamar could be a symptom of the anxiety in the Davidic family. But that act also generated further anxiety, which soon spiraled out of control. Absalom avenges Amnon's crime by having his half brother killed. Knowing that his own life was in some danger, Absalom flees from David's presence and withdraws from Judea to live with his maternal grandfather "Talmai son of Ammihud, king of Geshur" (2 Sam. 3:3; 13:37–39). For the next three years David and Absalom manage the anxiety in their relationship by the distance between them. The anxiety that stirred David's anger at Absalom and his grief over the death of Amnon eventually diminish sufficiently for Absalom to come home. Joab develops a ruse to persuade the king to grant amnesty to Absalom, allowing him to return (14:1–24). Although he does return to his own home, for two more years Absalom and David continue to experience the distance between them, not having a face-to-face encounter (vv. 24, 28). Finally, at Absalom's request (and with some serious effort to get Joab's attention), the young man secures an audience with his father (vv. 29–33). This reconciliation does not endure. Absalom soon orchestrates a rift between David and his own people, resulting in David's needing to leave Jerusalem and in a bloody rebellion that ends with Absalom's death (2 Sam. 15–18).

Overfunctioning and Underfunctioning

Saul demonstrates an underfunctioning posture on occasion, becoming the "identified patient" in his emotional system. His irrational paranoia about

David, who loyally served the king and repeatedly refused to do him harm; his jealousy over David's popularity with both the people of Israel (1 Sam. 18:7–9, 15–16) and his own children (18:1–3, 20, 28–29; 19:1–2); and his intermittent fits of depression (16:14–23; 19:9–10) might all be symptoms that allowed Saul to withdraw from responsibilities as king. The overfunctioners who took responsibility for the king in his unstable emotional condition included his children, who found ways to circumvent their father's murderous plans for David—warning him and providing him with protection.

David ordinarily appears as a highly responsible leader of his people and his troops. On several occasions, however, David's behavior suggests some underfunctioning. When he might have been out with his armies one spring ("the time when kings go out to battle," 2 Sam. 11:1), David instead sent Joab and his officers to fight while he remained at home. During those days he found himself caught up in a web of poor decisions: abusing his power by summoning Bathsheba, the wife of his soldier Uriah, and having sex with her; trying to cover up her subsequent pregnancy by bringing Uriah home from the front lines, hoping that he would sleep with her and then assume the child was his; and finally, when that ploy failed, ordering Joab to see to it that Uriah died in battle, even though the acts necessary to make that happen would cost the lives of some of his soldiers (2 Sam. 11). This irresponsible behavior cost several lives, including that of the child he conceived with Bathsheba (12:15–19). Since an overfunctioner reciprocally accompanies every underfunctioner, we might wonder who in the story plays that part. Perhaps Joab, David's general, fits the bill. At David's command, Joab sends Uriah home from the battle. He knowingly carries out the king's orders that will result in the death of Uriah and others. In this episode Joab does for David what David is unwilling to do for himself.

The story of Absalom's rebellion also reveals underfunctioning behavior on David's part. When the king became aware of the sexual assault of his daughter Tamar, he could have acted against his son Amnon, Tamar's half brother, who was guilty of this crime. Instead he gave in to the pressure of his relationship with his son: "When King David heard of all these things, he became very angry, but he would not punish his son Amnon, because he loved him, for he was his firstborn" (2 Sam. 13:21). What David would not do (deal with Amnon), his son Absalom takes into his own hands. David's underfunctioning is matched by the overfunctioning of Absalom, who carefully plots over two years to find a way to lure Amnon to his death (vv. 23–33).

When Absalom attempts a coup against David's government, David insists that his army spare his son in the battle (2 Sam. 18:5). Despite David's command, which his soldiers were careful to follow (vv. 9–13), Joab plays his overfunctioning role again, doing "for" David what David would not do for himself. Joab himself thrust three spears through Absalom, and the general's armor-bearers finished the job (vv. 14–15). Joab meets David's intense grief at the news of Absalom's death (vv. 19–33) with disgust (19:1–8). When David returns to Jerusalem from the imposed exile, he removes Joab from his role as commander of his armies, replacing him with Amasa, another nephew, who had joined Absalom in his coup but then sought forgiveness from the king (v. 13).

This same scenario had played out earlier in the relationship between David and Joab when David refused to deal violently with Abner, Saul's former general. Again, Joab does what David would not do, luring Abner to the cistern of Sirah and, with the help of his brother Abishai, taking Abner's life (2 Sam. 3:1–30). David's reaction to the news of this murder is like his response to the message that Absalom had died in battle. He called Israel to mourn Abner's death and buried him with honor (vv. 31–38). David says of his nephews who committed this act: "Today I am powerless, even though anointed king; these men, the sons of Zeruiah, are too violent for me" (v. 39). A reader can only wonder if David's attitude toward those who were threatening him is a principled act of differentiation or a passive, underfunctioning stance.

Projection

Rising anxiety in Saul's own life, generated in part by his religious and leadership failures that alienated him from the prophet Samuel (1 Sam. 13:5–14; 14:24–46; 15:1–35), led him to focus his attention on David as a potential threat. Projecting onto this third person his anxiety, which grew out of his own relationships to his children and to the nation he was attempting to lead, allowed Saul to identify an "enemy" on which to center himself.

Multigenerational Transmission Process

Bowen's concept of multigenerational transmission process is an attempt to explain how emotional processes move across generations, resulting in individuals within the system who are both higher and lower functioning. The concept takes the idea of the family projection process and applies it over time. As one generation after another focuses more on one child than on another, some individuals arise in that family who are high on the scale of differentiation and others emerge with a lower ability to function in life.

The biblical narrative records little of David's own ancestry. The book of Ruth contains a short-story account of his great-grandparents, Ruth and

Boaz, introducing us to people who faithfully follow God's instruction in the course of their ordinary lives. As Eugene Peterson observes, "There are no outstanding historically prominent figures in Ruth, no splendid kings, no charismatic judges, no fiery prophets; it is a plain story about two widows and a farmer whose lives are woven into the fabric of God's salvation through the ordinary actions of common life."[3] All we learn is that Boaz and Ruth settle in Bethlehem and have a child, Obed, who eventually fathers Jesse, whose youngest son is named David. Of Obed, David's grandfather, we know practically nothing. And of Jesse, David's father, we know only that he had eight sons. From the fact that Samuel went to this family to seek a faithful leader for Israel and found one in the youngest of the clan, we may infer that the family had preserved the importance of faith in God through the generations.

The entire Davidic dynasty, from his son Solomon down to Jesus himself, would become the focus of study if we were to examine David's multigenerational family. That same family tree that produced relatively high-functioning leaders like Uzziah, Hezekiah, and Josiah also generated relatively low-functioning leaders like Manasseh and Jehoiachin. The biblical narratives do not supply sufficient information about the families of these kings to allow us to confidently apply the concept specifically to each of David's descendants. However, BFST predicts that in a family we will observe such varied manifestations of emotional maturity over multiple generations.

In the generations that followed David, the biblical historians measured all other kings against David's reputation for faithfulness to God. These theological histories of Israel compare the kings of Davidic descent to their ancestor in this one specific matter (1 Kings 11:4, 6, 33; 14:8; 15:3, 5, 11; 2 Kings 14:3; 16:2; 18:3; 22:2; 2 Chron. 7:17; 28:1; 29:2; 34:2–3). By the eighth century BC, David came to represent the figure of the ideal, faithful king, anticipating the appearance of the messiah in the last days.[4] The intergenerational transmission of a faith in Israel's God shows up in some generations of the family but does not seem to be as present in others. Perhaps the multigenerational transmission process is at work in producing more principled leaders at some points and less-well-defined leaders at others.

Family Projection Process

The family projection process describes the way in which an anxious family passes its emotional immaturity along by means of an intense focus on one child, resulting in that child's ultimately leaving home with more emotional dependence on the parents than do other children in the family. All things being equal, the child on the receiving end of this projection process will develop a lower degree of differentiation of self and will predictably have fewer resources available to face life's problems, thereby living with a higher level of chronic anxiety.

Projection may have played a part in David's·family as his intense positive focus on his eldest son, Amnon, interfered with his willingness to act justly on the report of the rape of Tamar (2 Sam. 13:21). When Absalom murders Amnon, David deeply grieves (v. 36). In the same way, despite the murderous and rebellious acts of his son Absalom, David's intense positive focus on him remains (v. 39; 14:28–33; 18:5, 19–33). It would be possible, based on theory, to speculate as to whether both Amnon's sexual violence toward Tamar and Absalom's anger, violence, conflict, and cutoff might grow out of their being on the receiving end of an intense projection of the family's anxiety, however positive it might appear. We cannot demonstrate this conclusively with so little data, but such symptoms as these would be consistent with the impact of projection on these sons.

Sibling Position

Bowen's sixth concept, sibling position, is an ironic one in many biblical stories, including that of David and his family. Although eldest siblings in the family constellation often take charge and rise to positions of leadership in their systems, the frequently occurring biblical theme of the promotion of the younger over the older obtains in these narratives. Bowen suggests that when an oldest child reacts like a youngest and vice versa, we are likely seeing the result of the family projection process at work. The oldest has in some way attracted the worried focus of the parents and has emerged with more emotional dependence. The younger child, escaping that focus, may develop a higher level of functioning. David is the youngest of his family, and it does not seem to enter the mind of either his father, Jesse, or the prophet, Samuel, that God might choose the youngest to be king (1 Sam. 16:1–13). But, somewhat like Joseph before him, this younger brother ascends above his siblings to become their ruler. Like Joseph, his father dispatches him to visit his older brothers (Gen. 37:12–13; 1 Sam. 17:17–18). Neither Joseph nor David receive a warm welcome from their older siblings (Gen. 37:17–20; 1 Sam. 17:28–30). David comes to his brothers, who are cowering, along with Israel's King Saul and his armies, before the Philistine champion, Goliath (1 Sam. 17:4–11, 22–27). In the face of the giant, David, the youngest, demonstrates courage that they do not have and slays the Philistine with his sling and a stone (vv. 31–58).

When David grows old and approaches death, two of his sons and their supporters vie for the right to succeed him on the throne. With Amnon (first son) and Absalom (third son) out of the way, Adonijah, David's fourth-born son, exalts himself. Born to Haggith (2 Sam. 3:4), he makes a bid for his father's position (1 Kings 1:5).[5] He organizes support for himself, including Joab, who has again assumed authority as commander of the army by murdering Amasa (2 Sam. 20:9–20), and the priest Abiathar, who had once served as a kind of chaplain in David's army before he was king (1 Sam. 23:6–11). Another faction in David's court, however, prefers a different candidate: Solomon, the youngest of David's ten sons, born to Bathsheba (2 Sam. 12:24–25). The priest Zadok; Benaiah, one of David's "mighty men" (1 Chron. 27:6); the prophet Nathan; along with Shimei and Res, members of David's court, do not support the older Davidic son in his bid for the crown (1 Kings 1:8). Nathan approaches Bathsheba and persuades her to ask David to insert himself into this competition, naming her son, Solomon, as heir to the kingdom (vv. 11–31). David instructs Zadok, Nathan, and Benaiah to support and anoint Solomon in his place. Solomon publicly displays David's choice by riding about in procession on the king's mule while trumpets sound and people proclaim, "Long live King Solomon!" (vv. 32–40). David's voice in the matter has trumped Adonijah's attempt to assume power, forcing him and his faction to stand down (vv. 41–48). Once more, the youngest sibling ascends to prominence over the eldest.

Although this seems to contradict some of the claims of BFST and the research of Toman, there may be other ways to understand what is taking place. Other variables may be at work in the lives of these ascendant younger siblings beyond simply their location in the family constellation. Perhaps their level of differentiation is significantly higher than that of their siblings because of a family projection process that left them freer from the family's anxious focus. Or, as mentioned regarding the patriarchal family, perhaps this is a recurring theological theme in the biblical narrative that underscores God's ironic choices of the weaker, less privileged, or less powerful through whom to accomplish kingdom purposes (1 Cor. 1:26–31).

Emotional Cutoff

Emotional cutoff occurs in the Davidic story most prominently in the rebellion of Absalom, who first experiences a conflict with his doting father, then kills his half brother, and finally runs away from home to live with his maternal grandfather (2 Sam. 13:37–39). Although David later allows him to return to Jerusalem, the still unresolved attachment between father and son shows up in Absalom's undermining his father's position, leading a rebellion, and ultimately losing his life (14:21–18:18). David's deep grief at Absalom's death illustrates further the attachment at the root of the relationship (18:32–19:8).

Societal Emotional Process

The last of Bowen's eight interlocking concepts, societal emotional process, is rooted in Bowen's observation that society at large operates with the same emotional processes that occur in the nuclear family. Periods of heightened societal anxiety result in the family emotional process of conflict, distance, overfunctioning and underfunctioning, and projection playing out on the large stage of society.

This concept helps to make sense of David's story. Certainly, many aspects of the Davidic narratives are distinctive to a time and culture far removed from ours, such as the taking of multiple wives, often to seal political ties. But the story becomes more universally human when seen against the backdrop of an anxious, leaderless time. Friedman identifies five characteristics of chronically anxious families that show up as well in the greater society during chronically anxious times.

1. *Reactivity:* the vicious cycle of intense reactions of each member to events and to one another.
2. *Herding:* a process through which the forces of togetherness trump the forces for individuality and move everyone to adapt to the least mature members.
3. *Blame displacement:* an emotional state in which family members focus on forces that have victimized them rather than taking responsibility for their own being and destiny.
4. *A quick-fix mentality:* a low threshold for pain that constantly seeks symptom relief rather than fundamental change.
5. *Lack of well-differentiated leadership:* a failure of nerve that both stems from and contributes to the first four.[6]

These characteristics describe well the social setting that both Saul and David faced during their reigns.

The book of Judges closes with an observation about the leaderless condition of the people of Israel, in which the tribes found themselves fighting against both their external enemies, such as the Philistines or the Midianites, and their fellow Israelites in intertribal warfare (Judg. 21:25). Samuel functioned both as a prophet and as the last of the judges. Blaming Samuel and his sons, the people seek a quick fix by demanding a king like other nations (1 Sam. 8:5). They will not hear Samuel's warning about where such a choice will ultimately lead (vv. 11–22). Samuel (together with the Lord) accedes to their wishes, and Saul is anointed king. But anxious systems do not produce mature leaders.

Saul comes to power against the better judgment of the prophet Samuel, who, despite anointing him as king does little to support him and, in fact, contributes to his failure as a leader by not showing up on time to lead in public worship (underfunctioning?), forcing the king to act as priest and offer a sacrifice (overfunctioning?) (1 Sam. 13–15). Saul's character failure becomes obvious in a short time. He is not a king who will lead Israel back to faithfulness to their God. Saul's dynasty soon collapses, and he must operate as a lame-duck king, becoming increasingly unstable and paranoid. The regressive state of Israel's society takes its toll on both Saul's leadership and his family. David lives through this time of political and social instability and then inherits it as the context in which he will spend the last forty years of his life attempting to provide leadership to Israel.

David comes to power as the unexpected king. He was a mere shepherd and the youngest of Jesse's family. The one trait that marks David in the biblical narrative is his faithfulness to God. When Samuel examines Jesse's sons, looking for the chosen one, God warns the prophet, "Do not look on his appearance or on the height of his stature, because I have rejected him; for the Lord does not see as mortals see; they look on the outward appearance, but *the Lord looks on the heart*" (1 Sam. 16:7, emphasis added). Saul had a striking, powerful appearance (10:23), but his *heart* was not right. David, on the other hand, is "a man after [God's] own heart" (13:14). Whether facing off against a gigantic foe, fleeing from Saul and refusing to do him harm, or dancing in the streets when the ark of the covenant returns to Jerusalem, David appears as a leader who will point his nation back to the Lord. The narrative does not hide the facts of David's moral and spiritual failures (his assault of Bathsheba and murder of Uriah [2 Sam. 11] and his census of Israel [2 Sam. 24]). Nevertheless, Israel's historians regarded him as a leader who took the nation to a more stable place, at least for a time. The twelve tribes eventually unite under David's rule and continue as one nation through the next generation, the reign of Solomon. David establishes a political capital and religious center for the nation in Jerusalem. These accomplishments may imply a gradual lessening of the chronic anxiety of Israelite society for a time. David's son and successor, Solomon, becomes and does everything Samuel has warned the people of in his attempt to dissuade them from seeking a king. Societal reactivity increases during Solomon's reign, despite apparent prosperity, and his son Rehoboam witnesses the one nation become two as a result.

Conclusion

The Davidic stories illustrate well that when taken on its own terms as an interpretive perspective, BFST offers a robust set of questions and insights that can provide a distinctive understanding of biblical stories. Perhaps more than anything, Bowen theory helps to humanize the stories. Despite their seeming ancient and foreign in many ways to twenty-first-century readers, these accounts are about human beings like us. They struggle to survive. They engage in politics and intrigue. They act courageously and boldly in some instances, and weak and cowardly at other times. They give in to their worst impulses and exhibit unusual virtue. They react to anxiety in their world and in their families just as we do three thousand years later. Additionally, as we found to be true of the stories of Abraham, Bowen theory reminds us that the families that appear in the biblical narratives were as deeply flawed as any of ours. Yet these families sometimes produced men and women of deep faith and courage, who were willing to trust God and who made a lasting impact on their world.

Bowen Theory and Theological Language

I have been presenting Bowen Family Systems Theory (BFST) to pastors and lay leaders in congregations and to seminary students for more than a dozen years. I have regularly witnessed thoughtful Christians seek to bring the theory's ideas, which intuitively make good sense to them, into conversation with their understanding of the Bible and of Christian theology. Someone raises a hand and asks, "How does that idea relate to . . . ?" or "Isn't that in conflict with . . . ?"

My philosophy professor in college, Dr. Glen T. Cain, often assured us undergraduates that "all truth is God's truth." If something is true, then it will not conflict with something else that is true. We may need to refine our understanding of one or the other of the ideas, perhaps, or the ideas may stand in an authentic paradoxical relationship (some truth is like that). But two true things will not contradict each other. This understanding has helped free me to listen for God's truth in fields other than theology and to seek to bring them into conversation with my faith in Christ.

The Power of Assumptions

Sometimes two distinct disciplines simply ask different questions of the world. BFST is a scientific theory and operates with a characteristic set of assumptions and practices. Consequently, when we work with this theory, we must respect the boundaries these differences create. For example, Bowen insisted on working with *facts*, not with subjective opinions that could be neither verified nor disproved. In seeking to understand the way an emotional system operates, he encouraged the asking of questions but insisted on avoiding the "why" question: "Systems theory attempts to focus on the functional facts of relationships. It focuses on what happened, how it happened, and when and where it happened, insofar as these observations are based on fact. It carefully avoids . . . automatic preoccupation with why it happened. This is one of the main differences between conventional and systems theory."[1]

Bowen had issues with the "why" question because of its inherent subjectivity and its connection with cause-effect thinking (as opposed to systems thinking). He says,

> Why thinking has also been a part of cause-and-effect thinking because ever since man first became a thinking being he began to look around for causes to explain events that affected him. In reviewing the thinking of primitive man, we are amused at the various evil forces he blamed for his misfortunes, or the benevolent forces he credited for his good fortunes. We can chuckle at the causality that man in later centuries assigned to illness before he knew about germs and microorganisms. We can smugly assure ourselves that scientific knowledge and logical reasoning have now enabled man to go beyond the erroneous assumptions and false deductions of past centuries and that we now assign accurate causes for most of man's problems. However, an assumption behind systems theory is that man's cause-and-effect thinking is still a major problem in explaining his dysfunctions and behavior.[2]

The appropriate questions for science are "What?" "When?" "Where?" and "How?" The question "Why" is appropriate for theology and philosophy.

So, for example, BFST can help us see the emotional processes involved in a family or congregation, but it cannot help us discern the influence of the Holy Spirit, the working out of God's purposes in the system, or the spiritual experience of an individual or group. Bowen is interested, even regarding "supernatural" matters, in the "functional facts" that we can observe in a system. It may be a *fact* that the congregation believes God was at work through a crisis they faced. We could investigate that fact and its impact on the functioning of the congregation and of individuals. The belief, the *why*, is not in itself a *fact*, however. It can be neither proved nor disproved. As a scientific theory, BFST operates with an unprovable assumption: all that exists is the natural world and its order. Science, as science, does not have a place for the *super*natural. That is outside its methodology and knowledge.

Theological language and reasoning operate with a different set of assumptions that can be neither proved nor disproved. These assumptions might include the existence of God, the basic tenets of the Apostles' Creed, the inspiration and authority of the Bible, or a quite detailed confession of faith. To say we cannot prove these beliefs does not imply they are necessarily unreasonable, however. Christian theology and BFST operate on separate but parallel tracks when it comes to human behavior and relationships.[3] They share a common interest in many subjects but bring completely different perspectives to them.

As with other matters of faith and science, such as astrophysics or organic chemistry, Christian theologians can enter conversation with BFST by recognizing the separate and distinctive approaches, methodologies, and assumptions of each discipline. When Christian interpreters attempt to make the Bible speak scientifically rather than theologically, answering questions about the created order that the scientific method can appropriately answer, they often twist either the Bible or science. Augustine of Hippo cautioned about such approaches to the Christian Scriptures in the fourth century. He admonished Christians to be careful about using the Bible to justify ideas outside of theological matters, especially to unbelievers who may know the subject matter expertly.

> Whenever, you see, they catch some members of the Christian community making mistakes on a subject which they know inside out, and defending their hollow opinions on the authority of our books, on what grounds are they going to trust those books on the resurrection of the dead and the hope of eternal life and the kingdom of heaven, when they suppose they include any number of mistakes and fallacies on matters which they themselves have been able to master either by experiment or the surest of calculations?[4]

Making Room for Science in Our Theology

The different assumptions made by BFST and Christian theology will inevitably produce some genuine differences in understanding. For example, in chapter 8 we considered how sin and forgiveness are theological categories that do not exist in Bowen's theory, which speaks instead of such human behaviors as reactivity, conflict, distance, and cutoff. BFST understands human beings as merely biological organisms produced by evolution over eons of time. Christian theology, while capable of making space for evolution as a process, will nevertheless affirm that human beings, in addition to fully belonging to the biological world, distinctively bear "the image of God" (Gen. 1:26–27).[5]

Both BFST and Christian thought affirm the possibility that human beings can grow as persons, becoming a better version of themselves. Although Bowen believed that one could make some bit of progress toward a higher level of differentiation over many years of intentional work, Christian theology affirms the possibility that God's Holy Spirit works in us and with us in the process of spiritual formation and growth, which could possibly include our differentiation, since spiritual formation also affects our relationships.

Bowen hypothesized a "perfect human being," fully differentiated, but did not believe it was possible for a person to possess all the qualities he assigned to 100 on his scale of differentiation.[6] As argued in chapter 11, Christian theology makes a claim for Jesus as being the "last Adam," a fully human being (1 Cor. 15:45). Does that imply a level of differentiation that would be at the highest point on Bowen's scale, a notion that Bowen himself did not hold?

Bowen hypothesized that societal anxiety in the current regression originates in our becoming increasingly separated from nature. Scripture narrates our alienation from God, creation, and one another (Gen. 3:1–16). Both BFST and Christian theology see the human's connection to the natural or created order as important to human flourishing. Bowen moves from that belief to the hope that the human beings who survive this current crisis will be able to "live in better harmony with nature."[7] In Christian theology, the reconciliation of humanity to the created order is even part of the eschatological hope.[8]

The examples here attest to the way a faith perspective might need to *add* to the scientific perspective, *without denying it*, to accommodate scientific truth more fully to its theological truth. Such an approach does not see the science as incorrect but as in some sense incomplete, simply by the boundaries of its methods. A scientist, thinking as a scientist, would not make such an accommodation but would stop at the boundary line of the "functional facts." For Christian pastors and congregational leaders, BFST provides a fresh way to look at human relationships that is not exclusive of our theological foundations.

Coming to Terms with Bowen Theory

We use language "equivocally" when two people take a term that has more than one meaning and use it differently. They are not "coming to terms" with one another. They are not speaking "unequivocally." This often happens when people encounter the terms of BFST and try to reconcile them with familiar theological or biblical language. The words or terms sound similar, but they mean or imply very different things.

For example, much of BFST deals with the self. Bowen encourages those who would grow in emotional maturity to "define a self," to "take an I-position," to "focus on self." People familiar with the teaching of Jesus can sometimes recoil at all this talk about the self. Did Jesus not instruct his followers to "deny themselves" (Matt. 16:24; Mark 8:34; Luke 9:23)? How is the call to differentiation compatible with cross-bearing and discipleship?

To begin with, the New Testament does not have a word for "the self" as we use it in the modern world, probably because first-century culture did not have such a concept. In Jesus's instructions on self-denial, the Greek text has no noun, only a reflexive pronoun: "deny themselves." The biblical word for the interior life of a human is not "the self." Sometimes it is "heart" (*kardia*) or "mind" (*nous*) or "spirit" (*pneuma*), each of which seems to refer to the will or the decision-making control center of the human life. This is the dimension of human life that is "formed" in "spiritual formation."[9] A more comprehensive New Testament term for the inner life of a person is "soul" (*psychē*), which at times can simply refer to a person's life. Eugene Peterson charges the modern world with substituting the "self" for the "soul." "But in our current culture," Peterson writes, "'soul' has given way to 'self' as the term of choice to designate who and what we are. Self is the soul minus God. Self is what is left of soul with all the transcendence and intimacy squeezed out, the self with little or no reference to God (transcendence) or others (intimacy)."[10] "Self" is the modern, nontranscendent, scientific word for the interior life. To think of "defining a self" or "forming a soul" would be more of an equivalency. The "soul" in Jesus's teaching is not to be denied but to be preserved (Mark 8:36). "Denying oneself" would equate far more to learning to manage one's automatic reactivity, something we would attempt to control if we were working on "differentiating a self." The terms are more similar than contradictory.

Christian theology conceives of salvation as an act of God that reconciles previously alienated relationships between humans and God, humans and creation, and between humans themselves. The early church comprised people who were learning the life of reconciliation in community. The book of Acts describes what they were experiencing as "fellowship" (*koinōnia*), in which life and possessions were shared as the believers "were together" (Acts 2:42–47). This description of life matches the frequent appeals in the New Testament for unity and love among Christ's followers.[11]

Knowing of this call to fellowship and unity, Christian leaders sometimes balk at the concept of the togetherness force in BFST as something indicative of increasing anxiety. Is togetherness not a good thing in the church? Is that not what the earliest church enjoyed? Once again, we find ourselves up against an equivocal use of terms. The "togetherness" that Bowen identifies is an automatic, emotional response of human beings (and many other species) to the presence of a perceived threat. It pushes a flock of birds to fly near one another to avoid predators, fish to swim in schools, and wildebeests to travel in herds. Among humans it can take the form of enforced conformity: everyone speaking, thinking, and behaving alike. We grow more anxious when others who are important to us seem to think differently or behave differently. We are more comfortable with sameness, and so, when anxiety rises, we seek it. That is the togetherness force at work. It operates below the level of our awareness most of the time.

This is different from the experience described in Acts. The *koinōnia* (community) they experienced grew out of the willing choice to be together, to sacrifice possessions to meet the needs among them, to love one another as Jesus had commanded. The story of the early church reveals that the community did have boundaries that included both behaviors (Acts 5) and beliefs (Acts 10–11) and that these boundaries defined the early Christian movement vis-à-vis other sects of Judaism. Within the boundaries of that community existed diversity of both thought and practice, as witnessed by the canon of the New Testament itself.[12] Because they were human beings living in an anxious world, the togetherness force that Bowen describes would certainly have had its influence in those early congregations. That, however, is not what the New Testament writers are describing by unity and fellowship, which they understood to be gifts and creations of the Holy Spirit among God's people.

First-time encounters with Bowen's concept of marital fusion sometimes become an obstacle for people accustomed to the biblical language of husband and wife becoming "one flesh" (Gen. 2:24; Mark 10:8). The biblical metaphor expresses a blending of lives sexually and reproductively (as the union produces children), as well as practically (the departure from father and mother and striking out to live life together). The apostle Paul describes the sexual dimension of the one-flesh relationship as something spiritual, involving the inner person, and therefore not something people should treat casually (1 Cor. 6:16).

Although every marriage, Christian or not, is between two relatively emotionally immature people and will involve marital fusion as Bowen identified it, this is not the one-flesh relationship described in Scripture. Bowen observed that we marry someone who is at the same level of emotional maturity as we are and is willing to invest as much "self" in the inevitable fusion of life as we are. The fusion in a marriage is the part where one has no self but is simply reactive to the anxiety of the other. Defining a self requires pulling out of that fusion a bit, giving both partners a little more self to work with.

Bowen would characterize an ideal marriage as "open" (the two would be able to talk about literally any subject without fear of the other's anxiety), "equal" (one would not be subservient to the other; each would have a right to an opinion and input into decisions), and "separate" (each could have their own feelings, emotions, or thoughts without the other having to react to them).[13] Such marriages do not exist fully, except in theory. But nothing in this description of the "unfused" marriage would preclude it from being a one-flesh relationship.

"Love" is another term that shows up frequently in Bowen's work (167 times in *Family Therapy*). Bowen was not certain, he claimed, what we mean by the word "love," but he knew that people reacted emotionally to the word.[14] He said, "After much experience with family members, as they used the term and reacted to it, I arrived at the following functional definition of love as a relationship fact. It was, 'I am not able to accurately define love, but it is a fact that statements to another important person about the presence or absence of love in self, or in the other, predictably [result] in an emotional reaction in the relationship.'"[15] Bowen simply used a common term to describe a functional fact of human relationships. People talk about and react emotionally to "love" or its absence. This is not what Christians mean when we use that word.

"Love" is the biblical term that describes the desired relationship between believers and our God, our neighbor, and even our enemies. For Bowen, love is primarily an emotional reaction or a term that elicits emotional reaction. For biblical theology, love is a willful choice, a behavior that puts the other's well-being ahead of selfish reactions and agendas. As argued in chapter 12, the character of love described in 1 Corinthians 13 outlines the behavior of a well-differentiated life, in which one lives in relationships with others based on principles, not automatic reactions. Christian love flows from the principles and character of the one who practices it; it is not mere reactivity.

Christian leaders need not fear scientific theories, such as Bowen's approach to human behavior and natural systems. We can learn to think clearly about how our assumptions may differ from those of scientists and stick to questions that are appropriate to our theological sources and methods. We can learn to accommodate scientific learning and our theological constructs so that they can occupy space next to each other without having to reject one or the other. We can attend closely to the ways that theologians and scientists use language to describe their thinking and concepts, not assuming that the words all communicate the same things. The compatibility of BFST with historical Christian thought is one of the features that makes it a useful perspective for leaders of Christian congregations.

Important Terms in Bowen Family Systems Theory

anxiety—The emotional/physiological response to a threat that may be either real or perceived.

anxiety, acute—The response we have to a threat that is both real and time-limited.

anxiety, chronic—The reaction to a perceived, imagined, or exaggerated threat that is not time-limited.

autonomy force—The internal pressure we feel to express our individuality, to be for ourselves, to differentiate from others. Bowen also called this the "differentiating force." *See also* togetherness force.

basic self—Our considered beliefs, values, and principles that are not negotiable in a relationship.

Bowen Family Systems Theory (BFST)—The biologically based theory of human behavior, founded on natural systems, developed by Dr. Murray Bowen, comprising eight interlocking concepts. *See also* ninth concept.

coach—Someone outside our relationship system, trained in BFST, who offers a degree of objectivity about our lives, an "outside angle," with whom we can consult in our attempts to grow emotionally and spiritually.

conflict—A common symptom of anxiety in a system, in which people insist on their way as the only way and clash with others taking the same emotional stance.

cutoff—A common symptom of anxiety in a system; an extreme expression of distancing, in which people completely break off relationships, especially between generations. As a verb, the idea is expressed as "to cut off." *See also* distancing.

detriangling—The ability to remain connected to the other two parties in an emotional triangle in a one-to-one relationship while not taking on the anxiety that belongs to the two of them. *See also* emotional triangle.

differentiation of self—A person's capacity to remain true to their deepest principles, to be thoughtful rather than reactive, while remaining emotionally connected to others who are important to oneself. Differentiation is the capacity to separate our intellectual and emotional systems and to choose between them.

differentiation-of-self scale—Bowen's hypothetical scale, ranging from 0 to 100, intended to account for the full range of human functioning, from the least well-differentiated (0) to the most emotionally mature (100).

distancing—A common symptom of anxiety in a system, in which people withdraw from others emotionally, creating a superficial harmony. *See also* cutoff.

dysfunctional spouse—One of four symptoms of anxiety in the family emotional process, in which anxiety in a family focuses on one spouse's intense physical, emotional, or social dysfunction (also called "symptomatic spouse"). *See also* overfunctioning; underfunctioning.

emotion—As a technical term, "emotion" is not equivalent to "feelings." The term "emotion" refers to all the responses a human being makes to anxiety, most of which are outside our awareness, and includes our entire physiology (such as digestion, skin temperature, heart rate, blood pressure, etc.). *See also* feelings.

emotional cutoff—*See* cutoff.

emotional maturity—*See* differentiation of self.

emotional process—The constant interaction of emotional reactivity, the level of differentiation and the level of chronic anxiety, the interplay of the togetherness forces and the autonomy forces, and the emergence of symptoms within a relational system.

emotional reactivity—The automatic, unthinking, emotional response that human beings have to real or perceived threats in their environment. *See also* anxiety.

emotional system—The emotional connectedness that develops when people engage in relationships that are long-term, intense, and significant.

emotional triangle—The "molecule" of the emotional system, formed when one person becomes uncomfortable in relationship to another and so pulls in a third to manage the anxiety in the original relationship. Triangling is the act of forming such a triangle. *See also* detriangling.

extended family—One's family outside of the immediate, nuclear family of origin, including one's grandparents, uncles, aunts, and cousins, plus the multiple generations of one's ancestors.

family diagram—A representation of one's family in which we can chart the emotional processes of the family by use of symbols and abbreviations, sometimes referred to as a genogram. Bowen preferred the simpler term: family diagram.

family emotional process—The ways in which a family "binds" or focuses its anxiety in one of four symptoms: conflict, distance, overfunctioning/ underfunctioning (including "dysfunctional spouse"), and projection of the anxiety onto a child.

family of origin—The emotional unit in which a person is reared (not necessarily one's biological family).

family projection process—The intense positive or negative focus of parents on a child as a way of managing the anxiety of their own marriage, often resulting in the child's becoming more emotionally dependent or symptomatic.

feelings—Emotional responses that operate at the level of awareness, emotional responses of which we are conscious. *See also* emotion.

functional self—As opposed to "basic self," this refers to our capacity to function at a higher level when anxiety is relatively low in our emotional system.

interlocking triangles—The connection of emotional triangles within a relational system that permits anxiety to travel from one triangle throughout the entire system.

I-position—A differentiating move in which a person states clearly and calmly their own belief or commitment, what they will or will not do, and holds that position despite pressure from the system for conformity.

multigenerational transmission process—The way in which one generation transmits levels of emotional maturity and ways of responding to anxiety to the next generation, resulting in branches of the family that are increasing in differentiation over time and others that are regressing.

ninth concept—The concept of "the supernatural," which Murray Bowen began to talk about near the end of his life, involving such things as the way in which belief in the supernatural affects one's functioning, as well as the way such reported phenomena as extrasensory perception, healings, and other spiritual experiences impact individuals and families.

nuclear family—The family in which one lives, which may include husband, wife, and children or many other possible configurations.

nuclear family emotional process—*See* family emotional process.

overfunctioning—A common symptom of anxiety in a system, in which one member of the system takes on responsibilities that rightfully belong to others. *See also* underfunctioning.

process—*See* emotional process.

projection—A common symptom of anxiety in a system, in which portions of the system focus their attention on one part as "the problem." The part that receives the focus often agrees with this diagnosis. *See also* family projection process.

reactivity—*See* emotional reactivity.

reciprocal functioning—*See* overfunctioning; underfunctioning.

relational system—*See* emotional system.

sibling position—The unique place one occupies in the family of origin, based on one's birth order (for example, oldest, or older brother of sisters, or younger sister of sisters). This position teaches one about relationships with both sexes and affects the way one functions in the system.

societal emotional process—The ways in which anxiety and reactivity occur and function in a society, following the same pattern as in an individual family.

societal regression—The process of society's developing significant symptoms over time because of rising anxiety and reactivity, paralleling the kind of regression that a family can experience.

supernatural—*See* ninth concept.

systems thinking—The capacity to see the whole and the individual members of a system together, noticing the parts played by each and the effect of each on the other. This includes the ability to recognize the symptoms of increasing anxiety, to observe the emotional processes taking place, and to notice one's own part in the system's reactivity.

thinking systems—*See* systems thinking.

togetherness force—The pressure we experience from important relationships to be "for the system," to conform to others, to fit in, to be "we." *See also* autonomy force.

triangle—*See* emotional triangle.

underfunctioning—A common symptom of anxiety in a system, in which portions of the system fail to accept responsibility for functioning that is rightfully theirs, allowing others to take it up for them. *See also* dysfunctional spouse; overfunctioning.

watching process—The act of observing the ways in which emotional processes (conflict, distance, reciprocal functioning, projection, emotional triangles, reactivity) are occurring in a system while maintaining a relatively objective perspective.

Bowen-Based Training Programs

The Bowen Center for the Study of the Family
4400 MacArthur Boulevard NW, Suite 103
Washington, DC 20007
202-965-4400
www.thebowencenter.org
info@thebowencenter.org

The Center for Family Consultation
820 Davis Street, Suite 221
Evanston, IL 60201
847-251-7350
www.centerforfamilyconsultation.net
info@centerforfamilyconsultation.net

The Center for Family Process
10601 Willowbrook Drive
Potomac, MD 20854
301-983-9525
www.centerforfamilyprocess.com

The Center for Family Systems Theory of Western New York
1088 Delaware Avenue, Suite 9G
Buffalo, NY 14209
716-886-4594
www.familysystemstheory.org

The Center for the Study of Human Systems
PO Box 693
Stephens City, VA 22655
540-868-0866
www.hsystems.org
rgoffice136@gmail.com

The Center for the Study of Natural Systems and the Family
729 Rutland Street
Houston, TX 77007
713-790-0226
www.csnsf.org
vaharrison@sbcglobal.net

The Center for the Study of Natural Systems and the Family
Border Programs
El Paso, TX
915-726-5662
https://border.csnsf.org
theomead@yahoo.com

Faithwalking
P.O. Box 131074
Houston, TX 77219
Ken Shuman, Executive Director
http://www.faithwalking.us

Florida Family Research Network
2172 NW 99th Avenue
Doral, FL 33172
561-279-0861
www.ffrnbowentheory.org
egbfamilycenter@comcast.net

Healthy Congregations
3081 Columbus Pike
Delaware, OH 43015
740-803-2417
www.healthycongregations.com
office@healthycongregations.com

KC Center for Family Systems
3100 NE 83rd Street, Suite 2350
Kansas City, MO 64119
816-436-1721, ext. 4
www.kcfamilysystems.org
info@kcfamilysystems.org

The Leader's Edge
10601 Willowbrook Drive
Potomac, MD 20854
301-299-7475
www.coachingleadership.com
crimone@coachingleadership.com

Leadership in Ministry
701 S. Columbia Dr.
Decatur, GA 30030
404-378-8821
www.leadershipinministry.org
leadershipinministry@gmail.com

The Learning Space
4545 42nd St. NW, Suite 201
Washington, DC 20016
202-966-1145
www.thelearningspacedc.com

Living Systems
1500 Marine Drive
North Vancouver, BC V7P 1T7
604-926-5496
www.livingsystems.ca
info@livingsystems.ca

Lombard Mennonite Peace Center
101 West 22nd Street, Suite 206
Lombard, IL 60148
630-627-0507
www.LMPeaceCenter.org
Admin@LMPeaceCenter.org

Ministry Leadership Concepts
3623 Pavillion Circle
San Antonio, TX 78217
210-834-2731
www.ministryleadershipconcepts.com
rdhester@earthlink.net

New England Seminar on Bowen Theory
25 A Medway Street
Dorchester, MA 02124
617-312-8699 or 617-296-4614
www.bowentheoryne.org
annvnicholson@gmail.com

The Princeton Family Center for Education
PO Box 331
Pennington, NJ 08534
609-203-0162
www.princetonfamilycenter.org
leegardner@verizon.net

Programs in Bowen Theory
120 Pleasant Hill Avenue North, Suite 370
Sebastopol, CA 95472
707-823-1848
www.programsinbowentheory.org
info@programsinbowentheory.org

Southern California Training in Bowen Theory
625 Third Avenue
Chula Vista, CA 91910
619-525-7747
www.socalbowentheory.com
info@socalbowentheory.com

Vermont Center for Family Studies
PO Box 5124
Essex Junction, VT 05453
802-355-6241
www.vermontcenterforfamilystudies.org
Vfsoffice@gmail.com

Western Pennsylvania Family Center
733 North Highland Avenue
Pittsburgh, PA 15206
412-362-2295
www.wpfc.net
info@wpfc.net

APPENDIX E

Bowen Family Systems Theory and Ministry

A Bibliography

Anderson, Douglas. "Spirituality and Systems Therapy: Partners in Clinical Practice." In *Religion and the Family: When God Helps*, edited by Laurel Arthur Burton, 87–101. New York: Haworth Pastoral Press, 1992.

Anderson, Herbert, and C. George Fitzgerald. "Use of Family Systems in Preparation for Ministry." *Pastoral Psychology* 27 (1978): 49–61.

Armour, Michael C., and Don Browning. *Systems-Sensitive Leadership: Empowering Diversity without Polarizing the Church*. Joplin, MO: College Press Publishing, 2000.

Blessing, Kamila. "Differentiation in the Family of Faith: The Prodigal Son and Galatians 1–2." In *Psychology and the Bible: A New Way to Read the Scriptures*, vol. 3, *From Gospel to Gnostics*, edited by J. Harold Ellens and Wayne G. Rollins, 165–91. Praeger Perspectives: Psychology, Religion, and Spirituality. Westport, CT: Praeger, 2004.

———. *Families of the Bible: A New Perspective*. Psychology, Religion, and Spirituality. Santa Barbara, CA: Praeger, 2010.

———. "Family Systems Psychology as Hermeneutic." In *Psychology and the Bible: A New Way to Read the Scriptures*, vol. 1, *From Freud to Kohut*, edited by J. Harold Ellens and Wayne G. Rollins, 185–207. Praeger Perspectives: Psychology, Religion, and Spirituality. Westport, CT: Praeger, 2004.

———. "Murray Bowen's Family Systems Theory as Bible Hermeneutic Illustrated Using the Family of the Prodigal Son." *Journal of Psychology and Christianity* 19 (2000): 38–46.

Bohler, Carolyn Stahl. "Essential Elements of Family Systems Approaches to Pastoral Counseling." In *Clinical Handbook of Pastoral Counseling*, edited by Robert J. Wicks, Richard D. Parsons, and Donald Capps, 1:585–613. Expanded ed. New York: Paulist Press, 1993.

Bowen, Murray. *Family Therapy in Clinical Practice*. Lanham, MD: Jason Aronson, 1994.

Burton, Anne L., and Charles A. Weinrich. "So Great a Cloud of Witnesses: The Use of Family Systems Process in Forming Pastoral Identity and Facilitating Pastoral Functioning." *Journal of Pastoral Care* 44, no. 4 (1990): 331–41.

Creech, R. Robert. "Bowen Theory and a Pastoral Transition." *Family Systems Forum* 12, no. 3 (Spring 2010): 1–2, 8–10.

———. "Generations to Come: The Future of Bowen Family Systems Theory and Congregational Ministry." *Family Systems Forum* 16, no. 1 (Spring 2014): 3–8.

David, James R. "The Theology of Murray Bowen or the Marital Triangle." *Journal of Psychology & Theology* 7, no. 4 (1979): 259–62.

DeArment, Daniel C. "Families and Groups: Their Nature and Function from a Systems Perspective." *Journal of Pastoral Care* 41, no. 2 (June 1987): 111–18.

Deinhardt, Carol L., and Janice Hirst. "Family Systems in the Kingdom of God: Christian Counsellors/Therapists as Mediators of a New Reality." *Didaskalia* 8, no. 1 (September 1996): 73–93.

Ellens, Dale D. "Ministering to Families with a Retarded Child Using the Family Systems Model." *Military Chaplains' Review*, Fall 1990, 71–84. https://archive.org/stream/militarychaplain59unse/militarychaplain59unse_djvu.txt.

Farrell, Bruce David. "After the Church Split, Moving Forward the Family of Faith: An Application of Seven Principles of Peter Steinke." DMin diss., Gordon-Conwell Theological Seminary, 1996. Microform. Theological Research Exchange Network Series 068–0069.

Fischer, Kathleen R. "Spirituality and the Aging Family: A Systems Perspective." *Journal of Religious Gerontology* 8 (1992): 1–15.

Fortel, Deborah, and David R. Sawyer. "A Family Systems Approach to Building Healthy Relationships across Our Denomination." *Church and Society* 81, no. 1 (September 1990): 47–48.

Friedman, Edwin H. *A Failure of Nerve: Leadership in the Age of the Quick Fix*. Edited by Margaret M. Treadwell and Edward W. Beal. 10th anniversary rev. ed. New York: Church Publishing, 2017.

———. *Generation to Generation: Family Process in Church and Synagogue*. New York: Guilford, 1985.

Galindo, Israel, ed. *Leadership in Ministry: Bowen Theory in the Congregational Context*. North Charleston, SC: CreateSpace / Didache Press, 2017.

———. "What's Systems Theory Got to Do with It? Addressing Congregations' Emotional Processing in Our Preaching." *Congregations* 33, no. 2 (2007): 32–35.

Garland, Diana S. Richmond. "Understanding Clergy Misconduct in Religious Systems." *Journal of Family Ministry* 13, no. 4 (1999): 79–80.

Gilbert, Roberta M. *The Cornerstone Concept: In Leadership, in Life*. Falls Church, VA: Leading Systems Press, 2008.

———. *Extraordinary Leadership: Thinking Systems, Making a Difference*. Falls Church, VA: Leading Systems Press, 2006.

———. "Societal Regression and the Clergy." *Review & Expositor* 102, no. 3 (June 1, 2005): 445–59.

Hanisch, Rhonda R., and Anne Marie Nuechterlein. "Our Mission and Ministry: Differentiated and Connected Identity and Relationships." *Pastoral Psychology* 38 (1990): 205–12.

Harris, Jon R. "Dysfunction, Healing, and the Family of Origin." In *Handbook of Family Religious Education*, edited by Blake J. Neff and Donald Ratcliff, 188–206. Birmingham, AL: Religious Education Press, 1995.

Heaney-Hunter, JoAnn. "'Active Faith' in Christian Marriage: The Challenge of Family Systems." *Pastoral Psychology* 45 (1997): 261–75.

Heiden-Rootes, Katie M., Peter J. Jankowski, and Steven J. Sandage. "Bowen Family Systems Theory and Spirituality: Exploring the Relationship between Triangulation and Religious Questing." *Contemporary Family Therapy* 32, no. 2 (June 1, 2010): 89–101.

Herrington, Jim, R. Robert Creech, and Trisha Taylor. *The Leader's Journey: Accepting the Call to Personal and Congregational Transformation*. San Francisco: Jossey-Bass, 2003.

Hill, E. Wayne, and Carol Anderson Darling. "Using the Family Ecosystem Model to Enhance Pastoral Care and Counseling." *Journal of Pastoral Care* 55, no. 3 (September 2001): 247–57.

Howe, Leroy T. "Self-Differentiation in Christian Perspective." *Pastoral Psychology* 46 (1998): 347–62.

Ivy, Steven S. "Ministry to Persons with AIDS: A Family Systems Approach." *Pastoral Psychology* 43 (1994): 131–32.

Jankowski, Peter J., and Marsha Vaughn. "Differentiation of Self and Spirituality: Empirical Explorations." *Counseling and Values* 53, no. 2 (January 2009): 82–96.

Jensen, Carl A. "Toward Pastoral Counseling Integration: One Bowen Oriented Approach." *Journal of Pastoral Care & Counseling* 57, no. 2 (Summer 2003): 117–29.

Kisner, Jeffrey A. "A Family Systems Approach to Grief." *Pastoral Psychology* 28 (1980): 265–76.

Long, Janie K., and Jay A. Mancini. "Aging Couples and the Family System." In *Family Relationships in Later Life*, edited by Timothy H. Brubaker, 29–47. 2nd ed. Sage Focus Editions 64. Thousand Oaks, CA: Sage Publications, 1990.

Lyon, Steve M. "Leading in Congregational Conflict: A Family Systems Model." *Southwestern Journal of Theology* 43, no. 3 (2001): 37–56.

Majerus, Brian D. "Toward an Authentic Knowing of God: The Differentiation-of-Self Construct in Relational Spirituality." *Journal of Spirituality in Mental Health* 12, no. 4 (November 2010): 288–99.

Marcuson, Margaret. *Leaders Who Last: Sustaining Yourself and Your Ministry*. New York: Seabury Books, 2009.

Matthews, Lawrence E. "Bowen Family Systems Theory: A Resource for Pastoral Theologians." *Review & Expositor* 102, no. 3 (Summer 2005): 425–44.

Menking, Wayne L. *When All Else Fails: Rethinking Our Pastoral Vocation in Times of Stuck*. Eugene, OR: Wipf & Stock, 2013.

Mercurio, Andrew T. "A Family Systems Survey of Congregational Dysfunction." *Evangelical Journal* 19 (2001): 1–19.

Mitchell, Kenneth. "You Must Leave before You Can Cleave: A Family Systems Approach to Premarital Pastoral Work." *Pastoral Psychology* 30 (1981): 71–88.

Moon, Mi Sun. "A Pastoral Theology of Caring in Korea: Contributions from Marriage and Family Therapy." PhD diss., Southern Baptist Theological Seminary, 2000. Ann Arbor, MI: ProQuest Information & Learning, 2001.

Mullen, Paul M., and E. Wayne Hill. "A Family Systems Model for Pastoral Care and Counseling in Times of Crisis." *Journal of Pastoral Care* 44, no. 3 (September 1990): 250–57.

Natale, Samuel M. "A Family Systems Approach to Religious Education and Development." *Religious Education* 74, no. 3 (May 1979): 245–53.

Nessan, Craig L. "Surviving Congregational Leadership: A Theology of Family Systems." *Word & World* 20, no. 4 (September 2000): 390–99.

Nyengele, M. Fulgence. "Family Systems Theory and the Concerns of African Women Theologians: Pastoral Theological Reflections." *Africa Theological Journal* 25, no. 2 (2002): 71–98.

Ott, Emlyn. "Leaving as Process: Toward Differentiation of Self in Pastoral Transitions." *Trinity Seminary Review* 28, no. 1 (December 2007): 21–28.

Pattison, E. Mansell. "Systems Pastoral Care." *Journal of Pastoral Care* 26, no. 1 (March 1972): 2–14.

Richardson, Ronald W. *Becoming a Healthier Pastor*. Minneapolis: Fortress, 2004.

———. "Bowen Family Systems Theory and Congregational Life." *Review & Expositor* 102, no. 3 (2005): 379–402.

———. *Creating a Healthier Church: Family Systems Theory, Leadership, and Congregational Life*. Minneapolis: Fortress, 1996.

————. *Polarization and the Healthier Church: Applying Bowen Family Systems Theory to Conflict and Change in Society and Congregational Life*. CreateSpace Independent Publishing Platform, 2012.

Rock, Stanley A. "The Pastor, the Family, and the Congregation: Learning from Family Therapy." *Reformed Review* 35 (1982): 66–72.

Rogers, Martha L. "Some Bible Families Examined from a Systems Perspective." *Journal of Psychology & Theology* 7, no. 4 (1979): 251–58.

Royer, Kathryn. "Clergy Clinic in Emotional Process Family Systems Therapy." In *Foundation Theology 2007: Student Essays for Ministry Professionals*, edited by John H. Morgan, 111–21. South Bend, IN: Cloverdale, 2007.

Sandholm, Gayle L. "A Systems Perspective to Marriage Counseling." *Pastoral Psychology* 31 (1982): 118–28.

Shapiro, Tim. "Thinking about Congregations: Using Bowen Family Systems Theory." *Congregations* 37, no. 2 (Spring 2010): 27–28.

Steinke, Peter L. *Congregational Leadership in Anxious Times: Being Calm and Courageous No Matter What*. Herndon, VA: Alban Institute, 2006.

————. *A Door Set Open: Grounding Change in Mission and Hope*. Herndon, VA: Alban Institute, 2010.

————. *Healthy Congregations: A Systems Approach*. Herndon, VA: Alban Institute, 1996.

————. *How Your Church Family Works: Understanding Congregations as Emotional Systems*. Herndon, VA: Alban Institute, 2006.

Stevens, R. Paul. "Analogy or Homology? An Investigation of the Congruency of Systems Theory and Biblical Theology in Pastoral Leadership." *Journal of Psychology & Theology* 22, no. 3 (September 1994): 173–81.

Stevens, R. Paul, and Phil Collins. *The Equipping Pastor: A Systems Approach to Congregational Leadership*. Washington, DC: Alban Institute, 1993.

Thomasma, Norman. "Utilizing Natural Family Systems Theory to Foster Health in Congregations: Murray Bowen as Teacher of Congregations." *Reformed Review* 58, no. 2 (2005): 119–28.

Thompson, Robert. "Bowen and Volf: One White Man's Knapsack for His Journey with African-American Liberation." *Journal of Pastoral Theology* 14, no. 2 (Fall 2004): 31–47.

Van den Blink, A. J. "The Family and Pastoral Care." *Journal of Pastoral Care* 39, no. 2 (June 1985): 173–81.

Van Katwyk, Peter L. "A Family Observed: Theological and Family Systems Perspectives on the Grief Experience." *Journal of Pastoral Care* 47, no. 2 (1993): 141–47.

Vogelsang, John D. "Fostering Both a Healthy and Just Congregation: Family Systems and Social Systems Approaches." *Journal of Family Ministry* 10, no. 1 (1996): 3–15.

Notes

Preface

1. Francis Bacon, *The Essays*, ed. John Pitcher (New York: Penguin Classics, 1986), 209.
2. Jim Herrington, R. Robert Creech, and Trisha Taylor, *The Leader's Journey: Accepting the Call to Personal and Congregational Transformation* (San Francisco: Jossey-Bass, 2003). A new edition of this book will soon be forthcoming from Baker Academic.

Chapter 1 Always Take a Map

1. "World Population Projected to Reach 9.8 Billion in 2050, and 11.2 Billion in 2100," United Nations Department of Economic and Social Affairs," June 21, 2017, https://www.un.org/development/desa/en/news/population/world-population-prospects-2017.html.
2. Jeffrey S. Passel and D'Vera Cohn, "U.S. Population Projections: 2005–2050," *Pew Research Center's Hispanic Trends Project*, February 11, 2008, http://www.pewhispanic.org/2008/02/11/us-population-projections-2005-2050/.
3. "World's Population Increasingly Urban with More than Half Living in Urban Areas, United Nations Department of Economic and Social Affairs," July 10, 2014, world-urbanization-prospects-2014.html.
4. Wendell Berry, "The Unsettling of America," in *The Art of the Commonplace: The Agrarian Essays of Wendell Berry*, ed. Norman Wirzba (Emeryville, CA: Shoemaker & Hoard, 2003), 35–46.
5. Murray Bowen, *Family Therapy in Clinical Practice* (Lanham, MD: Jason Aronson, 1994), 281.

Chapter 2 Reading the Map

1. Murray Bowen, *Family Therapy in Clinical Practice* (Lanham, MD: Jason Aronson, 1994), 353.
2. *The American Heritage Dictionary of the English Language*, 5th ed. (New York: Dell, 2012), s.v. "theory."
3. Israel Galindo, "On BFST Orthodoxy," *Perspectives on Congregational Leadership*, March 16, 2011, http://perspectivesig.blogspot.com/2011/.
4. Bowen, *Family Therapy*, 305.
5. Edwin H. Friedman, *Generation to Generation: Family Process in Church and Synagogue* (New York: Guilford, 1985), 1.

6. Bowen, *Family Therapy*, 218. Bowen also refers to the individuality force as the "differentiating force."

7. Michael E. Kerr and Murray Bowen, *Family Evaluation: An Approach Based on Bowen Theory* (New York: Norton, 1988), 64.

8. Saul McLeod, "What Is the Stress Response?" *Simply Psychology*, 2010, https://www.simplypsychology.org/stress-biology.html.

9. Archibald Hart, *Adrenaline and Stress: The Exciting New Breakthrough That Helps You Overcome Stress Damage* (Nashville: Nelson, 1995), 19–30.

10. Bowen, *Family Therapy*, 425.

11. Roberta M. Gilbert, *The Eight Concepts of Bowen Theory* (Falls Church, VA: Leading Systems Press, 2006).

12. Bowen, *Family Therapy*, 415.

13. According to Friedman (*Generation to Generation*, 35–39), emotional triangles operate by the following seven laws:

1. The relationship of any two members of an emotional triangle is kept in balance by the way a third party relates to each of them or to their relationship.

2. If one is the third party in an emotional triangle, it is generally not possible to bring change (for more than a week) to the relationship of the other two parts by trying to change their relationship directly.

3. Attempts to change the relationship of the other two sides of an emotional triangle not only are generally ineffective but are often converted to their opposite intent due to homeostatic forces.

4. To the extent a third party to an emotional triangle tries unsuccessfully to change the relationship of the other two, it is more likely that the third party will wind up with the stress of the other two.

5. The various triangles in an emotional system interlock so that efforts to bring change to any one of them is often resisted by homeostatic forces in the others or in the system itself.

6. One side of an emotional triangle tends to be more conflictual than the others.

7. We can only change a relationship to which we belong.

14. For a more detailed investigation of emotional triangles, see Peter Titelman, *Triangles: Bowen Family Systems Theory Perspectives* (New York: Haworth, 2007).

15. Bowen, *Family Therapy*, 348.

16. Bowen, *Family Therapy*, 354. Friedman sometimes uses the term "self-differentiation," although Bowen does not. Note that Bowen deliberately chose a biological term for this concept. For focused analysis of the concept of differentiation, see Roberta M. Gilbert, *The Cornerstone Concept* (Falls Church, VA: Leading Systems Press, 2008); and Peter Titelman, ed., *Differentiation of Self: Bowen Family Systems Theory Perspectives* (New York: Routledge, 2015).

17. Some have attempted such instruments, however. See, for example, Carolyn Licht and David Chabot, "The Chabot Emotional Differentiation Scale: A Theoretically and Psychometrically Sound Instrument for Measuring Bowen's Intrapsychic Aspect of Differentiation," *Journal of Marital and Family Therapy* 32, no. 2 (April 1, 2006): 167–80; Richard B. Miller, Shayne Anderson, and Davelyne Kaulana Keals, "Is Bowen Theory Valid? A Review of Basic Research," *Journal of Marital and Family Therapy* 30, no. 4 (October 1, 2004): 453–66.

18. Bowen, *Family Therapy*, 160–64.

19. Bowen, *Family Therapy*, 91.

20. This idea of "fusion" differs drastically from the biblical concept of marriage as "one flesh" (see appendix B).

21. Bowen, *Family Therapy*, 322. See also Roberta M. Gilbert, *Extraordinary Relationships: A New Way of Thinking about Human Interactions* (New York: Wiley, 1992), 109–10.

22. Bowen, *Family Therapy*, 424.

23. Bowen, *Family Therapy*, 168–69.

24. Bowen, *Family Therapy*, xv.

25. Note that the field of epigenetics is investigating the relationship between genetics and the environment. See, for example, Michael J. Meaney, "Epigenetics and the Biological Definition of Gene × Environment Interactions," *Child Development* 81, no. 1 (January 1, 2010): 41–79.

26. Although Bowen preferred the simple and direct term "family diagram," others have employed the term "genogram" to describe the mapping out of a family's emotional process over several generations. Help for developing a family diagram can be found in Jack O. Bradt, *The Family Diagram: Method, Technique, and Use in Family Therapy* (Washington, DC: Groome Center, 1980); Israel Galindo, Elaine Boomer, and Don Reagan, *A Family Genogram Workbook* (Decatur, GA: Educational Consultants, 2006); Monica McGoldrick and Randy Gerson, *Genograms in Family Assessment* (New York: Norton, 1986); and Monica McGoldrick, Randy Gerson, and Sueli Petry, *Genograms: Assessment and Intervention*, 3rd ed. (New York: Norton, 2008).

27. Friedman, *Generation to Generation*, 32.

28. Bowen, *Family Therapy*, 203–4.

29. Walter Toman, *Family Constellation: Its Effects on Personality and Social Behavior*, 3rd ed. (New York: Springer, 1976). Toman uses these categories: (1) oldest brother of brothers; (2) youngest brother of brothers; (3) oldest brother of sisters; (4) youngest brother of sisters; (5) male only child; (6) oldest sister of sisters; (7) youngest sister of sisters; (8) oldest sister of brothers; (9) youngest sister of brothers; (10) female only child (141–85). He provides special interpretation to such situations as twins and middle children (185–94). In a larger family, it is worth noting, a family member may occupy more than one position. A girl, for example, can be a younger sister of one brother and the older sister of another.

30. Bowen, *Family Therapy*, 385.

31. Bowen, *Family Therapy*, 381–83. For more extensive research and application of the concept of emotional cutoff, see Peter Titelman, ed., *Emotional Cutoff: Bowen Family Systems Theory Perspectives* (New York: Routledge, 2003).

32. Bowen says, "The more intense the cutoff with the past, the more likely the individual to have an exaggerated version of his parental family problem in his own marriage, and the more likely his own children to do a more intense cutoff with him in the next generation" (*Family Therapy*, 382).

33. Murray Bowen, "On Emotional Process in Society," in *Bowen Theory and Practice: Feature Articles from the Family Center Report, 1979–1996*, ed. Ruth Riley Sagar (Washington, DC: Georgetown Family Center, 1997), 211.

34. Ronald W. Richardson has written a helpful book for congregational leaders who are trying to lead their churches through the conflictual and polarizing issues that plague society. See *Polarization and the Healthier Church: Applying Bowen Family Systems Theory to Conflict and Change in Society and Congregational Life* (CreateSpace Independent Publishing Platform, 2012).

35. In a letter to family members on April 27, 1980, Bowen wrote,

The nodal point is to conceptualize spiritual phenomena into systems theory. I know it is possible and achievable in perhaps 50 to 100 years. Do not know why it took me so long to recognize it, except that is the way heads work. The field is complex going all the way from simple things such as fairly routine spirituality, extrasensory perception, and telepathic communication, to magic and mysticism, and voodooism, etc. I do not know enough about it to do more than frame a stage for effort, but I do know enough to add it as a 9th concept in my total theory. Systems Theory deals only with function, carefully bypassing all "why" reasoning. ("Murray Bowen Archives Project, Archives by Topics: Systems Theory," http://murraybowenarchives.org/theme-SystemsTheory.html)

He spoke at some length about his thinking on this topic in a November 1980 recorded interview with Michael Kerr, "Towards a Systems Concept of Supernatural Phenomena," available through the Bowen Center for the Study of the Family (thebowencenter.org) at Washington, DC. Israel Galindo examines the potential of this ninth concept to bring BFST and faith into conversation in "Exploring the Ninth Concept: BFST and Faith in Dialogue," in *Leadership in Ministry: Bowen Theory in the Congregational Context*, ed. Israel Galindo (North Charleston, SC: CreateSpace / Didache Press, 2017).

36. Roberta Gilbert's oft-quoted mantra declares: "If you know theory, you can use it. If you don't, you can't." *Extraordinary Leadership: Thinking Systems, Making a Difference* (Falls Church, VA: Leading Systems Press, 2006), 179.

Chapter 3 Third-Way Leadership

1. Richard Robert Osmer, *Practical Theology: An Introduction* (Grand Rapids: Eerdmans, 2008), 4.

2. Volf and Bass define "Christian practices" as "patterns of cooperative human activity in and through which life takes shape over time in response to and in the light of God as known in Jesus Christ." Miroslav Volf and Dorothy C. Bass, *Practicing Theology: Beliefs and Practices in Christian Life* (Grand Rapids: Eerdmans, 2001), 3.

3. Volf and Bass, *Practicing Theology*, 3.

4. Eugene H. Peterson, *Christ Plays in Ten Thousand Places: A Conversation in Spiritual Theology* (Grand Rapids: Eerdmans, 2005), 5.

5. Peterson, *Christ Plays in Ten Thousand Places*, 6.

6. John Maxwell and Steven R. Covey, *The 21 Irrefutable Laws of Leadership: Follow Them and People Will Follow You*, rev. ed. (Nashville: Nelson, 2007).

7. Edwin H. Friedman, *A Failure of Nerve: Leadership in the Age of the Quick Fix*, ed. Margaret M. Treadwell and Edward W. Beal, 10th anniversary rev. ed. (New York: Church Publishing, 2017), 20.

8. William H. Willimon explains that he was never happy with the term "burnout" to describe why pastors leave ministry. This seems to imply that they simply lack energy for the task. He believes the problem is more like "blackout," which he describes as "the gradual dissipation of meaning in ministry, a blurring of vision, the inability to keep the theological rationale for ministry that is necessary to enliven our imagination. We wake up one day and no longer have a reason or purpose for doing the things the church expects us, as pastors, to do." *Pastor: The Theology and Practice of Ordained Ministry* (Nashville: Abingdon, 2009), 325–26.

9. Warren G. Bennis, *On Becoming a Leader* (New York: Perseus, 1989), 45.

10. Edwin H. Friedman, *Generation to Generation: Family Process in Church and Synagogue* (New York: Guilford, 1985), 224.

11. Patricia A. Comella, Joyce Bader, Judith S. Ball, Kathleen K. Wiseman, and Ruth Riley Sagar, eds., *The Emotional Side of Organizations: Applications of Bowen Theory* (Washington, DC: Georgetown Family Center, 1996).

12. Murray Bowen describes the family's process of resistance to a person who is working on differentiation: "When any family member makes a move toward differentiating a self, the family emotional system communicates a three-stage verbal and nonverbal message: (1) You are wrong. (2) Change back. (3) If you do not, these are the consequences. Generally, the messages contain a mixture of subtle sulks, hurt feelings, and angry exchanges, but some communicate all three stages in words." *Family Therapy in Clinical Practice* (New York: Jason Aronson, 1994), 216. Yet later he observes that change is possible: "When any key member of an emotional system can control his own emotional reactiveness and accurately observe the functioning of the system and his part in it, and he can avoid counterattacking when he is provoked, and when he can maintain an active relationship with the other key members without withdrawing or becoming silent, the entire system will change in a series of predictable steps" (436).

13. Everett M. Rogers, *Diffusion of Innovations*, 5th ed. (New York: Free Press, 2003).

14. Rogers, *Diffusion of Innovations*, 267–97.

15. Friedman, *Generation to Generation*, 47.

16. Friedman, *Failure of Nerve*, 68–69.

17. Friedman, *Generation to Generation*, 2–3.

18. Gene Klann, *Crisis Leadership: Using Military Lessons, Organizational Experiences, and the Power of Influence to Lessen the Impact of Chaos on the People You Lead* (Greensboro, NC: Center for Creative Leadership, 2003), 4.

19. Klann, *Crisis Leadership*, 20.

20. Note that everything stated in this section about congregational crises would be applicable to the pastoral care crises into which a pastor steps as a leader, helping others to negotiate a future that has been called into question by a family or individual crisis, such as the loss of a job, the death of a family member, or a threatening medical diagnosis. Some pastoral care crises can easily become congregational crises: the death or potentially fatal or severely limiting illness of a child or a parent of young children, for example, can stir people's worst fears. The death of a stalwart lay leader or a financial pillar may pose a threat to the congregation's survival.

21. Klann, *Crisis Leadership*, 11.

22. For further suggestions about developing crisis plans, see Otto F. Crumroy Jr., Stan Kukawka, and Frank M. Witman, *Church Administration and Finance Manual: Resources for Leading the Local Church* (Harrisburg, PA: Morehouse, 1998), 436–62.

23. Bowen, *Family Therapy*, 409–10.

24. Bowen wrote: "I believe that the level of differentiation of a person is largely determined by the time he leaves the parental family and he attempts a life of his own. Thereafter, he tends to replicate the lifestyle from the parental family in all future relationships. It is not possible ever to make more than minor changes in one's basic level of self; but from clinical experience I can say it is possible to make slow changes, and each small change results in the new world of a different lifestyle" (*Family Therapy*, 371).

25. In *The Leader's Journey: Accepting the Call to Personal and Congregational Transformation* (San Francisco: Jossey-Bass, 2003), Jim Herrington, Trisha Taylor, and I make the case that personal change in the life of the leader underlies the capacity to lead congregational transformation.

Chapter 4 The Future of Congregational Leadership

1. Murray Bowen, *Family Therapy in Clinical Practice* (Lanham, MD: Jason Aronson, 1994), 276.

2. Bowen, *Family Therapy*, 279–80.

3. C. Kirk Hadaway and Penny Long Marler, "How Many Americans Attend Worship Each Week? An Alternative Approach to Measurement," *Journal for the Scientific Study of Religion* 44, no. 3 (2005): 316.

4. Ronald W. Richardson, *Polarization and the Healthier Church: Applying Bowen Family Systems Theory to Conflict and Change in Society and Congregational Life* (CreateSpace Independent Publishing Platform, 2012).

5. Edwin H. Friedman, *A Failure of Nerve: Leadership in the Age of the Quick Fix*, ed. Margaret M. Treadwell and Edward W. Beal, 10th anniversary rev. ed. (New York: Church Publishing, 2017), 2.

6. Katharine Gratwick Baker, "Emotional Cutoff and Societal Process: Russia and the Soviet Union as an Example," in *Emotional Cutoff: Bowen Family Systems Theory Perspectives*, ed. Peter Titelman (New York: Routledge, 2003), 384.

7. Karl A. Menninger, *Whatever Became of Sin?* (New York: Hawthorn Books, 1973), 192–203.

8. Murray Bowen, "An Odyssey Toward Science," in *Family Evaluation: An Approach Based on Bowen Theory*, by Michael E. Kerr and Murray Bowen (New York: Norton, 1988), 342–43.

9. Bowen, *Family Therapy*, 378–79.

10. Friedman, *Failure of Nerve*, 4.

11. Friedman, *Failure of Nerve*, 60.

12. Friedman, *Failure of Nerve*, 60.

13. Friedman, *Failure of Nerve*, 89.

14. Murray Bowen, *Defining a Self in One's Family of Origin*, part 2, DVD, vol. 6 of 15 vols., Bowen-Kerr Interview Series (Washington, DC: Bowen Center for the Study of the Family, 1980), http://thebowencenter.org/media/.

15. "Scientific Consensus: Earth's Climate Is Warming," *Climate Change: Vital Signs of the Planet*, https://climate.nasa.gov/scientific-consensus.

16. Bowen, *Family Therapy*, 281.

17. Edward O. Wilson, *The Creation: An Appeal to Save Life on Earth* (New York: Norton, 2006), 5.

18. Wilson, *Creation*, 6.

19. Wilson, *Creation*, 8.

20. Ellen F. Davis, *Scripture, Culture, and Agriculture: An Agrarian Reading of the Bible* (Cambridge: Cambridge University Press, 2009). A growing bibliography of biblically centered ecotheology supports such a focus on creation care. See Fred Bahnson and Norman Wirzba, *Making Peace with the Land: God's Call to Reconcile with Creation* (Downers Grove, IL: InterVarsity, 2012); Richard Bauckham, *The Bible and Ecology: Rediscovering the Community of Creation* (Waco: Baylor University Press, 2010); Bauckham, *Living with Other Creatures: Green Exegesis and Theology* (Waco: Baylor University Press, 2011); Wendell Berry, "The Gift of Good Land," in *The Art of the Commonplace: The Agrarian Essays of Wendell Berry* (Emeryville, CA: Shoemaker & Hoard, 2002), 293–304; Steven Bouma-Prediger, *For the Beauty of the Earth: A Christian Vision for Creation Care*, 2nd ed. (Grand Rapids: Baker Academic, 2010); Pope Francis, *Laudato si': On Care for Our Common Home*, encyclical letter (Huntington, IN: Our Sunday Visitor, 2015); David G. Horrell, *Greening Paul: Rereading the Apostle in a Time of Ecological Crisis* (Waco: Baylor University Press, 2010); Horrell, *Bible and the Environment: Towards a Critical Ecological Biblical Theology* (Oakville, CT: Equinox, 2010); Mark Liederbach and Seth Bible, *True North: Christ, the Gospel, and Creation Care* (Nashville: Broadman & Holman Academic, 2012); Michael G. Maudlin, Marlene Baer, and Alison Petersen, eds., *The Green Bible* (San Francisco: HarperOne, 2008); J. Richard Middleton, *A New Heaven and a New Earth: Reclaiming Biblical Eschatology* (Grand Rapids: Baker Academic, 2014); Jürgen Moltmann, *God in Creation: A New Theology of Creation and the Spirit of God* (Minneapolis: Fortress, 1993); Matthew Sleeth, *The Gospel according to the Earth: Why the Good Book Is a Green Book* (New York: HarperOne, 2010).

21. Wendell Berry, "Christianity and the Survival of Creation," in *The Art of the Commonplace: The Agrarian Essays of Wendell Berry*, ed. Norman Wirzba (Emeryville, CA: Shoemaker & Hoard, 2003), 307–13.

22. Wendell Berry, "The Pleasures of Eating," in Wirzba, *Art of the Commonplace*, 322.

23. Berry, "Pleasures of Eating," 325.

24. Wilson, *Creation*, 12. Richard Louv coined the term "nature-deficit disorder," not as a medical diagnosis but as a way of calling attention to what social and medical research is discovering about the human costs of alienation from nature. Louv, *Last Child in the Woods: Saving Our Children from Nature-Deficit Disorder*, updated and expanded ed. (Chapel Hill, NC: Algonquin Books, 2008).

25. "World's Population Increasingly Urban with More than Half Living in Urban Areas," United Nations Department of Economic and Social Affairs," July 10, 2014, http://www.un.org/en/development/desa/news/population/world-urbanization-prospects-2014.html.

26. Daniel V. Papero, "A GPS for Troubled Times: Nature, Science, and Systems Thinking," presentation given at the Center for the Study of Natural Systems and the Family, El Paso, TX, 2009. A DVD of this presentation is available at https://www.csnsf.org/product/a-gps-for-troubled-times/.

Chapter 5 Proclamation

1. John Stott, "A Definition of Biblical Preaching," *Preaching Today* (newsletter), August 2, 2005, http://www.preachingtoday.com/skills/2005/august/2--stott.html.

2. Ronald E. Osborn, "Functional Definition of Preaching: A Tool for Historical Investigation and Homiletical Criticism," *Encounter* 37, no. 1 (1976): 53–72.

3. Israel Galindo, "What's Systems Theory Got to Do with It? Addressing Congregations' Emotional Processing in Our Preaching," *Congregations* 33, no. 2 (2007): 35.

4. William H. Willimon, *Pastor: The Theology and Practice of Ordained Ministry* (Nashville: Abingdon, 2016), 115.

5. Phillips Brooks, *Lectures on Preaching, Delivered before the Divinity School of Yale College in January and February, 1877* (New York: Dutton, 1877), 8.

6. For a discussion of pastoral affection as an ethical obligation, see Joe E. Trull and R. Robert Creech, *Ethics for Christian Ministry: Moral Formation for Twenty-First-Century Leaders* (Grand Rapids: Baker Academic, 2017), 79–82.

7. Edwin H. Friedman described the herding instinct in a system as "a process through which the forces for togetherness triumph over the forces for individuality and move everyone to adapt to the least mature members." *A Failure of Nerve: Leadership in the Age of the Quick Fix*, ed. Margaret M. Treadwell and Edward W. Beal, 10th anniversary rev. ed. (New York: Church Publishing, 2017), 54.

8. Edwin H. Friedman, *Generation to Generation: Family Process in Church and Synagogue* (New York: Guilford, 1985), 29.

9. Murray Bowen describes life at a "moderate" level of differentiation (25–50 on the scale), where most people, including pastors, would be presumed to fall.

> Lives are relationship oriented, and major life energy goes to loving and being loved, and seeking approval from others. Feelings are more openly expressed than in lower-level people. Life energy is directed more to what others think and to winning friends and approval than to goal-directed activity. Self-esteem is dependent on others. It can soar to heights with a compliment or be crushed by criticism. Success in school is oriented more to learning the system and to pleasing the teacher than to the primary goal of learning. Success in business or in social life depends more on pleasing the boss or the social leader, and more on who one knows and gaining relationship status than in the inherent value of their work. (*Family Therapy in Clinical Practice* [Lanham, MD: Jason Aronson, 1994], 367–68)

10. Bowen notes that the approach of coaching young adults toward differentiation has proved unsuccessful in cases where they remain financially dependent on their parents. "They have the aptitude for quickly understanding family emotional systems, but they lack the courage to risk family displeasure in the differentiation process" (*Family Therapy*, 235).

11. Wendell Berry, *The Hidden Wound* (Boston: Houghton Mifflin, 1970), 19.

12. Berry, *Hidden Wound*, 20–21.

13. Berry, *Hidden Wound*, 22.

14. Dan McBride, a church comedian in the 1960s, offered ministerial advice about this in musical form. *Tiptoe through the Tithers, and Other Good Advice by Dan McBride, M.R.E.* (Fort Worth: CHM Recordings, 1967), https://www.youtube.com/watch?v=5teAb-YtTMk.

15. Bowen, *Family Therapy*, 198.

16. Friedman, *Generation to Generation*, 37.

17. Bowen, *Family Therapy*, 199.

18. Frank A. Thomas approaches African American preaching from the perspective of BFST, analyzing the way in which it has engaged the emotional process of congregations. He identifies five elements that focus preaching on *emotional process* rather than on intellectual content, as most Western Euro-American preaching has done: (1) use of dialogical language, (2) appeal to core belief, (3) concern for emotive movement, (4) unity of form and substance, and (5) creative use of reversals. *They Like to Never Quit Praisin' God: The Role of Celebration in Preaching* (Cleveland: Pilgrim Press, 1997), 4–18.

19. Norman Thomasma, "Utilizing Natural Family Systems Theory to Foster Health in Congregations: Murray Bowen as Teacher of Congregations," *Reformed Review* 58, no. 2 (2005): 122, https://repository.westernsem.edu/pkp/index.php/rr/article/view/1520/1752.

20. Such requests imply not curiosity about what the pastor thinks on the matter but a demand for the preacher to tell everyone else how to think about the issue—namely, to proclaim the opinions of requesting members.

21. James E. Lamkin, "Systems Theory and Congregational Leadership: Leaves from an Alchemist's Journal," *Review & Expositor* 102, no. 3 (Summer 2005): 471 (emphasis original).

22. Murray Bowen, "An Odyssey Toward Science," in *Family Evaluation: An Approach Based on Bowen Theory*, by Michael E. Kerr and Murray Bowen (New York: Norton, 1988), 342–43.

23. Galindo, "What's Systems Theory Got to Do with It?," 33.

24. Reinhold Niebuhr, *The Nature and Destiny of Man: A Christian Interpretation* (Louisville: Westminster John Knox, 1996), 2:194; Calvin Miller, *Preaching: The Art of Narrative Exposition* (Grand Rapids: Baker Books, 2010), 41.

25. For a discussion of ethical issues surrounding plagiarism in preaching, see Trull and Creech, *Ethics for Christian Ministry*, 90–91.

26. Friedman suggests that preaching a sermon on a controversial subject is a way to assess the level of differentiation of one's congregation.

> All we have to do is give a talk in which we carefully differentiate ourselves—define clearly what we believe and where we stand on issues, in a way that is totally devoid of "shoulds" and "musts." The response of the congregational family, no matter what the faith, will always range along the following spectrum. Those who function emotionally toward the "better differentiated" end will respond by defining themselves: "Father, I agree"; "I disagree"; "I believe," etc.; or, "Ms. Jones, I like what you said, though I am not sure I can agree with you on . . ." Those at the "less well-differentiated" end will respond not by defining themselves but by continuing to define their clergyman or clergywoman: "Father, how can you say that when . . . "; "Ms. Smith, how do you reconcile this with what you said the other day when you . . . "; "Rabbi, sometimes I wonder if you are even Jewish." (*Generation to Generation*, 30)

27. Margaret Marcuson, "How to Preach Sermons That Make People Wiggle and Keep Your Job," *Margaret Marcuson* (blog), May 5, 2016, https://margaretmarcuson.com/sermons-that-make-people/.

28. Bowen described healthy emotional systems as being more "open." "An 'open' relationship system is one in which an individual is free to communicate a high percentage of inner thoughts, feelings, and fantasies to another who can reciprocate. No one ever has a completely open relationship with another, but it is a healthy state when a person can have one relationship in which a reasonable degree of openness is possible" (*Family Therapy*, 322).

29. Galindo provides a helpful table outlining the possible intersections between BFST and the functions of the pastoral sermon ("What's Systems Theory Got to Do with It?," 35).

Chapter 6 Pastoral Care

1. James Boyer offers BFST as a means of connecting to the emotional system of another person (heart) while simultaneously remaining outside it (mind). See his "Pastoral Care Triage: Bowen Theory and Leading with the Heart and Mind," in *Leadership in Ministry: Bowen*

Theory in the Congregational Context, ed. Israel Galindo (North Charleston, SC: CreateSpace / Didache Press, 2017).

2. William H. Willimon, *Pastor: The Theology and Practice of Ordained Ministry*, rev. ed. (Nashville: Abingdon, 2016), 61.

3. Willimon, *Pastor*, 60.

4. Flannery O'Connor, *The Habit of Being: Letters of Flannery O'Connor*, ed. Sally Fitzgerald (New York: Farrar, Straus & Giroux, 1988), 81.

5. Willimon, *Pastor*, 91.

6. Pastors should consider the extent of the boundaries of their pastoral care. Are pastors called to shepherd their flock, or does the entire community have some claim on them? We can easily become the community chaplain, responding to every pastoral care need in the neighborhood rather than fulfilling our full pastoral responsibilities to our congregations, which include preaching and leadership in addition to care. Less-well-differentiated pastors might find the incoming calls for help to be affirming, but maturity might call for us to exercise some discernment about which calls we respond to and which we find a way to delegate or refer. Even Jesus seemed to have drawn some boundaries on his ministry that he crossed only on occasion (Matt. 15:24).

7. David K. Switzer, *Pastoral Care Emergencies* (Minneapolis: Fortress, 2000), 13 (emphasis original).

8. Willimon, *Pastor*, 91.

9. Eugene H. Peterson, *The Contemplative Pastor: Returning to the Art of Spiritual Direction* (Grand Rapids: Eerdmans, 1993), 112.

10. Peterson, *Contemplative Pastor*, 65.

11. Wayne L. Menking, *When All Else Fails: Rethinking Our Pastoral Vocation in Times of Stuck* (Eugene, OR: Wipf & Stock, 2013), 26.

12. Switzer, *Pastoral Care Emergencies*, 20.

13. Steve Corbett and Brian Fikkert, *When Helping Hurts: How to Alleviate Poverty without Hurting the Poor . . . and Yourself* (Chicago: Moody, 2014).

14. Church consultant Margaret Marcuson has explored the idea of "invasive helping" in an unpublished paper presented to the Boston Theological Circle on October 6, 1997, titled "May I Help You? A Reflection on Bowen Family Systems Theory and Christian Ethics."

15. Willimon, *Pastor*, 60.

16. Edwin H. Friedman, *A Failure of Nerve: Leadership in the Age of the Quick Fix*, ed. Margaret M. Treadwell and Edward W. Beal, 10th anniversary rev. ed. (New York: Church Publishing, 2017), 133.

17. For this distinction, Menking relies on an article by Arthur J. Clark, "Empathy and Sympathy: Therapeutic Distinctions in Counseling," *Journal of Mental Health Counseling* 32, no. 2 (April 2010): 95–101.

18. Menking, *When All Else Fails*, 12.

19. Menking, *When All Else Fails*, 24–26.

20. Quoted in Willimon, *Pastor*, 60.

21. Willimon, *Pastor*, 108.

22. Murray Bowen, "An Odyssey Toward Science," in *Family Evaluation: An Approach Based on Bowen Theory*, by Michael E. Kerr and Murray Bowen (New York: Norton, 1988), 343.

23. Henri J. M. Nouwen, *The Wounded Healer: Ministry in Contemporary Society* (Garden City, NY: Image Books, 1979).

24. Switzer, *Pastoral Care Emergencies*, 20–21 (emphasis original).

Chapter 7 Spiritual Formation

1. Howard W. Stone and James O. Duke, *How to Think Theologically*, 2nd ed. (Minneapolis: Fortress, 2006), 127.

2. Dallas Willard's primary works in the area of spiritual formation include the following: *Hearing God: Developing a Conversational Relationship with God* (Downers Grove, IL: InterVarsity, 1983); *The Spirit of the Disciplines: Understanding How God Changes Lives* (San Francisco: HarperSanFrancisco, 1990); *The Divine Conspiracy: Rediscovering Our Hidden Life in God* (San Francisco: HarperSanFrancisco, 1998); *Renovation of the Heart: Putting On the Character of Christ* (Colorado Springs: NavPress, 2002); *The Great Omission: Reclaiming Jesus's Essential Teachings on Discipleship* (New York: HarperOne, 2007); and *Knowing Christ Today: Why We Can Trust Spiritual Knowledge* (New York: HarperOne, 2009). Additional bibliography including many of Willard's articles and lectures can be found at http://www.dwillard.org.

3. Willard, *Renovation of the Heart*, 19.

4. Willard, *Renovation of the Heart*, 22. While acknowledging Willard's distinction between the spiritual formation that all people undergo and the specifically Christian spiritual formation that seeks conformity to the character of Christ, I will use the terms "formation" or "spiritual formation" from this point only in reference to Christian spiritual formation.

5. Willard, *Great Omission*, 80.

6. Willard, *Divine Conspiracy*, 347–48.

7. Other authors categorize the classical disciplines in distinctive ways. Richard J. Foster separates them into inward disciplines (meditation, prayer, fasting, study), outward disciplines (simplicity, solitude, submission, service), and corporate disciplines (confession, worship, guidance, celebration). *Celebration of Discipline: The Path to Spiritual Growth* (San Francisco: Harper & Row, 1978).

Eugene H. Peterson regards the study of the Word of God, the practice of common worship, the praying of daily psalms, and recollected prayer (personal prayer) as the essential spiritual practices. He lists fourteen other disciplines that he regards as tools to be used as needed in our formation: spiritual reading, spiritual direction, meditation, confession, bodily exercise, fasting, Sabbath-keeping, dream interpretation, retreats, pilgrimage, almsgiving or tithing, journaling, sabbaticals, and small groups. *Under the Unpredictable Plant: An Exploration in Vocational Holiness* (Grand Rapids: Eerdmans, 1992), 108–10.

Douglas J. Rumford identifies twenty spiritual practices and organizes them functionally, based on the role each plays in our formation. He groups them as practices that help us grow in our awareness of God's presence (repentance, confession, preview, review, prayer, worship), practices that shape an eternal perspective in our minds (Bible study, meditation, spiritual reading), practices that break the power of evil in our lives (fasting, silence, solitude, battling temptation, prayer for spiritual battle), and practices that help us align our lives with God's purpose in the world (building character, building relationships, spiritual direction, spiritual friendship, stewardship, spiritual service through spiritual gifts). *SoulShaping* (Wheaton, IL: Tyndale House, 1996).

8. Willard, *Divine Conspiracy*, 417–18n18.

9. Joan Chittister, *The Rule of Benedict: A Spirituality for the 21st Century* (New York: Crossroad, 2010), 26.

10. Willard, *Spirit of the Disciplines*, 8–9.

11. Willard, *Renovation of the Heart*, 83–91.

12. Leroy T. Howe, "Self-Differentiation in Christian Perspective," *Pastoral Psychology* 46, no. 5 (May 1998): 347–62.

13. Willard, *Renovation of the Heart*, 159 (emphasis original).

14. Willard, *Renovation of the Heart*, 162.

15. Willard, *Spirit of the Disciplines*, 84–85.

16. "The spiritual and the bodily are by no means opposed in human life—they are complementary. We here explicitly disown and condemn any suggestion to the contrary, because it is the spiritual life alone that makes possible fulfillment of bodily existence—and hence human existence." Willard, *Spirit of the Disciplines*, 75–76.

17. See chap. 6 of Willard, *Spirit of the Disciplines*, "Spiritual Life: The Body's Fulfillment," 75–94.

18. Murray Bowen, *Family Therapy in Clinical Practice* (Lanham, MD: Jason Aronson, 1994), 407.

19. Willard says,

> Somewhat ironically, perhaps, *all* of the "spiritual" disciplines are, or essentially involve, bodily behaviors. But really, that makes perfect sense. For the body is the first field of energy beyond our thoughts that we have direction over, and all else we influence is due to our power over it. Moreover, it is the chief repository of the wrong habits that we must set aside, as well as the place where new habits are to be instituted. We are, within limits, able to command it to do things that will transform our habits—especially the inner habits of thought and feeling—and so enable us to do things not now in our power. (*Divine Conspiracy*, 353–54, emphasis original)

20. Bowen, *Family Therapy*, 371.

21. Bowen, *Family Therapy*, 202.

22. Bowen, *Family Therapy*, 436.

23. See the final three chapters in *Family Therapy*: "Toward the Differentiation of Self in Administrative Systems" (461–66), "On the Differentiation of Self" (467–528), and "Toward the Differentiation of Self in One's Family of Origin" (529–46).

24. Bowen, *Family Therapy*, 539.

25. Bowen, *Family Therapy*, 540.

26. Bowen, *Family Therapy*, 541.

27. Bowen, *Family Therapy*, 542.

28. Murray Bowen, *Defining a Self in One's Family of Origin*, part 2, DVD, vol. 6 of 15 vols., Bowen-Kerr Interview Series (Washington, DC: Bowen Center for the Study of the Family, 1980), http://thebowencenter.org/media/.

29. Bowen, *Family Therapy*, 371.

30. Willard, *Renovation of the Heart*, 126.

31. Willard, *Renovation of the Heart*, 127.

32. Peter J. Jankowski and Marsha Vaughn, "Differentiation of Self and Spirituality: Empirical Explorations," *Counseling and Values* 53, no. 2 (January 2009): 82–96; on 95–96 see the extensive bibliography on studies related to BFST and spirituality.

33. Louise Rauseo, "The Mystic and Differentiation of Self" (unpublished paper, Wisdom of the Ages Conference, Houston, 1998), 1. Rauseo expanded her work on mystics and differentiation in a recent pair of articles. See Louise Rauseo, "Mystics: On Being Human and Being a Self, Part I," *Family Systems Forum* 18, no. 4 (Winter 2016): 3–11; and "Mystics: On Being Human and Being a Self, Part II," *Family Systems Forum* 19, no. 1 (Spring 2017): 3–10.

34. Doug Hester, "Differentiation of Self and Spirituality" (unpublished paper, The Facts of Life, Houston, 2000), 7.

35. Willard, *Spirit of the Disciplines*, 76.

36. Willard, *Spirit of the Disciplines*, 86.

37. Willard, *Renovation of the Heart*, 134 (emphasis original).

38. Bowen, *Family Therapy*, 361–62.

39. Willard, *Renovation of the Heart*, 134. Victoria Harrison has studied the impact of contemplative prayer practices on levels of anxiety by using biofeedback equipment and has identified a positive connection between prayer and decreased levels of anxiety in her subjects; see her "Prayer and Emotional Reactivity," in *The Cornerstone Concept: In Leadership, in Life*, by Roberta M. Gilbert (Falls Church, VA: Leading Systems, 2008), 191–206.

40. Jannel Glennie affirms a strong connection between BFST and these spiritual practices.

> It seems to me that the spiritual disciplines serve the same purpose as the eight Bowen Concepts. Both models give form and substance to essential yet complex, challenging

human relations and then can be extended to broader—even cosmic—dimensions. Both systems are hard to maintain in the midst of so many other superficial quick solutions and societal norms. Both require stamina, resilience and a willingness to change. Both provide roots and boundaries for the persistent practitioner that stabilizes life and brings joy and humor with it. And both produce fruit that benefits those around us. Both are meant to set one free. Both promote health and a less fearful, less anxious life. ("Connecting Bowen Natural Systems Theory to an Intentional Spiritual Life, or, How Does the 9th Concept Fit?" [unpublished paper, Advanced Clergy Clinic in Family Emotional Process, Lombard Mennonite Peace Center, Chicago, 2012], 15–160)

41. Rauseo, "The Mystic and Differentiation of Self," 1.

42. Willard, *Divine Conspiracy*, 353.

Chapter 8 Christian Community

1. Scot McKnight, *The Jesus Creed: Loving God, Loving Others* (Brewster, MA: Paraclete, 2014).

2. This truth became a principle for John Wesley. According to Augustine Birrell, "Wesley's motive never eludes us. In his early manhood, after being greatly affected by Jeremy Taylor's *Holy Living and Dying* and the *Imitatio Christi*, and by Law's *Serious Call* and *Christian Perfection*, he met 'a serious man' who said to him, 'Sir, you wish to serve God and go to heaven. Remember you cannot serve Him alone. You must therefore find companions or make them. The Bible knows nothing of solitary religion.'" *Journal of John Wesley*, Christian Classics Ethereal Library, https://www.ccel.org/ccel/wesley/journal.iv.html.

3. Henri J. M. Nouwen, *The Way of the Heart: Connecting with God Through Prayer, Wisdom, and Silence* (San Francisco: HarperSanFrancisco, 1991), 20.

4. Mark 9:50; John 13:34–35; 15:12, 17; Rom. 12:10, 16; 13:8; 14:13, 19; 15:5, 7, 14; 1 Cor. 6:7; 7:5; 11:33; 12:25; Gal. 5:13, 15, 26; Eph. 4:2, 25, 32; 5:19, 21; Phil. 2:3; Col. 3:9, 13, 16; 1 Thess. 3:12; 4:9, 18; 5:11, 13, 15; 2 Thess. 1:3; Heb. 3:13; 10:24–25; James 4:11; 5:9, 16; 1 Pet. 1:22; 4:8–10; 5:5, 14; 1 John 1:7; 3:11, 23; 4:7, 11–12; 2 John 5.

5. Matt. 5:21–26; 6:12–16 (cf. Mark 11:25–26); 18:21–35; Luke 17:3–5; 23:34; 2 Cor. 2:7–10; Eph. 4:32; Col. 3:13.

6. Miroslav Volf, *Free of Charge: Giving and Forgiving in a Culture Stripped of Grace* (Grand Rapids: Zondervan, 2006), 181.

7. L. Gregory Jones calls this "cheap forgiveness," since it is rooted not in the costly grace of the cross, but in the therapeutic culture. L. Gregory Jones and Célestin Musekura, *Forgiving as We've Been Forgiven: Community Practices for Making Peace*, Resources for Reconciliation (Downers Grove, IL: InterVarsity, 2010), 41.

8. For a thorough theological discussion of what it means for God to forgive us in Christ and for the believer to receive God's forgiveness, see L. Gregory Jones, *Embodying Forgiveness: A Theological Analysis* (Grand Rapids: Eerdmans, 1995), 101–62; Volf, *Free of Charge*, 127–56.

9. Jones, *Embodying Forgiveness*, 163.

10. Jones, *Embodying Forgiveness*, 163–204.

11. Volf, *Free of Charge*, 189–90.

12. Frederick William Danker et al., *A Greek-English Lexicon of the New Testament and Other Early Christian Literature* (Chicago: University of Chicago Press, 2000), 156.

13. Volf, *Free of Charge*, 162.

14. Volf, *Free of Charge*, 130.

15. Richard J. Foster, *Prayer: Finding the Heart's True Home* (San Francisco: HarperOne, 2002), 188.

16. Elisabeth Elliot, *Love Has a Price Tag* (Ventura, CA: Regal Books, 2005), 68.

17. Murray Bowen, *Family Therapy in Clinical Practice* (Lanham, MD: Jason Aronson, 1978), 382.

18. Peter Titelman, ed., *Emotional Cutoff: Bowen Family Systems Theory Perspectives* (Binghamton, NY: Hayworth, 2003), 52–57.

19. Titelman explains, "In order to bridge emotional cutoff, not just make perfunctory or formalized contact with family members from whom one is cut off, one must define self in the extended family [by] using three main principles and techniques: (1) working toward person-to-person relationship; (2) becoming a better observer and managing one's own emotional reactiveness; and (3) detriangling self in emotional situations." He also recommends gathering family history, meeting unknown family members, expanding contact and visits with extended family members and members of the family of origin, and attending important family events such as weddings, funerals, and graduations (*Emotional Cutoff*, 54).

20. Bowen, *Family Therapy*, 540.

21. Elliot, *Love Has a Price Tag*, 72.

Chapter 9 Bowen Family Systems Theory and Biblical Interpretation

1. For a thorough approach to biblical hermeneutics from an evangelical perspective, see Grant R. Osborne, *The Hermeneutical Spiral: A Comprehensive Introduction to Biblical Interpretation*, rev. ed. (Downers Grove, IL: IVP Academic, 2007).

2. The Society of Biblical Literature has had a scholarly group devoted to psychology and biblical studies for over twenty years. See Walter Brueggemann, "Psychological Criticism: Exploring the Self in the Text," in *Method Matters: Essays on the Interpretation of the Hebrew Bible in Honor of David L. Petersen*, ed. David L. Petersen, Joel M. LeMon, and Kent Harold Richards, Resources for Biblical Study 56 (Atlanta: Society of Biblical Literature, 2009), 213–32; J. Harold Ellens, Donald Capps, and Wayne G. Rollins, eds., *Psychology and the Bible*, 4 vols. (Westport, CT: Praeger, 2004); J. Harold Ellens, "The Bible and Psychology: An Interdisciplinary Pilgrimage," *Pastoral Psychology* 45, no. 3 (January 1997): 193–208; M. Scott Fletcher, *The Psychology of the New Testament*, 2nd ed. (New York: Hodder & Stoughton, 1912); D. Andrew Kille, *Psychological Biblical Criticism*, Guides to Biblical Scholarship: Old Testament Series (Minneapolis: Fortress, 2001); Wayne G. Rollins and D. Andrew Kille, eds., *Psychological Insight into the Bible: Texts and Readings* (Grand Rapids: Eerdmans, 2007); Wayne G. Rollins, "Psychology, Hermeneutics, and the Bible," in *Jung and the Interpretation of the Bible*, ed. David LeRoy Miller (New York: Continuum, 1995), 9–39; Rollins, "Rationale and Agenda for a Psychological-Critical Approach to the Bible and Its Interpretation," in *Biblical and Humane: A Festschrift for John F. Priest*, ed. John F. Priest et al., Scholars Press Homage Series 20 (Atlanta: Scholars Press, 1996), 153–72; Rollins, "The Bible and Psychology: New Directions in Biblical Scholarship," *Pastoral Psychology* 45, no. 3 (1997): 163–79.

3. Kamila Blessing, "Murray Bowen's Family Systems Theory as Bible Hermeneutic Illustrated Using the Family of the Prodigal Son," *Journal of Psychology and Christianity* 19, no. 1 (Spring 2000): 38–46; Blessing, "Differentiation in the Family of Faith: The Prodigal Son and Galatians 1–2," in *Psychology and the Bible: A New Way to Read the Scriptures*, vol. 3, *From Gospel to Gnostics*, ed. J. Harold Ellens and Wayne G. Rollins, Praeger Perspectives: Psychology, Religion, and Spirituality (Westport, CT: Praeger, 2004), 165–91; Blessing, "Family Systems Psychology as Hermeneutic," in *Psychology and the Bible*, vol. 1, *From Freud to Kohut* (Westport, CT: Praeger, 2004), 185–207; Blessing, *Families of the Bible: A New Perspective*, Psychology, Religion, and Spirituality (Santa Barbara, CA: Praeger, 2010).

4. Blessing, *Families of the Bible*, 207.

5. Murray Bowen, *Family Therapy in Clinical Practice* (Lanham, MD: Jason Aronson, 1978), 423.

6. Note the deliberate omission of the "why" question. This question for Bowen was too subjective to be considered a "fact" of human behavior (*Family Therapy*, 261).

7. Brueggemann, "Psychological Criticism," 15.

8. Others such as Edwin H. Friedman have applied this concept to impersonal subjects as well. See Friedman, *Generation to Generation: Family Process in Church and Synagogue* (New York: Guilford, 1985), 35.

9. American Psychiatric Association, *Diagnostic and Statistical Manual of Mental Disorders*, 5th ed. (Washington, DC: American Psychiatric Publishing, 2013), 298.

10. Other examples of Blessing's departure from BFST can be mentioned: Bowen's "Scale of Differentiation of Self" becomes Blessing's "Differentiation Continuum" (*Families of the Bible*, 40); the term "manifest level of differentiation" (40) is introduced, apparently as a synonym for "pseudo-self." She describes Bowen's concepts of "Family Projection Process" and "Multigenerational Transmission Process" as the way families pass their family emotional system on to their children or to other generations (206). Bowen used Family Projection Process to describe how a family "picks out" a child to focus on, projecting their anxiety onto that one, resulting in that child's being a bit more dependent, a bit less differentiated than his or her siblings (*Family Therapy*, 127–31). Multigenerational Transmission Process describes how that projection process plays out over several generations, resulting in branches of the family tree that are much more or much less well-differentiated (168–69). Blessing turns Bowen's eight "concepts" into eight "characteristics" (*Families of the Bible*, 207).

11. Israel Galindo, "On BFST Orthodoxy," *Perspectives on Congregational Leadership* (blog), March 16, 2011, http://perspectivesig.blogspot.com/2011/.

Chapter 10 Mapping the Family of Abraham

1. This study will not attend to the historical issues related to these accounts, such as how they were preserved, their historical setting, or their value as historical materials. Neither will we focus on the literary features of these narratives, such as characters, plot, and themes. Instead we are looking at these as accounts of human behavior—how the emotional system of this family over several generations is described in behavioral terms. The questions we ask are "Who?" "What?" "When?" "Where?" and "How?" The stories will simply be taken at face value in their canonical form, without regard to theories of their origin, preservation, or redaction along the way.

2. As the story opens, the main character is named Abram and his wife, Sarai. In Gen. 17:1–16 their names are changed to Abraham and Sarah. The significance of the name change involves a play on the Hebrew words. Abram means "exalted father," while Abraham means "father of a multitude." Sarai has her name changed to Sarah, but both are forms of a word for princess. To avoid confusion, the names Abraham and Sarah will be used regardless of the place in the story to which they refer.

3. Victoria Harrison, "Patterns of Ovulation, Reactivity, and Family Emotional Process," *Annals of the New York Academy of Sciences* 807, no. 1 (January 1, 1997): 522–24; Harrison, "Bowen Theory and the Study of Reproduction and Evolution," *Family Systems Forum* 5, no. 3 (Fall 2003): 5.

4. The recurrence of childlessness as a symptom in the patriarchal stories will be taken up later in this chapter.

5. "The basic building block of any emotional system is the 'triangle.' When emotional tension in a two-person system exceeds a certain level, it 'triangles' a third person, permitting the tension to shift about within the triangle. Any two in the original triangle can add a new triangle. An emotional system is composed of a series of interlocking triangles. The emotional tension system can shift to any of the old preestablished circuits." Murray Bowen, *Family Therapy in Clinical Practice* (Lanham, MD: Jason Aronson, 1978), 174.

6. God is identified as "the God of . . . Abraham" (Gen. 24:12, 27, 42, 48; 26:24). To Jacob he is the God of Abraham and Isaac (28:13; 31:42, 53; 32:9; 48:15). To Joseph and his brothers, he is the God of Abraham, Isaac, and Jacob (50:24). This identity continues in the theological

tradition of Israel (Exod. 2:24; 3:6, 15, 16; 4:5; 6:3, 8; 32:13; 33:1; Lev. 26:42; Num. 32:11; Deut. 1:8; 6:10; 9:5, 27; 29:13; 30:20; 34:4; 1 Kings 18:36; 2 Kings 13:23; 1 Chron. 29:18; 2 Chron. 30:6).

7. Although not to be identified as an emotional process as much as a literary theme, the stories also contain repeated accounts of people deceiving and being deceived by disguise or by clothing. Jacob deceives Isaac with Esau's clothing (Gen. 27:1–40). Laban deceives Jacob by presenting him with Leah, veiled, rather than Rachel (29:15–27). Jacob's sons deceive their father with Joseph's bloody coat (37:29–35). Tamar deceives Judah by dressing as a prostitute (38:12–30). Joseph deceives his brothers by dressing and speaking as an Egyptian (42:6–8; 45:1–3).

8. Bowen began to describe the concepts of his theory as "interlocking" as early as 1963 (*Family Therapy*, 358).

9. Bowen acknowledged Walter Toman's study (*Family Constellation: Its Effects on Personality and Social Behavior*, 3rd ed. [New York: Springer, 1976]) of the effect of the projection process on a child, which could affect the way the constellation of siblings functioned and could change the functioning of one or more of the children. Bowen said: "The original profiles were developed from the study of 'normal' families. They are remarkably close to the observations in this research, except [that] Toman did not include the predictable ways that profiles are skewed by the family projection process. Knowledge gained from Toman, as modified in this concept, provides important clues in predicting areas of family strength and weakness for family therapy. This is so important [that] it has been included as a separate concept" (*Family Therapy*, 308).

10. Bowen, *Family Therapy*, 382.

11. See David E. Garland and Diana R. Garland, *Flawed Families of the Bible: How God's Grace Works through Imperfect Relationships* (Grand Rapids: Brazos, 2007).

Chapter 11 Mapping the Character of Jesus

1. Murray Bowen, *Family Therapy in Clinical Practice* (Lanham, MD: Jason Aronson, 1994), 472.

2. Bowen writes, however, "In considering the over-all scale, it is essentially impossible for anyone to have all the characteristics I would assign to 100" (*Family Therapy*, 164).

3. Note the way Luke inserts the genealogy of Jesus between the accounts of his baptism and his temptation in the wilderness (Luke 3:21–4:13). In each of the three passages—the baptismal narrative, the genealogy, and the temptation narrative—the phrase "my Son" or "son/Son of God" appears. Luke uses the genealogy to define what he means by the phrase "son of Enos, son of Seth, son of Adam, son of God" (3:38). Jesus is the new Adam, the Son of God, who receives God's blessing (v. 22) and successfully faces off against the tempter (4:13). Luke, a fellow worker of Paul, may have learned his second/new/last Adam theology from the apostle, who developed that concept as part of his soteriology and his eschatology (Rom. 5:12–21; 1 Cor. 15:20–28, 45–49). The writer of Hebrews also reflects a second-Adam Christology (Heb. 2:5–9).

4. John W. Miller's extensive psychohistorical study of Jesus from the perspective of Freudian developmental psychology depends on a presumed knowledge of Jesus's early life even more than does a study from a family systems perspective. Miller makes a valiant effort to derive as much information as possible from the Gospel texts. See Miller, *Jesus at Thirty: A Psychological and Historical Portrait* (Minneapolis: Fortress, 1997), 32–41.

5. For a recent scholarly evaluation of the Gospels as reliable testimony to the life of Jesus, see Richard Bauckham, *Jesus and the Eyewitnesses: The Gospels as Eyewitness Testimony* (Grand Rapids: Eerdmans, 2017).

6. N. T. Wright regards discerning the psychology of Jesus (or Abraham or David or Paul, for that matter) as "impossible." He says, "After all, as pastors, psychiatrists and psychotherapists know, it is hard enough to understand the inner workings of someone's psyche (even supposing we could define such a thing with any precision) when they share one's own culture and language, and when they co-operate with the process and answer one's questions. How much

harder when none of these things are the case." *Jesus and the Victory of God*, 3rd ed. (Minneapolis: Fortress, 1997), 479.

7. If Joseph had chosen to disgrace Mary, charging her with adultery, she could have been subjected to a public stoning (Lev. 20:10; Deut. 22:23–24; Matt. 1:19; John 8:1–11).

8. The question of Jesus's relationship to his siblings remains in debate (François Rossier, "The 'Brothers' and 'Sisters' of Jesus: Anything New?," *Marian Studies* 58 [2007]: 101–14). Some Roman Catholic scholars have concluded that Jesus's siblings were in fact children born to the union of Joseph and Mary after Jesus's birth—the "Helvidian" view (John P. Meier, "The Brothers and Sisters of Jesus in Ecumenical Perspective," *Catholic Biblical Quarterly* 54 [1992]: 1–28). At the same time, a Protestant historian, Richard Bauckham, finds himself more persuaded by the "Epiphanian" view that the siblings were the children of Joseph by a previous marriage ("The Brothers and Sisters of Jesus: An Epiphanian Response to John P Meier," *The Catholic Biblical Quarterly* 56, no. 4 [October 1994]: 686–700). Most Protestant scholars espouse the Helvidian view. Most Roman Catholic interpreters support either the Epiphanian view or the Hieronymian view (that those called "brothers" and "sisters" were cousins rather than siblings), since these perspectives are consistent with the doctrine of Mary's perpetual virginity. I join the majority of Protestant readers in understanding these siblings to be children of Mary and Joseph.

9. Miller argues that it is the mother who engenders confidence and "trust" in a son, ultimately releasing him from herself so that he can pursue an increasingly important relationship with his father. Miller observes evidence of the way in which, by the time Jesus is an adult, he and his mother have successfully resolved the emotional attachment, resulting in his deep capacity to live with trust in God. "In any case," he writes, "there is ample evidence for asserting that one of the outstanding characteristics of the *adult* Jesus was the evocative power of his faith (trust) and an equally remarkable capacity for uninhibited, autonomous action" (*Jesus at Thirty*, 51).

10. Miller places enormous weight on the significance of Joseph's life and death on Jesus (*Jesus at Thirty*, 31–45).

11. Miller notes that Joseph's death would have meant that Jesus, following his father's trade, would have been the chief means of financial support for the family. The emotional, social, and spiritual leadership of the family would have gravitated to him as well (*Jesus at Thirty*, 52–53).

12. Miller, from a Freudian developmental perspective, hypothesizes that Mary, having to cope with the loss of her husband, likely began to depend increasingly on the resourcefulness of her eldest son. When Jesus does leave home, choosing God over family, he makes a break with the "network of pseudo-obligations in which his life to this point has been enmeshed." So, when the break occurs, the strong reactivity of his family is understandable (Mark 3:19–21) (*Jesus at Thirty*, 53).

13. The term "Synoptics" in biblical studies refers to the first three Gospels in the New Testament: Matthew, Mark, and Luke. They are Synoptics because they tend to view the life of Jesus in a similar though not identical manner. Some degree of literary dependency exists among these three writings. Efforts to explain that dependency address what is known as the "Synoptic problem." For many years, the most widely accepted theory has been that Mark wrote first (the priority of Mark) and became a source for both Matthew and Luke. Interpreters think Matthew and Luke used another source in common, referred to as "Q" (for the German *Quelle*, or "source"). They believe this hypothetical source to consist primarily of sayings of Jesus. Additionally, both Matthew and Luke have material unique to themselves, indicating that other sources were available to them as well. Alternatively, some have argued for the priority of Matthew, who then became a source for Luke. Mark then produced his Gospel last as a kind of condensed version of the other two. Biblical scholars continue to investigate these issues. In contrast to the Synoptics, the Gospel of John is often referred to as "the Fourth Gospel" because it represents a perspective and a set of traditions independent of the other three.

14. For the Davidic hope, see 2 Sam. 7:1–17; Pss. 89; 132; Isa. 9:6–7; 11:1–16; 32:1–2; Jer. 33:20–22; Ezek. 34:22–24; 37:24–28; Hosea 3:4–5; Amos 9:11–12; Mic. 5:2–5; Zech. 9:9–10. The suffering servant poems are found in Isa. 42:1–4; 49:1–6; 50:4–9; 52:13–53:12.

15. For helpful theological treatments of Jesus's wilderness temptations, see Donald B. Kraybill, *The Upside-Down Kingdom*, 5th ed. (Harrisonburg, VA: Herald Press, 2011), 33–83; and Henri J. M. Nouwen, *In the Name of Jesus: Reflections on Christian Leadership* (New York: Crossroad, 1992). For a psychological perspective on that experience, see Miller, *Jesus at Thirty*, 55–64.

16. Although the Gospel of John does not contain an account of the temptations as found in the Synoptics, these same temptations recur throughout the story in the Fourth Gospel. See Raymond E. Brown, "Incidents That Are Units in the Synoptic Gospels but Dispersed in St. John," *Catholic Biblical Quarterly* 23, no. 2 (April 1961): 152–55.

17. Miller, *Jesus at Thirty*, 53. See note 10 above.

18. When Murray Bowen describes the differentiation process in a nuclear family, it sounds much like this experience in Jesus's family. The family system is also disturbed when any family member moves toward a slightly higher level of differentiation, and it will counter automatically to restore the family system to its former equilibrium. Thus, any small step toward differentiation is accompanied by a small emotional upheaval in the family system. This pattern is so predictable that absence of an emotional reaction is good evidence that the differentiating effort was not successful. There are three predictable steps in the family reaction to differentiation: (1) "You are wrong," or some version of that; (2) "Change back," which can be communicated in many different ways; and (3) "If you do not, these are the consequences." If the differentiating one can stay on course without defending self or counterattacking, the emotional reaction is usually brief, and the other then expresses appreciation (Bowen, *Family Therapy*, 495).

19. According to Martin Copenhaver, Jesus asked 307 questions in the Gospel accounts, while being asked 183 and only answering 3. See *Jesus Is the Question: The 307 Questions Jesus Asked and the 3 He Answered* (Nashville: Abingdon, 2014).

20. Andreas J. Köstenberger, *Encountering John: The Gospel in Historical, Literary, and Theological Perspective* (Grand Rapids: Baker Academic, 2002), 35–36.

21. In fact, people in the Fourth Gospel know little about Jesus's background (John 7:15, 27, 42, 52). He is the "son of Joseph from Nazareth" (1:45). His mother (unnamed in this Gospel) is present at a wedding in Cana of Galilee and witnesses his crucifixion (2:1–11; 19:25–27). Jesus has several brothers, also unnamed (2:12; 7:3–5, 10). Other than this, his background is a mystery.

22. Miller sees a tension in Jesus's relationship with Mary that reveals itself in her anxious seeking to "restrain" him (Mark 3:19–21), in his addressing her at the wedding (John 2:4) and from the cross (19:26) as "Woman" rather than "Mother," and in the fact that mothers do not appear explicitly in Jesus's teaching (John 3:4 is an implicit reference) or parables even though fathers do. In the few parables in which women do appear, they do not do so in their role as mother (Miller, *Jesus at Thirty*, 48–49).

On the one hand, the Gospel of John never refers to her as "Mary." She is "the mother of Jesus," which sounds more like a respectful title. Raymond Brown argues that the Johannine community seemed fond of using such titles for its leaders: "the Disciple Jesus Loved," "the Elder," "the Elect Lady" (Brown, *The Epistles of John*, Anchor Bible 30 [Garden City, NY: Doubleday, 1982], 647). What may seem like distance in Jesus's relationship with his mother in the Fourth Gospel may reflect more the esteem of the community to whom Jesus entrusted her from the cross (John 19:25–27). On the other hand, the expression "Woman" may have been a respectful address placed on Jesus's lips by the Gospel writer.

23. N. T. Wright, *How God Became King: The Forgotten Story of the Gospels* (New York: HarperOne, 2012).

24. Raymond E. Brown, *The Gospel according to John I–XII*, Anchor Bible 29 (Garden City, NY: Doubleday, 1966), cx, 535.

25. R. Robert Creech, "Christology and Conflict: A Comparative Study of Two Central Themes in the Johannine Literature and the Apocalypse" (PhD diss., Baylor University, 1984), 88–89.

26. Bowen, *Family Therapy*, 472.

Chapter 12 Mapping the Teaching of Paul

1. Werner Georg Kümmel, *Römer 7 und die Bekehrung des Paulus*, Untersuchungen zum Neuen Testament 17 (Leipzig: J. C. Hinrichs, 1929; repr., Lexington, KY: American Theological Library Association, 1965).

2. For a thorough review of the state of the question, see Ben Witherington with Darlene Hyatt, *Paul's Letter to the Romans: A Socio-Rhetorical Commentary* (Grand Rapids: Eerdmans, 2004), 179–206, esp. 185n21.

3. "It is important to give a modern audience a sense of caution about over-psychologizing the text and especially about using it as a way to deal with modern psychological dilemmas of moral impotence or schizophrenia or the like. Reading this text through the eyes of Freud is about as unhelpful as reading it through the eyes of Augustine or Luther" (Witherington with Hyatt, *Romans*, 205).

Gerd Theissen, although sensitive to the hermeneutical difficulties with psychological criticism, nevertheless says, "Chapters 7 and 8 of the Epistle to the Romans are the most intense presentation in Paul of a transformation in human life. If any Pauline texts can be interpreted psychologically, it is these chapters." *Psychological Aspects of Pauline Theology*, trans. John P. Galvin (Edinburgh: T&T Clark, 1987), 222.

4. Theissen, *Psychological Aspects of Pauline Theology*, 205–6.

5. Theissen writes: "There are of course many statements in Paul that one can interpret along the lines of a theory of drives. In Romans 7:14ff., sin is traced back to the flesh, and flesh is a characteristic of all living things. The 'drive' that contradicts the law appears as something rooted in nature. And as in some modern theories of drives, the drive contrary to the norm is hypostatized: sin lives within the human being and occupies the place of the I" (*Psychological Aspects of Pauline Theology*, 223).

6. James D. G. Dunn, *The Theology of Paul the Apostle* (Grand Rapids: Eerdmans, 1998), 62–73.

7. Dunn, *Theology of Paul the Apostle*, 67.

8. Although writers frequently use the term "reactivity" in discussions of Bowen Family Systems Theory, it is not a term that Bowen himself used frequently. When he used it, he usually modified the term by the adjective "emotional." Synonyms for emotional reactivity include emotional reactiveness, emotional response, emotional reflex, and anxiety.

9. Murray Bowen, *Family Therapy in Clinical Practice* (Lanham, MD: Jason Aronson, 1994), 158.

10. Bowen, *Family Therapy*, 321.

11. Bowen, *Family Therapy*, 422.

12. Bowen, *Family Therapy*, 228.

13. Bowen, *Family Therapy*, 203.

14. Roberta M. Gilbert, *Extraordinary Relationships: A New Way of Thinking about Human Interactions* (New York: Wiley, 1992), 38.

15. Bowen, *Family Therapy*, 425.

16. Karl Menninger, renowned psychiatrist and founder of the Menninger Clinic, where Murray Bowen worked from 1946 to 1954, argued for something like the concept of sin to call human beings to responsibility in relationships. See *Whatever Became of Sin?* (New York: Hawthorn Books, 1973).

17. One of the theological issues raised by human evolution is how to reconcile the doctrine of the fall with a story of human origins that does not read Gen. 3 literally. In a project known

as the Colossian Forum, a community of Christian scholars from a variety of disciplines addressed this question: "If humanity emerged from nonhuman primates (as genetic, biological, and archeological evidence seems to suggest), then what are the implications for Christian theology's traditional account of origins, including both the origin of humanity and the origin of sin?" The results of their thoughtful work are found in *Evolution and the Fall*, ed. William T. Cavanaugh and James K. A. Smith (Grand Rapids: Eerdmans, 2017).

18. Dallas Willard, *Renovation of the Heart: Putting On the Character of Christ* (Colorado Springs: NavPress, 2002), 167.

19. Dallas Willard, *The Spirit of the Disciplines: Understanding How God Changes Lives* (San Francisco: HarperSanFrancisco, 1990), 72 (emphasis original).

20. See Rom. 12:9, 10; 13:8–10; 14:15; 1 Cor. 8:1; 13:1–14:1; 16:14; 2 Cor. 2:8; 6:6; 8:7–8, 24; Gal. 5:6, 13, 14, 22; Eph. 1:15; 3:17; 4:2, 15–16; 5:2, 25–33; Phil. 1:9; 2:1–2; Col. 1:4, 8; 2:2; 3:14, 19; 1 Thess. 1:3; 3:6, 12; 4:9–10; 5:8, 13; 1 Tim. 1:5; 2:15; 4:12; 6:11; 2 Tim. 1:7, 13; 2:22; Titus 2:2, 4; Philem. 5, 7.

21. Bowen did not find the word "love" useful in his work because of the subjectivity that surrounds it. He wrote, "Positive statements about the presence or absence of 'love,' with reactions and counterreactions, can occupy the scene while there is no objective evidence of change in 'love' within the family. Whatever love is, it is factual that many family members react strongly to statements about it" (*Family Therapy*, 154). See appendix B.

22. This choice is interesting primarily because the word group *agapan/agapē* was relatively weak in meaning. According to Ethelbert Stauffer, "In the Greek writers the word is colorless. It is often used as a variation for *erán* or *philein* and commands no special discussion. The noun *agápē* occurs very seldom." *Theological Dictionary of the New Testament*, ed. Gerhard Kittel and Gerhard Friedrich, trans. Geoffrey W. Bromiley (Grand Rapids: Eerdmans, 1985), s.v. "*agapáō* [to love], *agápē* [love], *agapētós* [beloved]."

23. In fact, Paul describes such behaviors as "the works of the flesh" (Gal. 5:19).

24. Bowen, *Family Therapy*, 161–64.

25. Bowen, *Family Therapy*, 164.

26. Bowen, *Family Therapy*, 164.

Appendix A Mapping the Family of David

1. Murray Bowen, *Family Therapy in Clinical Practice* (Lanham, MD: Jason Aronson, 1994), 111–12.

2. Depending on how thoughtfully chosen David's retreats were, they could have been either a principled act of differentiation or a reactive flight response.

3. Eugene H. Peterson, *Five Smooth Stones for Pastoral Work* (Atlanta: John Knox, 1980), 77.

4. See 2 Sam. 7:1–17; Pss. 89; 132; Isa. 9:6–7; 11:1–16; 32:1–2; Jer. 33:20–22; Ezek. 34:22–24; 37:24–28; Hos. 3:4–5; Amos 9:11–12; Mic. 2:2–5; Zech. 9:9–10; Matt. 1:1–25; Luke 1:32–33, 68–71; 2:10–12; John 7:41; Acts 2:29–32; 15:15–18; Rom. 1:3; Rev. 3:7; 5:5; 22:16.

5. We do not know what became of Chileab, David's second son, born in Hebron to Abigail, former wife of Nabal of Carmel (2 Sam. 3:3). In 1 Chron. 3:1, his name is Daniel.

6. Edwin H. Friedman, *A Failure of Nerve: Leadership in the Age of the Quick Fix*, ed. Margaret M. Treadwell and Edward W. Beal, 10th anniversary rev. ed. (New York: Church Publishing, 2017), 53–54.

Appendix B Bowen Theory and Theological Language

1. Murray Bowen, *Family Therapy in Clinical Practice* (Lanham, MD: Jason Aronson, 1994), 261.

2. Bowen, *Family Therapy*, 261.

3. Both theologians and scientists have thoughtfully considered the relationship between science and faith and have produced a formidable bibliography. Lay science readers can find a helpful survey by biologist Darrel R. Falk, *Coming to Peace with Science: Bridging the Worlds between Faith and Biology* (Downers Grove, IL: IVP Academic, 2004). Lay theological readers might begin with Georgetown theologian John F. Haught, *Is Nature Enough? Meaning and Truth in the Age of Science* (New York: Cambridge University Press, 2006).

4. Augustine of Hippo, *On Genesis*, in *The Works of Saint Augustine: A Translation for the 21st Century*, I/13, ed. John E. Rotelle, trans. Edmund Hill (Hyde Park, NY: New City Press, 2004), 187. Alister E. McGrath reports that John Calvin issued similar warnings. See McGrath, *The Foundations of Dialogue in Science and Religion* (Malden, MA: Wiley-Blackwell, 1991), 124–25.

5. See, for example, William T. Cavanaugh and James K. A. Smith, eds., *Evolution and the Fall* (Grand Rapids: Eerdmans, 2017); Francis S. Collins, *The Language of God: A Scientist Presents Evidence for Belief* (New York: Free Press, 2007); Dominic Johnson et al., "Adaptive Faith: Religion in Evolutionary Perspective," *Christian Century*, February 20, 2013, 34–49, http://dominicdpjohnson.com/media/pdf/2013ChristianCenturyAdaptiveFaith.pdf; John F. Haught, *God after Darwin: A Theology of Evolution* (Boulder, CO: Westview, 2007); Haught, *Making Sense of Evolution: Darwin, God, and the Drama of Life* (Louisville: Westminster John Knox, 2010); Matthew Levering, *Engaging the Doctrine of Creation: Cosmos, Creatures, and the Wise and Good Creator* (Grand Rapids: Baker Academic, 2017); Jürgen Moltmann, *God in Creation* (Minneapolis: Fortress, 1993).

6. Bowen, *Family Therapy*, 163, 474.

7. Bowen, *Family Therapy*, 281.

8. J. Richard Middleton, *A New Heaven and a New Earth: Reclaiming Biblical Eschatology* (Grand Rapids: Baker Academic, 2014).

9. Dallas Willard, *Renovation of the Heart: Putting On the Character of Christ* (Colorado Springs: NavPress, 2002), 27–44.

10. Eugene H. Peterson, *Christ Plays in Ten Thousand Places: A Conversation in Spiritual Theology* (Grand Rapids: Eerdmans, 2005), 37.

11. See, for example, John 17:11, 21–23; Rom. 12:4–5; 1 Cor. 10:17; 12:5, 12–13, 26, 27; Gal. 3:26–28; Eph. 1:10; 2:14–19, 21; 3:6, 15; 4:4–6, 12–13, 16, 25; Col. 3:11, 15.

12. James D. G. Dunn, *Unity and Diversity in the New Testament: An Inquiry into the Character of Earliest Christianity* (Philadelphia: Continuum, 1990).

13. Roberta M. Gilbert, *Extraordinary Relationships: A New Way of Thinking about Human Interactions* (New York: Wiley, 1992), 98–112.

14. Bowen, *Family Therapy*, 154.

15. Bowen, *Family Therapy*, 419.

Index

Abraham, family of, 125–36
abuse, 42
acute anxiety, 17, 159, 185
administration, 35
agapē, 158, 221n22
"all truth is God's truth," 177
Amnon, 166, 167, 168, 172, 173
anxiety, 9–11, 17–18, 35–37,
   96–97, 111, 120, 156,
   181–82, 185
  acute, 17, 159, 185
  in biblical texts, 122
  chronic, 18, 54, 174, 185
  of Mary, 140
approval, desire for, 66
Augustine, 153, 179
autonomy force, 185

Bacon, Francis, ix
basic self, 185
Bass, Dorothy, 32, 206n2
Bauckham, Richard, 218n8
beliefs and practices, 32
Berry, Wendell, 59–60, 67
Bible
  interpretation of, 117–24
  literary genres of, 117, 123
  social science interpreters
   of, 118
Birrell, Augustine, 214n2
birth order, 25–26. *See also*
  sibling position
blackout, 204n8
blame disposition, 174
Blessing, Kamila, 119–21,
  216n10
body, and spirituality, 96
Bowen, Murray, 6, 14–15
Bowen Family Systems The-
  ory (BFST), ix, 7, 185
  on anxiety, 18, 97, 156, 180

in biblical interpretation,
  118–24
and Christian community,
  159–60
and clarity of preaching, 63
on differentiation of self, 92,
  94, 137–38
on emotional cutoff, 121
on family leader, 70
and family of David, 163–76
on harmony with nature,
  58, 61
humanizes the stories of the
  Bible, 176
key concepts, 19–28
lack of category for sin, 93,
  105, 152, 155
on love, 183, 221n21
as map, 5, 161
on nuclear family, 167
and pastoral care, 78
popularity among clergy, 7–8
on progress in differentiation, 45, 97–98
on relationships, 99, 102
on scale of differentiation,
  148, 166, 180
as scientific theory of
  human behavior, 118
on the self, 181
in seminary training, 14
set of assumptions and
  practices, 177–78
on spiritual formation, 90
on supernatural, 27, 205n35
on symptoms of regres-
  sion, 51
and teaching of Paul, 151–62
Boyer, James, 210n1
Brooks, Phillips, 65
Brown, Raymond, 219n22

Brueggemann, Walter, 120
burnout, 204n8

Cain, Glen T., 177
calm leader, 39–40, 44
care, 42, 44
caregiver, vulnerability of, 80
caring for vs. taking care of, 83
change, resistance to, 35–37, 38
cheap forgiveness, 214n7
Christian practices, 206n2
Christlikeness, 90–91, 92, 98
chronic anxiety, 18, 54, 174,
  185
church, as community, 102
churches, add to society's regression, 51
cities, population of, 8–9
climate change, 9, 57
clinical pastoral education,
  6, 14
coaching, 185
  in differentiation, 94
  in spiritual direction, 100
Colossian Forum, 221n17
communication, 42–43
community, 101–102, 159–60
confession, 53
conflict, 22, 52, 179, 181
  in Abraham's family, 128–29
  and anxiety, 36
  in biblical texts, 122
  in life of David, 167–68
conflict management, 22
conformity, 182
congregations, 101–113
  diverse and unpredictable, 5
  as emotional systems, 14–16
  leadership, 34, 50
  as set of relationships, 103–4
consumption, 61

contemplative prayer prac-
    tices, 213n39
Corbett, Steve, 80–81
core beliefs, 55–56
Covey, Steven, 33
creation, care of, 57–61
crisis, 10–11
crisis leadership, 40–45
crisis management, 42
crisis plan, 42–43
culture war, 51
cutoff, 26, 110–11, 121, 179, 186
    in Abraham's family, 134–35
    in biblical texts, 123
    in stories of David, 173–74

David
    emotional triangles, 165–66
    mapping the family of,
        163–76
    scale of differentiation,
        166–67
detriangling, 20, 69–70, 94,
    186, 215n19
differentiation of self, 18, 33,
    45, 54, 132, 186
    in biblical texts, 123
    and clarity on beliefs, prac-
        tices, and principles, 55
    and effective leadership, 46
    and forgiveness, 108–12, 113
    in life of Jesus, 138, 139–46,
        148, 219n18
    minor changes in, 45, 207n24
    in pastoral care, 81–86
    and Paul, 161
    in preaching, 70–74
    scale of, 20–21, 137–38,
        166–67, 186
    and spiritual disciplines,
        96–98
    in spiritual formation, 92–95
disciplines
    of abstinence, 91
    of engagement, 91
distancing, 22, 110, 179, 186
    in Abraham's family, 129
    in biblical texts, 122
    in life of David, 168
Dittes, James, 78
Duke, James O., 89
Dunn, James, 154
dysfunctional spouse, 186

earth, stewardship of, 58–59
Elliot, Elisabeth, 108–9, 113

Elliot, Jim, 108
emotion, 155, 186
emotional cutoff. See cutoff
emotional maturity. See differ-
    entiation of self
emotional process, 5, 10, 20,
    186. See also family emo-
    tional process; societal
    emotional process
emotional reactivity, 17, 39, 66,
    93, 174, 179, 186, 220n8
    and Paul, 123, 152–57, 161
    and "the flesh," 155–56
emotional system, 15, 186
emotional triangles, 19–20,
    22–23, 112, 187, 204n13
    in Abraham's family, 130
    in biblical interpretation,
        120–21
    Jesus refuses to be drawn
        into, 144
    in the patriarchs, 126–28
    in preaching, 67–69
    in stories of David, 165–66
emotions vs. feelings, 155, 186
empathy, 82–83
environment, fragility of, 9, 57
epigenetics, 205n25
eschatology, 58
evolution, 179
extended family, 102, 187

facts, 178
faith and science, 58, 179, 183,
    222n3
fall, 220n17
family, as emotional system,
    15–16
family constellation, 25, 133
family diagram, 187, 205n26
family emotional process,
    21–23, 187
    in Abraham's family, 128–30
    in biblical texts, 122
    in family of David, 167
family of origin, 187
family projection process,
    24–25, 187
    in Abraham's family, 131–33
    in stories of David, 171–72
Fant, Clyde, 102
feelings, 155, 187
fellowship, 181–82
Fikkert, Brian, 80–81
fleeing, 22

forgiveness, 104
    and differentiation of self,
        108–12, 113
    as interpersonal, 104
    as intrapersonal, 104–5
Foster, Richard J., 106, 212n7
Freudian theory, 121, 218n12
Friedman, Edwin H., ix, 6, 8,
    24, 33, 38, 54–55
    on chronically anxious fami-
        lies, 174
    on differentiation of self, 55
    on emotional triangles,
        204n13
    on empathy, 82
    on enduring pain, 38
    on herding instinct, 209n7
    on leadership-toxic climate,
        52
    on preaching on controver-
        sial subject, 210n26
    on resistance to change, 35
    on self-differentiation,
        204n16
fruit of the Spirit, 159
fugue, 121
functional self, 187

Galindo, Israel, 7, 14, 65, 70
genetics, and environment,
    205n25
genogram, 205n26
Gilbert, Roberta, 6, 158,
    206n36
Glennie, Jannel, 213–14n40
Golden Triangle of Spiritual
    Growth (Willard), 90, 97
Goliath, 172
Goodall, Jane, 60
Gospels, on character of
    Jesus, 137–49
grace, in families, 136

Hagar, 126–27, 128, 131, 134
Harrison, Victoria, 213n39
Hauerwas, Stanley, 83
Hebrew prophets, 53
herding, 55, 66, 174, 209n7
hermeneutics, 117–19
Herrington, Jim, x, 7
Hester, Doug, 6, 95
holy habits, 92
Holy Spirit
    indwelling power of, 159
    influence of, 178

and spiritual disciplines, 93
and spiritual formation,
90–91, 180
hope, 56
hospital visits, 84
human behavior, 14
human relationships, 5

"I am" sayings, 146–47
image of God, 179
individuality force, 16–17
industrial eating, 59
indwelling sin, 157, 161
infertility, in Abraham's family, 131
innovation, 37
interlocking triangles, 52, 107,
127–28, 187, 216n5
I-position, 73, 74, 181, 187
Isaac, 127, 129, 131
Ishmael, 127, 128, 131, 134

Jackson, Wes, 60
Jacob and Esau, 127–28, 129,
130, 132, 134
Jeremiah, 53
Jesus
baptism of, 141
commitment to relationships, 148–49
death of, 147
differentiation of self, 138,
139–46, 148
genealogy of, 139, 141, 217n3
as last Adam, 180
relationship to siblings,
218n8
spiritual formation of, 140
teaching of, 142–44, 145–46
temptations of, 140–42,
219n16
John, Gospel of, 146–48,
218n13, 219n22
Jones, L. Gregory, 105, 106,
214n7
Joseph and his brothers, 128,
129, 130, 132–33, 134–35
Joseph and Mary, 140
Judges, 163, 174
justice, 56

Kerr, Michael, 17
Kierkegaard, Søren, 56
Kingsolver, Barbara, 60
Klann, Gene, 41–42
Kümmel, W. G., 153

Lamkin, James, 69–70
language, used equivocally,
180–81
leaders
as agents of change, 35
fears and anxieties of, 51
vulnerability of, 37–38
leadership, 11, 32–34, 50
and congregational ecology, 46
in crisis, 40–45
as relational, 34–37
well-differentiated, 174
leadership theory, 10
leadership-toxic climate, 52
less anxious presence, 39–40,
41, 45, 146
Louv, Richard, 208n24
love, 157–58, 183, 221n21
Luther, Martin, 153

management, 35
map, usefulness of, 3–4
Marcuson, Margaret, 7, 73
marriage, 21, 24, 182–83
Mary, mother of Jesus, 140
Mary and Martha, 19, 144
Matthews, Larry, 6
maturity, 111. See also differentiation of self
Maxwell, John, 33
McBride, Dan, 209n14
Menking, Wayne, 78–80, 82
Menninger, Karl, 53, 220n16
mercy, 56
Miller, John W., 217n4,
218nn9–12, 219n22
ministry, sustainable, 33
multigenerational transmission process, 23–24, 111,
187, 216n10
in Abraham's family, 130–31
in stories of David, 170–71

nature, alienation from,
58–60, 180, 208n24
nature-deficit disorder, 208n24
ninth concept, 187–88. See
also supernatural
nonanxious presence, 38–39
Nouwen, Henri, 101
nuclear family, 21, 68, 102, 188

"one flesh," 182–83
open relationship system,
210n28

ordinary, and pastoral care, 79
ordinary events of life, 90
organic production, 60
Osborne, Ronald E., 64
Osmer, Richard, 31
overfunctioning, 22, 107, 129,
188
in biblical texts, 122
of Rebekah, 129–30
in stories of David, 168–70

pain, endurance of, 38
palliative care, 52, 83
Papero, Dan, 60
parables, 144
pastoral affections, 37–38
pastoral care, 44, 77–88
boundaries of, 211n6
and differentiation of self,
81–86
helping and not hurting,
80–81
pastors, own emotional needs,
86
pastors vs. therapists, 78–79
patriarchs, 125–36
Paul, 151–62
on the flesh, 154
on love, 157–58
on relationships, 159–60
on sin, 123, 157, 162
on the Spirit, 159
on weak and strong, 111
peace, 56
Peterson, Eugene, 32, 79, 171,
181, 212n7
phenomenological language,
154
plagiarism in preaching, 72
planned discipline, 90–91
Pollan, Michael, 60
population growth, 8–9, 60
practical theology, 31–32
practices, 32
preaching, 63–65
on controversial issues, 73,
210n26
as detriangling, 69–70
and differentiation of self,
70–74
and emotional triangles,
67–69
personality in, 65
as relational task, 64–67
presence, 38

principles, thoughtful focus on, 54–57
process. *See* emotional process
projection, 22, 188
  in Abraham's family, 130
  by Saul, 170
promiscuous ministry, 82
prophetic preaching, 73
psychology, and biblical studies, 120, 215n2

Quelle (Gospels source), 218n13
quick-fix mentality, 174
racism, 67
Rauseo, Louise, 95, 213n33
reactivity. *See* emotional reactivity
Rebekah, 129–30, 132, 134
reciprocal functioning, 22, 188
  in Abraham's family, 129–30
reconciliation, 110, 181–82
regression, 51, 180. *See also* societal regression
relationships, 11, 99, 101, 102
renovation of the heart, 90
repentance, 52, 56
Richardson, Ronald W., 7, 205n34
righteousness vs. legalism, 142
rights vs. responsibilities, 51
Rogers, Everett M., 37
Rumford, Douglas J., 212n7
rural populations, 9
Ruth, 170–71

Salatin, Joel, 60
Samuel, 164–65, 171, 172, 175
Sarah, 126–27, 128, 131
Saul, 164–66, 168–69, 170, 175
scale of differentiation. *See* differentiation of self, scale of
science, and supernatural, 178
self
  basic vs. pseudo, 142
  responsible focus on, 53–54
self-denial, 181
self-management, 53
Sermon on the Mount, 142–43
sibling position, 25–26, 121, 188
  in Abraham's family, 133
  in stories of David, 172–73

sibling rivalry, 121
sin, 105, 220n16
  as broken relation with God, 123
  power of, 53, 93, 161
slavery, 67
SLOW (seasonal, local, organic, and whole) eating, 60
social change, 8
social justice, 63
social media, 50
societal anxiety, 58, 61, 174, 180
societal emotional process, 26–27, 50–52, 188
  in Abraham's family, 135
  in stories of David, 174–76
societal regression, 7, 10, 53, 60, 112, 204
solitude, 101
Solomon, 171, 173, 175–76
soul, and self, 181
spiritual disciplines, 100
  and differentiation of self, 96–98
  reduces anxiety, 99
spiritual formation, 89–100, 212n4
  and differentiation of self, 92–95
  Willard on, 90–92
spiritual progress, 98
spiritual theology, 32
Stauffer, Ethelbert, 148, 221n22
Steinke, Peter, 6, 7
Stevens, R. Paul, 6
stewardship of creation, 59–60, 61
Stone, Howard W., 89
Stott, John, 64
strategic leadership, 40
"stretching the triangle," 121
suffering, 79, 85
supernatural, 27, 96, 161, 178
Switzer, David K., 79, 86
sympathy, 82–83
Synoptic Gospels, 141, 218n13
systems theory
  as basis for reading biblical texts, 119
  vs. conventional theory, 178
systems thinking, 13, 188

Taylor, Trisha, x, 7
Ten Commandments, 55
texts, limited information from, 122
Theissen, Gerd, 220n3, 220n5
theological language, assumptions of, 179
theology, making room for science, 179–80
theories, 14
third-way leadership, 32–34, 36, 43, 44
Thomas, Frank A., 210n18
Titelman, Peter, 110, 215n19
togetherness force, 16–17, 37, 66, 181–82, 188
  in biblical texts, 122
  in death of Jesus, 144
  and kingdom of God, 145
Toman, Walter, 25, 121, 205n29, 217n9
triangle. *See* emotional triangles; interlocking triangles

underfunctioning, 22, 107, 129, 189
  in biblical texts, 122
  of Isaac, 129–30
  in stories of David, 168–70
undifferentiation, 137
urban agrarianism, 59
urban crowding, 9
Uriah, 166, 167, 169

VIM (vision, intention, and means), 92
vision and values, 42, 43
Volf, Miroslav, 32, 104, 106, 206n2

watching process, 189
Wesley, John, 214n2
Willard, Dallas, 90–92, 96–97, 98, 157, 212n2, 212n16, 213n19
Willimon, William H., 65, 78, 79, 82, 85, 206n8
Wilson, E. O., 58
worldview, naturalistic and theistic, 123
Wright, N. T., 217n6

younger brother over the older, 131